Sociology
as
Social Criticism

by the same author

Classes in Modern Society
Critics of Society
Sociology: A Guide to
  Problems and Literature

Sociology
as
Social Criticism

T. B. Bottomore

PANTHEON BOOKS
A Division of Random House, New York

Library of Congress Cataloging in Publication Data

Bottomore, T. B.
Sociology as Social Criticism.

Includes bibliographical references.
    1. Sociology—Addresses, essays, lectures.
I. Title.
HM51.B753 1975   301   74-4759
ISBN 0-394-46889-9

Manufactured in the United States of America

FIRST AMERICAN EDITION

For Katherine
Stephen
and Eleanor

Contents

Sociology
as
Social Criticism

Introduction

Conservatism and Radicalism in Sociology

The pervasive presence of conservative and radical ideas in socio-logical thought, and the historically changing relationships be-tween them, are at once obvious and difficult to interpret. One source of difficulty is the uncertain and variable meaning of 'conservative' and 'radical'. Some writers, perhaps, would still want to contrast 'bourgeois sociology' (which is conservative) with 'Marxist theory' (which is radical), but this view is no longer widely held. At the present time Marxism may serve in some societies to uphold a particular *status quo* and to inhibit criticism. Elsewhere, at least in its more orthodox forms, it may be seen as having lost some of its radical thrust, because it no longer bears upon the major conflicts and problems of the age and, by ignoring certain issues, has forfeited its liberating character.[1]

Those writers who have doubts about the radical nature of Marxist thought in the late twentieth century have often attempted to define the conservative and radical tendencies in sociology in other ways; for example, by making a distinction such as that of C. Wright Mills between 'celebrating society as it is' and 'criti-cising society', or by opposing, as Alain Touraine has done, a 'sociology of policy-making' and a 'sociology of contestation'. The trouble with such formulations is that they are, in general, less precise in their analysis of existing society, of the radical social forces at work in it, and of the goals of a radical movement, than Marx appeared to be in his account of capitalist society, the role of the working class, and the advent of socialism. But

[1] There is a good account of the recent development of radical ideas in France, in opposition to the Marxism of the Communist Party, in Richard Gombin, *Les origines du gauchisme* (Paris, 1971); and an analysis of the work of some major American social critics in relation to Marxist thought, in Peter Clecak, *Radical Paradoxes* (New York, 1973). To my knowledge there has not been any similar examination of radical thought in Germany, but the ideas of the later Frankfurt School are clearly expounded in Albrecht Wellmer, *Critical Theory of Society* (New York, 1971).

this indefiniteness may be inescapable, and may reflect the confused social conditions of the present time. There is no great virtue, after all, in having a precise and definite theoretical scheme which is quite disconnected from reality. In any case, the meaning of Marx's own social theory, as it was developed over several decades, has become a subject of controversy and of diverse interpretation; and many radical critics of Marxism in fact ground their criticism in some particular conception of the intention of Marx's thought. The extent to which social development is determined, and can be explained, by the growth of the productive forces; the significance of the working class as an agent of social transformation, as against the influence of what Marx himself designated the progress of the 'general intellect'; the necessary and appropriate social institutions of a socialist society—all these are matters for argument and interpretation.[1] It is not at all certain that there is a fundamental incompatibility with Marx's own thought, though there is clearly a different emphasis, in such a reformulation of the preconditions for socialism as that which Wellmer presents: 'the criticism and alteration of the "superstructure" have a new and decisive importance for the movements of liberation ... it would be necessary to include socialist democracy, socialist justice, socialist ethics and a "socialist consciousness" among the components of a socialist society to be "incubated" within the womb of a capitalist order.'[2]

If the radicalism of Marxism, in some of its principal versions, has been questioned, so too has the conservatism of sociology. In this case, also, there are conflicting interpretations of the development of thought. Sociology has often been described as the 'science of social crisis', and it emerged originally from the social and cultural crisis accompanying the decline of the *ancien régime* and the rise of industrial capitalism. But this intellectual response can be viewed in two different ways. Sociology may be seen from one aspect as developing out of the critical social thought of the Enlightenment and eventually assuming a thoroughly radical form in the thought of Karl Marx. Or, on the contrary, it may be conceived as a reaction against the Enlightenment by the conservative thinkers of the early nineteenth century,[3]

[1] I have discussed some of these questions more fully in my Introduction to *Karl Marx* (Englewood Cliffs, N.J., 1973).

[2] Wellmer, op. cit., pp. 121–2.

[3] See especially the discussion in R. A. Nisbet, *The Sociological Tradition* (New York, 1966), pp. 16–18.

whose ideas, greatly admired by Comte, entered profoundly into the constitution of his own sociological system.

Even if we were to accept one or other of these accounts it would still not be necessary to suppose that the orientation of sociological thought had remained quite unchanged over a period of nearly two centuries. Radical critics of sociology have often argued that the 'golden age' of sociological thought—the period between the 1880s and the 1920s when Max Weber, Durkheim and Pareto were writing their major works—had pre-eminently the character of a conservative reaction against Marxism. It is undoubtedly the case that these thinkers were particularly concerned, in different contexts, to criticise the Marxist theory,[1] and that they contributed important elements of a conservative theory of society. But the debate with Marxism in which they engaged itself helped to maintain a current of Marxist thought in sociology, and at certain times (as in the 1930s and the 1960s) there was a revival of radical thought which drew to a large extent upon Marxist ideas.

There is, however, a more thoroughgoing critique of the conservative orientation of sociology, which denies altogether the radicalism of Enlightenment thought in the form which it assumed in sociology, and which questions those elements of Marx's theory that were derived from the same source. This critique, undertaken mainly by the Frankfurt School, and especially by Max Horkheimer, sees the scientific rationalism of the Enlightenment as embodying a conception of nature as an object for human manipulation and control which led necessarily to a similar view of man himself, in his social relationships, as an object of domination.[2] Marx's own theory, especially because of its emphasis upon labour as the human mode of self-realisation—and more generally because of Marx's obvious approval of the development of modern science and industry—is criticised as belonging to the Enlightenment tradition.[3]

From this standpoint the whole early development of sociology —whether it is the intellectual contributions of the conservative romantics, or those of the Enlightenment thinkers, that are

[1] H. Stuart Hughes, in his *Consciousness and Society* (New York, 1958) quite rightly sees the critique of Marxism as one of the principal elements in the reorientation of European thought during this period.

[2] Max Horkheimer, *Eclipse of Reason* (New York, 1947); Theodor Adorno and Max Horkheimer, *Dialektik der Aufklärung* (Amsterdam, 1947).

[3] Later studies by members of the Frankfurt School have extended and deepened this criticism; see Wellmer, op. cit., Chapter 2, 'The latent positivism of Marx's philosophy of history'.

emphasised—is regarded as the elaboration of a conservative view of society which opposes in one way or another the doctrines that would make possible human liberation. The thinkers of the Frankfurt School seemed to be saying in the end that a bourgeois society could only produce, as a general cultural phenomenon, bourgeois conservative social theories. When this critical reflection was extended to Soviet thought, which was regarded as having elaborated above all the elements of scientific rationalism in Marxist theory, the pessimistic conclusion was reached that the most widely diffused styles of social thought in the principal modern civilisations all tended to uphold a system of domination, and were contested only by the few surviving representatives of 'critical reason'.[1]

These arguments bring to light another aspect of the development and orientation of sociological thought. There is on one side an inner connection of ideas which, according to how it is interpreted, reveals the tendency of a particular sociological outlook to reinforce or oppose an existing form of social life. On the other side, sociological thought derives its preoccupations and some part at least of its general framework of presuppositions, its criteria of what is significant or valid, from the form of society in which it is carried on. As Robert Lynd once observed: 'Social science is not a scholarly arcanum, but an organised part of the culture which exists to help man in continually understanding and rebuilding his culture'.[2] Lynd emphasised the 'rebuilding' of the culture, and advocated a more critical social science which would show the way to a radical transformation of American society in the decade of the depression. But sociology as a part of the culture cannot easily escape the influence of what is dominant in a given culture; and it is in those periods when there is manifest conflict and contestation in society itself that, in the first place, the distinction between a conservative and a radical sociology is sharply delineated, and secondly, a radical sociology assumes a growing importance in the whole field of social thought.

Only to the extent that modern societies are not harmonious wholes, that conflicts between major social groupings exist within them, can a radical sociology be constituted and continually recreated. The depiction of the whole post-Enlightenment period as a 'bourgeois' epoch, in which only bourgeois social thought,

[1] See especially the final chapter of Herbert Marcuse, *One-Dimensional Man* (New York, 1964).
[2] Robert S. Lynd, *Knowledge for What?* (Princeton, 1939), p. ix.

in however many different guises, could flourish, ignores the extent of the oppositions in modern societies, on the basis of which Marxism itself developed. It is in fact the apparent decline of such opposing forces, especially as they were manifested in the conflicts between clearly demarcated classes, that has led to new conceptions of modern society as 'industrial society' or 'scientific-technological society'; but the notion of a general 'pacification' of social life, of the emergence of a 'consensus' in the conditions of democracy and affluence, has not survived the radical upheavals of the 1960s.

Yet it would be a mistake, in my view, to give an exclusive importance to this aspect, and to represent sociological thought as the mere reflection of a particular balance of social interests. Within a given system of social relations and cultural norms there remains a sphere in which the relatively autonomous intellectual development of sociology is possible. If this is so then we can ask what the tendency of this development has been and is likely to be; whether it sustains or brings into question the established form of life. Two features of sociological thought seem to me to justify speaking of an inherently radical orientation. In the first place, I would emphasise as the principal legacy of the Enlightenment in sociological thought, and in Marxism as one of its forms, the critical outlook of science, rather than the idea of the domination of nature and its extension to social practice in the domination of men. It is one of the positive, and radical, features of sociology considered as a science that it involves a continuous criticism of all extant theories of society, including those everyday conceptions of the social world which shape practical life. At present, the general unease about the social consequences of advanced science and technology gives some encouragement, and justification, to the critics of scientific rationalism, but I cannot see that the cause of human liberation will be greatly helped by forsaking this for the religious mysticism that grows so luxuriantly among the exponents of a non-scientific counter culture.

The second feature of sociology to which I would draw attention has to do with its social consequences and how these are conceived within sociological thought. If the aim of sociology is taken to be the discovery of the hidden mechanism of social life, which is then communicated in the training of a small elite of 'social engineers', this does entail the production and reproduction of a form of domination. But if the aim is seen as the diffusion through society of an understanding of how social relationships are established, persist, or can be changed—as a kind of public enlightenment—then its effects can well be seen as liberating.

The essays which follow discuss more fully, and from various perspectives, the issues I have raised here. They have been selected and arranged in accordance with my view of the major concerns of a radical sociology: namely, to criticise social theories in terms of the view of the social world that they impose; to investigate the inequalities and constraints embedded in the structure of classes and elites, which obstruct the growth of human freedom; and to examine the character and prospects of those social movements which contest the existing structure of society. A radical sociology in this sense brings together three elements: it is at the same time theoretical, empirical and political.

PART I

Social Theories

Chapter 1

Conservative Man[1]

'The year 1968 marks a watershed in the history of democratic mass politics: the quiet years of accommodation, integration and domestication were finally over, new waves of mobilisation and counter-mobilisation brought a number of Western democracies out of equilibrium, a new generation challenged the assumptions and the rhetoric of the old.

The year 1968 also marks a watershed in the history of the international discipline of political sociology: the violent eruption of new forces did not only challenge the models and the theories of the fifties and the early sixties, but also forced a revaluation of data-gathering techniques and analysis strategies.'

This is not criticism but self-criticism, formulated in a preface by S. M. Lipset and Stein Rokkan to a collection of conference papers on political sociology, published in 1968.[2] It provokes a number of interesting questions. What kind of science is it, one may ask, that can be so easily overthrown, in the space of a few months, by a student revolt? And if it has been overthrown, if the events of 1968 do really oblige us to revise fundamentally the theories, models, and methods of research in political sociology, what new ideas and approaches are to be discovered in the work of Lipset himself, who was, in the 1950s and the early 1960s, one of the chief exponents of those notorious doctrines, proclaiming the 'end of ideology' and the achievement of 'stable democracy' in the Western industrial countries,[3] which are now

[1] Reprinted, with minor revisions, from the *New York Review of Books*, XV (6) (8 October 1970).

[2] Otto Stammer (ed.), *Party Systems, Party Organisations, and the Politics of New Masses* (Berlin: Institut für politische Wissenschaft an der Freien Universität, 1968).

[3] In the concluding chapter of *Political Man* (New York, 1959) he wrote: '... the fundamental political problems of the industrial revolution have been solved ... This very triumph of the democratic social revolution in the West ends domestic politics for those intellectuals who must have ideologies or utopias to motivate them to political action.' Similarly, in an essay on 'The Changing Class Structure and Contemporary European Politics'

to be abandoned? More widely, what alternative theories have emerged in the social sciences to take the place of the discredited views which Lipset once propounded?

The growing dissatisfaction with the state of sociological and political theory at the present time is unmistakable. Lipset alludes to it in one of his most recent papers—the introduction to *Politics and the Social Sciences* (1969)—where he writes: '. . . some now see in system theory only another variant of a conceptual scheme whose basic utility is as an intellectual organising framework, but which in fact does not submit itself to the cardinal test of science—empirical verification.' But although system theory, especially in its sociological version—functionalism—may in this way provide mainly a set of categories for classifying social phenomena, rather than a body of explanatory propositions, it does nonetheless convey a particular interpretation of the nature of human society. The essential idea upon which it rests is that every society should be conceived as a system in equilibrium; and that any disturbance of this equilibrium, if it occurs at all, should be seen as provoking a responsive adaptation, so that equilibrium is restored and the society is maintained in its original, or a slightly modified, form. This idea found its strongest expression in that version of functionalism (expounded principally by Talcott Parsons) in which the force that brings about equilibrium, adaptation and integration is defined as a 'central value system'; that is, a set of fundamental values, presumed to be accepted by all or most members of a society, which determine the form of each particular social system.

It is easy to see how the ideas of 'stable democracy' and the 'end of ideology' fit into this functionalist scheme. A 'stable democracy' can be represented as a well-nigh perfect example of a society in equilibrium, while the cessation of ideological conflict —notably in the specific form of the conflict between classes— can be interpreted as the culmination of a process of adaptation and integration, which is accomplished through the working of the central, democratic values. In Lipset's words: '. . . the workers have achieved industrial and political citizenship',[1] 'class conflict is minimised', and 'the history of changes in political ideologies

---

in S. R. Graubard (ed.), *A New Europe?* (Boston, Mass., 1964) he claimed that '. . . instead of European class and political relationships holding up a model of the United States' future, the social organisation of the United States has presented the image of the European future'—in the sense of a reduction, and eventual disappearance, of ideological conflict.

[1] Lipset (1959), op. cit., p. 406.

in democratic countries, from this point of view, can be written in terms of the emergence of new strata, and their eventual integration in society and polity'.[1] In *The First New Nation*, Lipset formulates his method explicitly in terms of 'equilibrium' and 'values': 'For the purposes of this book, I have tried to think in terms of a dynamic ... equilibrium model, which posits that a complex society is under constant pressure to adjust its institutions to its central value system, in order to alleviate strains created by changes in social relations ...'[2]

But it would be a mistake to regard the particular ideas which Lipset expounded at that time as simple inferences from a functionalist view of society. These ideas depended to a large extent, as did functionalism itself, upon the political climate of the age. The heyday of functionalism in sociology coincided with the period in which social conflict assumed predominantly the character of a conflict between nations, and especially between different types of social system. In the 1940s and 1950s the Western democracies were engaged in conflict first with the Fascist states, and afterwards with the USSR and the newly created communist states of Eastern Europe, and democracy as a form of society was sharply contrasted with these other forms. In these conditions it is comprehensible that the sources of conflict within societies should have been overshadowed and largely neglected. Indeed, the importance of such conflicts may actually have diminished in some societies, not only because the sense of national unity was enhanced by their involvement in external conflicts, but also because, in the postwar period, the Western democracies (as well as the countries of Eastern Europe) entered upon a period of exceptionally rapid and sustained economic growth, which has undoubtedly affected in various ways the relations between classes and between political groups. Thus the idea of the democracies as stable social systems which had attained their definitive form (and by implication a similar view of the communist societies) took root in fertile soil.

The crucial defect of this functionalist conception was that it reflected uncritically the features of a particular historical conjuncture. The source of this failing was its own unhistorical character, not only in the sense that it did not include a historical

---

[1] Graubard, op. cit., pp. 337–8.
[2] S. M. Lipset, *The First New Nation* (New York, 1963), pp. 8–9. It should be noted that Lipset does not distinguish very clearly between different senses of 'equilibrium'; his failure in this respect is well criticised by Brian Barry, *Sociologists, Economists and Democracy* (London, 1970), Chapter VIII.

theory (as has often been said), but more significantly in my view, that it produced in its adherents an extreme insensitivity to the potentialities for change in human society and encouraged a propensity to regard the fleeting present as an eternal order. The shock produced by the new radical movements, culminating in the political crises of 1968, was correspondingly great, and it plunged the social sciences into an intellectual disarray which still largely persists.

But what positive results came out of the crisis? In general, it may be said, a more critical outlook has developed, but in Lipset's own recent work there is little evidence of the radical reconstruction of political sociology which he was urging in 1968. The most significant change is the appearance of a new subject matter; the preoccupation with political immobility has given way to a concern with political movements. Much of Lipset's recent writing, from the time of the Berkeley Free Speech Movement at the end of 1964, but more particularly since 1968, has been devoted to the student movements and to some other manifestations of dissent and opposition in the Western industrial societies. But the manner in which he treats these subjects remains substantially unaltered. In his essay (with Philip Altbach) 'Student Politics and Higher Education in the United States', in the volume which he edited on *Student Politics* (1967), he is still largely engaged in establishing a descriptive classification, this time of various elements in the student movement—the family backgrounds of radicals, the situation of faculty, the characteristics of different universities—and he discusses the development of the radical movement solely in terms of these internal features of the university, without any reference to the sources of radicalism in the condition of American society as a whole. Moreover, he remains quite convinced that American society is unchangeable and does not need to change.

Basically, in the United States, with its relatively stable social system and a fairly long tradition of political tranquillity, radical social movements of any kind have had difficulty in establishing themselves. . . . It is possible that the new student left of the mid 1960s may imply some changes in American society. On the other hand, it is much more likely that it is one of many unsuccessful attempts in the United States to create a radical movement in an essentially infertile environment.'

Only in a later essay on the student movement does this conviction momentarily waver. In *Students in Revolt* (1969), following the rapid growth of radicalism on most university campuses, Lipset is forced to abandon his attempt to analyse it purely in terms of internal university influences. He quotes some research which, he says '. . . sheds strong doubt upon the hypotheses that relate American activism to characteristics of different types of universities or administration policies'—that is to say, upon the very hypotheses which he had advanced two years earlier. And he now relates student radicalism explicitly to the wider society:

'. . . the sources of political activism among students must be found in politics, in the factors associated with different types of politics. . . . one should learn to expect a sharp increase in student activism in a society where, for a variety of reasons, accepted political and social values are being questioned, in times particularly when events are testing the viability of a regime and policy failures seem to question the legitimacy of social and economic arrangements and institutions' (pp. 497–8).

This, however, represents the high point of Lipset's excursion into criticism of the established order. In his latest book (with Earl Raab), *The Politics of Unreason* (1970), he reverts to a pre-occupation with 'stable democracy', in the context of a study of right-wing extremist movements in America. The stage is set by defining democracy as 'pluralism', and extremism as '. . . that impulse which is inimical to a pluralism of interests and groups'. From this point of view, left-wing extremism and right-wing extremism are 'very much the same', since they both have an anti-pluralistic orientation. I think it is very doubtful whether 'extremism', without some more precise qualification, is a useful term in political analysis, but this is not the aspect of the natter which concerns me here; it is rather the nature of Lipset's discussion of extremism in relation to democracy. Like all conservative thinkers, he is anxious to emphasise the formal structure of checks and balances in a democratic system (without inquiring too closely into how it actually works), and to obscure or eliminate the more radical idea of democracy as a political movement of subject classes and groups against their rulers, which seeks to establish as fully as possible government *by* the people. From the latter standpoint there is nothing at all undemocratic in popular movements which aim to get rid of those interest groups whose activities are harmful to a majority of the population, even if this involves reducing somewhat the 'plurality of interest groups' which Lipset so much admires. In this sense, for example, American populism was a profoundly democratic movement which developed from earlier agrarian radical movements directed against the growing power of the banks, the railroads and big business. One of these, the Granger movement, transmitted to Populism an interest in co-operatives and contributed later to what Lipset himself once called 'agrarian socialism'.[1] The Populist movement, especially in the South, took up the cause of industrial workers and Negroes, and established relations with the Knights of Labor.[2] More generally, the socialist movement of the early twentieth century seems to have enjoyed its greatest success in those areas which had previously been strongholds of Populism. Lipset and Raab, however, follow the conservative interpretation of Populism in which the anti-industrial, anti-liberal elements in some sections of the movement are given undue prominence, and so they are led to include Populism among their 'extremist' movements: 'Doctrinal populism thus becomes a seductive form of political moralism, inimical to pluralistic politics'.

The results of a study conceived on these lines are predictable. Since left-wing and right-wing movements are equated as enemies of democracy the distinction between left and right vanishes; the important question of how some popular movements of opposition to the ruling minority become perverted into supporters of the established order is never even formulated; the 'American political system' is restored as the model of a democratic order; and the growing disaffection with the two established parties in the United States is regarded as dangerous and undemocratic extremism, which threatens the supreme values of pluralism and stability. The idea of pluralism itself is treated in a curious fashion which seems to imply that every interest group which happens to exist

[1] *Agrarian Socialism: The Cooperative Commonwealth Federation in Saskatchewan* (Berkeley, 1950; revised edn 1968). In his foreword to the original edition Robert Lynd indicated a fruitful line of inquiry which might have emerged from this study (but which had to wait for the work of other thinkers in the late 1960s) when he wrote: 'No phenomenon is more urgently in need of study today than the conditions under which new social movements may emerge ... The recovery of democracy, if indeed it can occur, can happen only through men thinking together of what it is they want and organising to move together.'

[2] These aspects of Populism are well described, and illustrated from the documents of the movement, in Norman Pollack, *The Populist Mind* (New York, 1967). See also the discussion in Michael P. Rogin, *The Intellectuals and McCarthy: The Radical Specter* (Cambridge, Mass., 1967), especially Chapter 6.

in American society—from commercial television to the Mafia—
must be carefully preserved as an element in a democratic order.

What has happened, then, to the challenge presented in the
heady days of 1968 by the 'violent eruption of new forces'?
What has become of the pressing need for a revaluation of concepts and methods in political sociology? One is tempted to
answer by saying that Lipset has behaved rather like the ideal
social system imagined by the functionalists. He has restored his
equilibrium by integrating an interpretation of the new radical
movements into his established scheme of thought, with a few
minor adaptations, and in this way has averted any fundamental
change in his outlook. With the balance thus re-established he
can take the field again as a leading defender of the American
status quo.

The importance of functionalist ideas for a conservative
interpretation of society can be seen clearly in another study
which appeared just at the time when Lipset was temporarily
voicing the dissatisfaction of political sociologists with the
explanatory powers of their science. Samuel P. Huntington's
Political Order in Changing Societies is based firmly upon the
concept of political stability, and extends its use in order to make
a sharp distinction between the industrial societies and the
developing countries. According to Huntington:

'The most important political distinction among countries concerns not their form of government but their degree of government. . . . Communist totalitarian states and Western liberal
states both belong generally in the category of effective rather than
debile political systems . . . (they) differ significantly from the
governments which exist in many, if not most, of the modernising
countries of Asia, Africa, and Latin America.'

But why is this the 'most important' distinction? And for
whom? Certainly not for the great majority of men, who in
modern times at least are more apt to engage in struggles for
independence from colonial rule, for democracy against dictatorship, for socialism against capitalism, even at the cost of disorder,
than they are to do battle for political order as such. In short,
they want other things besides, or more than, efficient government. Is it then the most important distinction for political scientists, because it enables them to understand better, to explain
more convincingly, the processes of politics? That seems unlikely
in principle, when the distinction corresponds so ill with the

distinctions which men make in actual political life. In any case it would have to be demonstrated, and Huntington's own book, though it provides much interesting information systematically arranged (which can, of course, be done with the aid of any conceptual scheme whatsoever) concludes with considerably less than a half-truth; namely, that '. . . he controls the future who organises its politics'. The real question which needs to be answered lies behind this statement. What is it—what economic conditions, what relations between classes, what external influences—that enables one group of men rather than another to organise a country's politics and to determine the kind of regime it shall have?

In fact, Huntington's assertion is neither empirical nor methodological; it is a value judgement. Its object is to persuade us to view the world in a particular way; to place a very high value upon political stability, and to conceive the political problems of developing countries not in terms of a choice among alternative regimes but in terms of how order can be established. The solution which Huntington himself would prefer is indicated later, when he refers to the possibility that '. . . there may be some evolution toward an American-type system'; in the western European countries at first, as they rid themselves of class conflict, and eventually in those developing countries which have 'become more fully modern'. Like Lipset, Huntington sees the American political system as a model for stable democracy.

This scheme of analysis, though it is based upon a valuation, has nevertheless an empirical aspect. The sharp contrast which Huntington tries to establish between political order in one type of society and political disorder in another depends upon the judgement, derived from the ideas of Parsons and Lipset, that the industrial countries possess stable political systems. Thus, after remarking that politics in these countries '. . . . embodies consensus, community, legitimacy, organisation, effectiveness, stability' he describes the condition of the developing countries in the following way:

'With a few notable exceptions, the political evolution of these countries after World War II was characterised by increasing ethnic and class conflict, recurring rioting and mob violence, frequent military coups d'etat, the dominance of unstable personalistic leaders who often pursued disastrous economic and social policies, widespread and blatant corruption among cabinet ministers and civil servants, arbitrary infringement of the rights and liberties of citizens, declining standards of bureaucratic efficiency and performance, the pervasive alienation of urban political groups, the loss of authority by legislatures and courts, and the fragmentation and at times complete disintegration of broadly based political parties.'

Within the last few years, however, a good number of the phenomena thus listed have made their appearance in the 'stable' industrial societies (both Western and Soviet), and it seems doubtful whether the term 'political stability' can any longer be applied accurately to most of these societies. On the contrary, they may be on the threshold of great political transformations. It would be more realistic then to look at global politics from the point of view of the radical changes which are being advocated and prepared in both the industrial and the developing societies, taking into account at the same time the ways in which the changes in the two parts of the world react upon each other.

To say this, however, is to raise a further problem. Social thought, at the present time, is strongly affected by the revival of radicalism, especially in the universities; just as it was affected in the 1950s by the prevailing conservative mood. The idea of a 'critical sociology' which has grown out of various strands of social criticism in the past decade, and especially out of the work of C. Wright Mills, expresses this radical orientation. But it has not yet been embodied in a new social theory. The principal alternative to the conservative sociology of the 1950s, as represented notably by Parsons and Lipset, is still some version or other of Marxism, which stands at the opposite pole from functionalism by virtue of its central concern with the conflict of interests and values in society, with the rise and development of social movements, and with the social forces which produce large-scale historical changes; and which is radical in its vision of a future egalitarian society. But Marxism too is experiencing a crisis as the discrepancy has grown between the theoretical ideas and political ideals of classical Marxism and the social realities of the twentieth century. Revolutions, unimagined by Marx, have taken place in peasant countries. The working class in capitalist societies has lost something of its pre-eminence as a force for change; nowhere is it revolutionary, everywhere its declining significance in the process of production and its changing social situation pose the question whether it can any longer perform the role which Marx assigned to it. Finally, socialism— the society of liberated, co-operative and joyful men which Marx envisaged—has turned out to be, in many countries, a bureau-cratic nightmare.

The attempts by Marxist thinkers to deal with these difficulties have not led to a reconstruction of Marxism as a social theory capable of explaining the events of the twentieth century. Indeed, that may not be possible. The proliferation of conceptual and methodological disputes, and the increasing uncertainty about the exact boundaries of Marxist thought in relation to other philo-sophical and sociological ideas (for instance, those of existential-ism, phenomenology, or structuralism), are suggestive rather of the breakdown of a distinctive intellectual tradition. In this process, various Marxist ideas have been absorbed, though in an unsystematic way, into the new 'critical sociology'. The most important of these, in the present state of the social sciences, is the historical conception which requires that particular events should be studied in their wider context, as occurrences within long-term processes of economic and social change. If the 'critical sociologists' do not fashion their studies in this way—if, let us say, they treat the upheavals of the late 1960s as unique events, or timeless phenomena of revolt, which they are disposed to applaud—they will be adopting substantially the viewpoint of those they criticise, who conceived 'stable democracy' in just the same way as an unhistorical absolute. Their moral response will be different, but they will arrive at no better understanding of the course of events, and they will have little of value to com-municate to those who are engaged in practical struggles to create a new society.

Chapter 2

Out of This World:
The Sociological Theory of
Talcott Parsons[1]

In 1937, during the decade of the Depression and the New Deal, of the revival of intellectual radicalism and left-wing social movements, of the Spanish Civil War and the approaching conflict with the Fascist states, Talcott Parsons published a study in social theory, *The Structure of Social Action*, which turned resolutely aside from any concern with the contemporary economic and political crisis in order to expound the ideas of some earlier European thinkers, and to distil from them a very general and abstract scheme of sociological thought. The main theme of the book, as Parsons notes in his Introduction to the paperback edition, was that the works of Alfred Marshall, Pareto, Durkheim and Max Weber represented, against the background of two preceding styles of social thought—utilitarian positivism and German idealism—a 'major movement in the structure of theoretical thinking' and 'an altogether new phase in the development of European thought about the problems of man and society'.

This 'major revolution', as Parsons calls it elsewhere,[2] was supposed to consist in the fact that the four thinkers whose work he examined, in spite of their apparently diverse concepts, methods, and interests, had all contributed elements of a 'theory of social action' which amounted to a new conception of man and society and formed the core of modern sociological thought. (I shall examine this idea of 'social action' in a moment.)

Initially, therefore, Parsons's book appears as an interpretation of a phase in European intellectual history. As such it is sadly deficient, because it ignores almost completely the work of two

[1] Reprinted, with minor revisions, from the *New York Review of Books*, XIII (8) (6 November 1969).
[2] In his preface to the second edition of *The Structure of Social Action* (New York, 1949).

thinkers—Marx and Freud—who were above all responsible for a revolution in men's conceptions of their individual and social life. From this point of view a much more illuminating history of the period is given by Karl Löwith[1] in his account of the movement of thought from Hegel to Nietzsche, and by H. Stuart Hughes[2] in his study of the controversy over Marxism, the revolt against positivism, and the attempt by Max Weber to reconcile or transcend the positivist and idealist traditions in social science.

Even if Parsons's book is regarded as dealing with the narrower subject of the formation of academic sociology, it still omits or misrepresents too many important aspects of this development, as some recent histories of sociological thought[3] have made plain. The influence of the conservative thinkers, de Bonald and de Maistre, the contributions of Saint-Simon and Tocqueville, find no place in Parsons's study. Herbert Spencer is peremptorily dismissed, although in more recent work Parsons has rehabilitated much of Spencer's theory of social evolution.[4] In his Introduction to the paperback edition of *The Structure of Social Action* Parsons acknowledges some of these omissions; but he has not yet arrived at a point where he would concede that his whole interpretation of the formation of modern sociology needs to be drastically revised.

In any case, it was by no means Parsons's intention simply to contribute a chapter to the history of ideas. '*The Structure of Social Action*', he wrote in the Preface to the second edition, 'was intended to be primarily a contribution to systematic social science and not to history, that is the history of social thought'. Parsons's aim was to make explicit, and to develop, the distinctive body of concepts upon which, in his view, the new science of society—sociology—rested. The progress of this undertaking over the past thirty years may be followed in a series of major works which include *The Social System* (1951), *Toward a General Theory of Action* (with Edward A. Shils and others, 1951), and *Economy and Society* (with Neil J. Smelser, 1956); and in several volumes of essays, the most recent being *Sociological Theory and Modern*

[1] Karl Löwith, *From Hegel to Nietzsche: The Revolution in 19th Century Thought* (New York, 1964).

[2] H. Stuart Hughes, *Consciousness and Society: The Reorientation of European Social Thought, 1890–1930* (New York, 1958).

[3] See, in particular, Raymond Aron, *Main Currents in Sociological Thought* (New York, 1965 and 1967), Vols. I and II; Robert A. Nisbet, *The Sociological Tradition* (New York, 1966).

[4] Parsons, *Societies: Evolutionary and Comparative Perspectives* (New York, 1966), Chapter 2.

Society (1967) and *Politics and Social Structure* (1969).[1] In the two volumes of 1951 Parsons first set out in a fully independent way his 'theory of action', and in the work of 1956 on the economic system he introduced some important modifications of it. He has recently summarised the leading ideas of this theory in the following way:

'Action consists of the structures and processes by which human beings form meaningful intentions and, more or less successfully, implement them in concrete situations. The word "meaningful" implies the symbolic or cultural level of representation and reference. Intentions and implementation taken together imply a disposition of the action system—individual or collective—to modify its relation to its situation or environment in an intended direction. . . . The classification of four highly general sub-systems of human action—the organism, personality, social system and cultural system—is an application of a general paradigm which can be used throughout the field of action. . . .

This paradigm analyses *any* action *system* in terms of the following four categories: (1) that concerned with the maintenance of the highest "governing" or controlling patterns of the system; (2) the internal integration of the system; (3) its orientation to the attainment of goals in relation to its environment; (4) its more generalised adaptation to the broad conditions of the environment—e.g., the non-action, physical environment.' (*Societies: Evolutionary and Comparative Perspectives*, pp. 5, 7.)

Parsons has never provided, so far as I know, a thorough analysis of the concept of 'action'; nor has he discussed the implications of this concept for the character of the explanations which may be possible, and should be sought, in sociology and other social sciences. His references, in the passage I have quoted, to 'meaningful intentions' and their implementation, and in *The Structure of Social Action* to 'normative orientations', or 'purpose', or the 'means-end schema', as being essential to the concept of action, suggest that he would align himself with those thinkers—ranging from the Hegelian Marxists (Marcuse) to the Marxist Existentialists (Sartre), the philosophical historians (Collingwood), and certain Wittgensteinians (Winch)—who reject the idea of a *science* of society and see the social studies as philosophical or historical disciplines.

[1] The contents of these two volumes overlap and some of the most important essays, which I shall discuss below, appear in both volumes.

But this is not the course which Parsons follows. In *The Structure of Social Action* his implicit argument (derived from Max Weber) seems to be that the theory of action occupies some middle ground between the positivist or natural science conception of sociology and the idealist view which emphasises the role of 'intuition' in the understanding of society; and he continues to argue from this position in a recent essay on Marx (in *Sociological Theory and Modern Society*). He does not, however, explore the nature of this middle ground, and the seeker after methodological enlightenment will have to turn elsewhere for an analysis of the concept of action; for instance, to the recent study by A. R. Louch, *Explanation and Human Action*, where ad hoc explanation of human *action* in particular contexts is opposed to attempts to subsume human *behaviour* under general laws, and some of Parsons's own generalisations are critically examined.

Adopting the notion of 'action', therefore, Parsons has devoted himself mainly to working out elaborate classifications of the types and structures of social action, in a language which is a genuinely original creation. The 'paradigm' set forth in the passage which I have quoted above is applied by Parsons to the social system in order to distinguish four sub-systems of society. The first sub-system is that which is formed by the institutions responsible for 'pattern-maintenance', or, in other words, for sustaining the general cultural values of a society; these are pre-eminently religious institutions. The second is that composed by the institutions concerned with 'integration', or the maintenance of differentiated norms and rules; these are primarily legal institutions—courts, the legal profession, the police. The third is the political system, which has responsibility for collective goal attainment (national interest or the destiny of a people?); and the fourth is the economy, which has the function of adaptation to the physical environment (i.e. production).

Each of these sub-systems, in turn, may be analysed with the help of the paradigm. The economy as a sub-system, for example, has four sub-sub-systems which are concerned with pattern-maintenance, integration, goal attainment, and adaptation within the economic sphere. The economic system is actually studied in this fashion in *Economy and Society* (Chapter IV), and Parsons's essays on political power and influence in *Sociological Theory and Modern Society* represent preliminary attempts to make a similar analysis of the political system. It is not clear to me how far this process of sub-division might eventually be carried, or with what results.

The 1950s, which saw the elaboration of these classificatory schemes, were a very productive period in Parsons's work, in which his influence began to be widely felt in both American and European sociology. Politically it was, of course, a conservative and uncreative period, dominated, especially in the United States, by the rigid attitudes and relationships of the Cold War, and by naive ideologies of economic growth and affluence, which found a somewhat more sophisticated expression in such writings as W. W. Rostow's *The Stages of Economic Growth* and J. K. Galbraith's *The Affluent Society*.

Parsons's sociology accorded well with this general state of mind. It posed no fundamental questions about the structure of American society, but provided a set of categories within which some of the elements of that structure could be neatly and intelligibly arranged. For example, in *The Social System* Parsons distinguishes a type of social structure which he calls the 'universalistic-achievement pattern', and he illustrates his description of this type by fitting various aspects of American society—occupational structure, the family, religious diversity, economic individualism—into the categories which he elaborates. In this way Parsons's conceptual scheme conveys a view of the society as a stable and enduring structure, while paying little attention to the factors of strain, conflict, and change which appear in it.

With the re-emergence everywhere, in the 1960s, of flux and uncertainty in social and political life, the interest in Parsons's theory has diminished, notwithstanding the effort he has made in recent writings to connect it more closely with the events and concerns of the present time. Young American sociologists seem to be turning to more radical sources for their ideas, while in Europe it is quite plainly the new versions of Marxism, the structuralism of Lévi-Strauss, ideas derived more immediately from the writings of the classical sociologists (above all, from Max Weber), and diverse philosophical criticisms of the social sciences, which now provide the intellectual setting in which the fundamental issues of sociological theory are posed and debated.

Even at the time when Parsons's ideas were being more widely discussed among sociologists they seem to have had curiously little impact upon broader social thought, or upon controversies about public policy. It is true that some American social scientists who were active in proclaiming the 'end of ideology' and in supporting the Congress for Cultural Freedom began to make reference to Parsons's sociology, and in one case (Edward Shils) became directly associated, for a short time, with Parsons's work.

Nevertheless, the idea of the 'end of the ideological age' seems to have originated in Europe, with Raymond Aron's attack upon Stalinism in *The Opium of the Intellectuals*,[1] and with the writings of Camus; and when the theme was taken up by American writers, particularly Daniel Bell and S. M. Lipset, its source was evidently not Parsons's social theory, but rather the disillusionment of these writers with their own earlier Marxist or socialist beliefs, reflecting, perhaps in an exaggerated form, a general malaise in radical thought. Parsons's ideas simply did not enter, as did the ideas of Weber and Durkheim, or of Veblen and Dewey in the United States, into the realm of general political discussion and policy making. On the contrary, they have tended to reflect in a passive way, and in a limited sphere of the social sciences, a mood which was already established in the society at large.

This intellectual isolation can be explained only in part by the difficulties which arise from Parsons's literary style, although what was said falsely of Condorcet may be said truly of him, that he 'writes with opium on a page of lead'. A deeper reason perhaps is that Parsons's work generally fails to arouse any intellectual excitement or sense of discovery, and this failure is certainly connected with the fact that much of what he actually says about social life, when expressed in ordinary language, proves to be commonplace. The point was made, publicly and irreverently, by C. Wright Mills in *The Sociological Imagination*, with the aid of some 'translations' of propositions taken from Parsons's 'grand theory'. It would be tedious to reproduce here, at length, the passages which Mills translates, but I will quote one paragraph by way of illustration. In *The Social System* (p. 41) Parsons writes:

'Attachment to common values means, motivationally considered, that the actors have common "sentiments" in support of the value patterns, which may be defined as meaning that conformity with the relevant expectations is treated as a "good thing" relatively independently of any specific instrumental "advantage" to be gained from such conformity, e.g. in the avoidance of negative sanctions. Furthermore, this attachment to common values, while it may fit the immediate gratificational needs of the actor, always has also a "moral" aspect in that to some degree this conformity defines the "responsibilities" of the actor in the wider, that is,

---

[1] See also his later reflections on the subject: Raymond Aron, *The Industrial Society* (New York, 1967), pp. 143–83.

social action systems in which he participates. Obviously the specific focus of responsibility is the collectivity which is constituted by a particular common value-orientation.'

Mills translates thus: 'When people share the same values, they tend to behave in accordance with the way they expect one another to behave. Moreover, they often treat such conformity as a very good thing—even when it seems to go against their immediate interests.' And he concludes: 'In a similar fashion, I suppose, one could translate the 555 pages of *The Social System* into about 150 pages of straightforward English. The result would not be very impressive.'

A. R. Louch, in his *Explanation and Human Action*, voices some similar conclusions even more sharply. He quotes from Parsons's essay 'General Theory in Sociology', published in R. K. Merton *et al.*, *Sociology Today* (1958), and comments:

'"The two main axes of differentiation . . . could also be identified in the generation and sex of the nuclear family." The roles of various members in the family can be talked about by reference to the internal–external axis, if we are organising the family by generations; to the instrumental–consummatory axis if we are thinking of differentiation by sex. I think this means that parents have authority over children, and that men tend to be the wage-earners. Once again, what's the news? Parsons's elaborate structure turns out to be a way of classifying the various interactions among individuals and groups, and any surprise arises only in that what we know already about human activities can be re-phrased in this terminology and classificatory system.'

This dressing-up of the dull and commonplace in pretentious language seems to me to result in some degree from Parsons's insensitivity to real social and political issues. In striking contrast with the thinkers whose ideas he set out originally to interpret— Marshall, Pareto, Durkheim, and Weber—he appears to have no sustained interest in political life and no great insight into its problems. Even when he embarks upon the study of an important political question, as he has done increasingly in the last few years, apparently in response to external pressures, his natural inclination is simply to restate, where possible according to his own conceptual scheme, some conventional and generally accepted judgements upon the subject.

There are several examples in his recent essays, but his paper on Negro Americans ('Full Citizenship for the Negro American?') shows this tendency particularly well. It was first published in 1965 and it formulates, in this instance with the help of ideas drawn from thinkers in another tradition (notably T. H. Marshall and Gunnar Myrdal) rather than from Parsons's own ideas, a view of the problem of Negro citizenship which was becoming widespread among American sociologists in the early days of the civil rights movement—a liberal view which saw Negroes merely as the last ethnic minority to qualify for the melting-pot and for complete inclusion in American society. In no way does Parsons contribute fresh insights into the history and conditions of Black Americans, or foresee the new directions which the Negro movement would take in the next few years; and his bland optimism about the resolution of a problem which he sees one-sidedly as a moral debate rather than a clash of interests now appears excessively naive.[1]

Another recent essay, on the universities and the student movement,[2] illustrates the same approach. Here, too, Parsons expounds a conventional view, describing the structure and development of American universities without even posing the question whether the crisis through which they are now passing does not call for fundamental reforms of their structure. In considering university government, for example, he distinguishes four principal elements in it—trustees, administrations, faculties, students—and likens their interrelations to the separation of powers in the governmental sphere (but without any attempt to show that the analogy makes sense). He goes on to argue that 'administrations and trustees must clearly have certain kinds of authority over both faculty and students', although this authority 'is (or should be) limited by the academic freedom of the other two groups'. But what are the grounds for asserting that administrators and trustees (especially the latter) should have any such authority in the university? What, indeed, is the case for having trustees at all?

Parsons does not argue these points, and it is all too evident

[1] Two earlier essays on 'Democracy and Social Structure in Pre-Nazi Germany' and 'Some Sociological Aspects of the Fascist Movements' (reprinted in *Politics and Social Structure*) can be assessed in a similar way. Parsons did not analyse the rise of Fascism, and the consolidation of its power, at the time when these events were taking place. He published his essays in 1942, when the ideas which he formulated had already become common currency. For this sociology, as for Hegel's philosophy, the owl of Minerva spreads its wings only with the falling of the dusk.

[2] 'The Academic System: A Sociologist's View', *The Public Interest*, No. 13 (Fall, 1968).

that they simply do not occur to him. Thus, at a time when one of the most explosive issues on American campuses is precisely that of the power (frequently seen as arbitrary and irresponsible) concentrated in the hands of trustees or regents, Parsons accepts uncritically the present structure of American universities and offers no more than a descriptive account of the traditional arrangements.

The propensity, in Parsons's approach to the study of social and political issues, to regard the present structure of American society as unalterable, or as at most capable of a gradual development along a very narrowly circumscribed path, does not arise solely, or in any simple fashion, from a conservative ideology. It has its source also in Parsons's specific conception of the nature of sociological theory, which was present in his work from the beginning, and which is clearly expressed in the opening pages of *The Social System*:

'The subject of this volume is the exposition and illustration of a conceptual scheme for the analysis of social systems in terms of the action frame of reference. It is intended as a theoretical work in a strict sense. Its direct concern will be neither with empirical generalisation as such nor with methodology, though of course it will contain a considerable amount of both. Naturally the value of the conceptual scheme here put forward is ultimately to be tested in terms of its usefulness in empirical research. But this is not an attempt to set forth a systematic account of our empirical knowledge, as would be necessary in a work on general sociology. The focus is on a theoretical scheme. The systematic treatment of its empirical uses will have to be undertaken separately.'

Parsons, therefore, excludes from the domain of theory 'in a strict sense' two elements which have usually been regarded, on the contrary, as vital in all theoretical sociology. The first of these is the attempt to formulate empirical generalisations and to establish systematic connections between them. In the history of sociological thought such attempts have been made in various ways. They have arisen in some cases from the direct confrontation with a puzzling social phenomenon or event, which provokes a search for some explanation. The phenomenon may either be one which has not hitherto attracted much attention (until its significance is revealed by the imaginative powers of a creative thinker), or it may be something genuinely new and distinctive in social life. Marx's attempt to explain the French Revolution and the rise of socialist movements belongs to this last category. In other cases it is the dissatisfaction with the generalisations or explanatory schemes of earlier thinkers which gives rise to new theories; as when Max Weber embarked upon a revision of the Marxist theory of the origins of capitalism, or when Durkheim proposed a sociological explanation of suicide in opposition to the diverse explanations (psychological and other) which were current at the end of the nineteenth century.

There is a common feature in all these cases; namely, that a problem is seen and formulated, and an explanation is proposed which will resolve it. In Parsons's work it is just this focus of attention which is lacking from the outset, since in his original interpretation of the classical sociologists he disregards the question of the validity of their explanations in order to concentrate upon the nature of the concepts which they employ.

In his most recent studies of social issues he follows a similar course by presenting a descriptive classification of the phenomena within a particular field, or an analysis of the concepts used in that field, rather than an explanation of events in relation to a clearly stated problem. I have already illustrated this last point from the essays on the American Negro and the American University, but another very striking example is to be found in the essay 'On the Concept of Political Power' (in *Sociological Theory and Modern Society*). This essay is devoted entirely to conceptual analysis, clarification, and revision, and it excludes rigorously any attempt to explain political events. After developing an analogy between 'money' and 'power', Parsons refers to phenomena which he calls 'power inflation' and 'power deflation'. His descriptions of these phenomena suggest weaknesses in his analogy, particularly since the conditions associated with power *deflation* seem to resemble those associated with currency *inflation*.[1] But it is more important here to note that he offers no indication at all of the possible causes of these political fluctuations. Thus he describes McCarthyism as a 'deflationary spiral in the political field', but he does not explain what caused this spiral. In the end, therefore, we understand McCarthyism no better than we did before; we simply have a new name for it.

[1] That is, according to Parsons, power deflation undermines 'the essential basis of trust on which the influence of many elements bearing formal and informal leadership responsibilities, and which in turn sustained "power-credit", necessarily rested.' [p. 343]. See, for a more comprehensive criticism of Parson's concept the essay by Anthony Giddens, '"Power" in the Recent Writings of Talcott Parsons', *Sociology*, 2 (3) (September 1968).

The second element which Parsons excludes from his view of theory is 'methodology', or the logic of the subject. This, it is true, does not belong strictly in the sphere of theory, but in that of meta-theory, inasmuch as it comprises reflection upon the character and status of sociological propositions and theories themselves. Nevertheless, the nature of sociology and its subject matter has always made unfruitful a complete separation between the two spheres. To be continually aware of the peculiar difficulties encountered by any attempt to explain social action, behaviour, or events is, in effect, to be a better, a more subtle, theorist. The fact is witnessed by the work of the major sociological thinkers from Marx to Durkheim, not one of whom elaborated his social theory without analysing, at the same time, its foundations and its formal structure.

All of them raised in some fashion a fundamental question (which has assumed great importance again in present controversies) about the status and limits of generalisation and causal explanation in sociology; and on the other side, about the nature, the reliability, and the value of an intuitive and imaginative comprehension of social life, such as one finds, for example, in Tocqueville's *Democracy in America*, or in Max Weber's *The Protestant Ethic and the Spirit of Capitalism*, or in the naturalistic novel and the novel of social criticism—for example, in Zola's *Germinal*, or in Dos Passos's USA. They raised, too, a series of more or less closely related questions about the validity of universal as against historical categories (or analytical as against dialectical reason) in social theory, and about objectivity and ideology.

Parsons has adhered firmly to his own rule in not dealing at any length, or in any systematic way, with such problems. Thus, although he often refers to positivism, it is always in the sense in which positivism is associated with utilitarianism as a conceptual scheme based upon the idea of individual rational action; not in the sense in which positivism, as a philosophy of science which affirms the appropriateness of causal explanation in the social sciences, can be opposed to another philosophy of science which asserts that social phenomena have to be related to one another and understood in a non-causal way (for example, by the operation of *Verstehen* or 'comprehension of meaning', as Dilthey and Max Weber described it).

Again, as I noted earlier, although Parsons expounds his concept of 'action' as involving 'meaningful intentions' in such a way as to appear to range himself against the positivists and behaviourists, and on the side of those who believe that the social sciences depend upon a distinctive type of knowledge and understanding, he still employs causal language on many occasions, and he has not thought it necessary to give an extended account of his views or methods. It is evident that his own theoretical 'goal-orientation' would have become a good deal clearer had he undertaken, at some stage, to examine the logical foundations of his theory.

Renouncing on one side empirical generalisation and on the other side methodological inquiry, Parsons confines himself largely to the analysis and classification of concepts; that is to say he works in a sphere which is, according to R. B. Braithwaite and others, characteristic of sciences at an early stage of their development, in which theory involves no more than classifying the phenomena with which the subject deals, mapping out the problem area, defining rules of procedure and schemes of interpretation. But this limitation seems unnecessary and undesirable in a subject which has advanced beyond this early stage, at least in the sense that the classical sociologists themselves put forward explanatory generalisations and theories which we can accept, correct, refute, or discard, according to our view of the empirical evidence and of the proper mode of explanation in sociology, but which we must in any case confront.

It should be said that on a few occasions Parsons has not restricted himself entirely to conceptual analysis, and from this point of view it is instructive to compare his essay on Marx with his essays on Durkheim and Weber in *Sociological Theory and Modern Society*. In discussing Durkheim and Weber he is chiefly concerned with their conceptual schemes, along the lines of his earlier work on the alleged revolution in thought which produced the idea of 'social action', but in examining Marx's thought (for the first time at any length) he devotes only a brief space to defining Marx's place in the intellectual movement which led from the two streams of utilitarian positivism and German idealism to modern sociology, and concentrates instead upon criticising Marx's explanatory generalisations. This difference in treatment seems to me to arise from the fact that while Parsons finds the explanations put forward by Durkheim and Weber ideologically acceptable, Marx's explanations are distasteful and so call for refutation. It should be added that Parsons does not independently refute them in his essay; he only summarises various criticisms of Marx's theory which are by now very familiar, and he does not present them in a way that shows how they could have derived from an alternative theory of his own.

It is only with respect to his preference for regarding society from the point of view of its normative elements or 'cultural codes'—such as religious and moral beliefs—rather than material interests, in the determination of action, that Parsons clearly establishes his opposition to Marx. The most important point of criticism, he says, is 'the untenability of Marx's attempt to rule the ideal and normative factors out of 'basic' significance in the determination of social process'. Parsons states this view again in *Societies: Evolutionary and Comparative Perspectives*, where he asserts, first, that no 'single-factor' theory of social development is acceptable, then goes on to say that 'this elementary truth does not, however, preclude the hierarchical ordering of the factors', and concludes: 'I believe that, within the social system, the normative elements are more important for social change than the "material interests" of the constitutive units.'

Thus Parsons asserts, just like Marx, the primacy of certain elements in social life, but unlike Marx, who set out to demonstrate empirically that profound changes in European society had resulted from changes in the mode of production, from the rise of new classes, and from class conflicts, Parsons does not consider it necessary to bring any evidence in support of his own belief that normative elements are more important. Elsewhere in the same work, in discussing the general course of social development, he refers to a 'tendency of societies to differentiate into four *primary* sub-systems' (the sub-systems of his model which I discussed above), but he does not even raise the question of the causes of such a tendency, let alone demonstrate that, if it exists, it is in any way dependent upon the supposed pre-eminence of normative elements in social life.

Parsons's work is dominated by this belief in the primary influence of values and norms (especially religious values) as against 'interests'. In his analysis of the concept of power, for example, he opposes what games theorists call the 'zero-sum' conception (particularly as it was used by C. Wright Mills in *The Power Elite*), according to which the power of some men involves the powerlessness of others, because this view implies the existence of divided interests and conflict in a society. He chooses to define power as the 'capacity of a social system to get things done in its collective interest'; this puts the emphasis upon an overriding collective interest, and upon the *integration* of the system through common values, while playing down any discordant interests or internal conflict.

This is just as one-sided a view as that of Marx, and perhaps even more one-sided, since Marx acknowledged the strength of the unifying forces in society which arose from the influence of 'ruling ideas', whereas Parsons will not admit the notion of 'power over others' (that is, the existence of ruling and subject groups) at all. Apart from the fact that Parsons's concept of power seems even plausible only in the case of democratic societies (not, surely, in the case of dictatorships or colonial regimes), and so cannot be universally employed, there is a more serious objection to the manner in which this definition is set up against others. How do we decide between definitions? Only by seeing how they work in explaining events, or in understanding a situation. Parsons, however, relates his concept of power only to other concepts in his general analysis of society. Where Weber and Mills, for example, used the concept of power, as they defined it, to explore and explain real political processes—the development of bureaucracy, the growth of modern political parties, the creation of a power elite—Parsons turns endlessly in a circle of concepts and analogies. Until such time as his concept of power has been tried out, let us say in studies of the formation of new nations, of twentieth-century revolutions, of the Black Power movement, its value cannot be determined.

Most sociologists, I think, have found it extraordinarily difficult to deal with Parsons's thought, even when they have penetrated the obscurity of the language. The repetitive conceptual explorations, the elaborate classifications which formulate in other terms elementary distinctions which have long been made between economic, political, religious, and other institutions, do not seem to lead in a definite direction, toward explaining the crucial forces at work in modern society. What is most obviously lacking is a focus, a constellation of problems, around which sociological theory might be constructed, as it has been constructed by others who have directed their thought to the problems of class and inequality, science and industrialism, rationalism and bureaucracy.

Parsons's general ideas convey a profoundly conservative outlook in which belief in stability, integration, order, and the determining influence of religious values, plays a large part. But even this is not an active conservatism such as might lead to a distinctive interpretation of the dangers and opportunities which confront men, individually and collectively, in the modern world. It is a detached, diffuse, unexamined, and undeclared conservative predisposition which reveals itself more in Parsons's whole approach to the subject than in any empirical statements about actual societies.[1] The very concept of 'human action', which others have seen as implying a 'project'—that is, a perpetual tension in human affairs between an existing situation and a future possibility—is devitalised by Parsons; and action just as it appears in a moment of time, without any orientation to the future, lies embalmed in a classification of the types of social action.

Nowhere is this remoteness from the real world of action more evident than in *Sociological Theory and Modern Society*. One of the oddest characteristics of the book is that it does not seem to be about modern society at all, in any serious way. Science, industry, population growth, starvation, revolution, race prejudice and conflict, nuclear war, are either not mentioned at all or get only the most fleeting attention. The events and issues which agitate, confuse, infuriate, or frighten men in present-day society, which engender revolt and repression, are left out of account, and the sociologist's contribution to practical wisdom and understanding is reduced to such fatuous proposals as that '... every effort be made to promulgate carefully considered statements of value commitments which may provide a basis for consensus among both have and have-not nations'.[2] How is it possible to discover a vital interest and concern, a clear direction, in thought which is so wilfully irrelevant?

[1] Parsons's outlook on particular social problems is often liberal, though never radical; but in these cases it usually results from having adopted some other thinker's definition of the situation.

[2] *Sociological Theory and Modern Society* (New York, 1967), p. 475.

Chapter 3

The Crisis in Sociology[1]

The 'new sociology' was proclaimed some years ago. Growing mainly out of the work of C. Wright Mills it was connected, through him, with the doctrines and movements of the New Left in the later 1950s and early 1960s. But just as the New Left grew old quite quickly and was supplanted by still newer movements so also the new sociology, without ever having established itself properly as a distinct style of social thought, has been pushed aside by yet more recent attempts to give the discipline a fresh orientation. In less than a decade we have had 'critical sociology', 'radical sociology', and such innovations, less closely tied to political commitments, as ethnomethodology and structuralism—not to speak of the Sociology Liberation Movement, which is perhaps more a mode of feeling than of thinking. Now Alvin Gouldner offers us yet another diversion in the shape of 'reflexive sociology', or the sociologist contemplating his own navel.[2]

This proliferation and rapid circulation of doctrines can easily be taken as the sign of an intellectual crisis, accompanying a crisis in social life which manifests itself in diverse movements of protest and opposition and in sporadic rebellions. The nature of such a situation is well described by Norman Birnbaum in an essay on the crisis in Marxist sociology:

'A doctrinal or theoretic crisis in a system of thought occurs when either of two sets of abstract conditions obtains. In one case the possibilities of internal development of a system exhaust themselves; the system's categories become incapable of transformation; the discussion generated by the system becomes scholastic, in the pejorative sense of the term. In the other case the realities apprehended by the system in its original form change, so much so that the categories are inapplicable to new conditions. It is clear

[1] Reprinted, with minor revisions, from the *New York Review of Books* XVI (4) (11 March 1971).

[2] Alvin Gouldner, *The Coming Crisis of Western Sociology* (New York, 1970).

that these two sets of conditions often obtain simultaneously; particularly for systems dealing with the historical movement of society, the two sets of conditions of crisis are often quite irseparable.'[1]

Sociology has quite frequently experienced crises of this kind. Considering only its recent history we can see how the 'progressive' sociology of the 1930s (represented by the work of Robert Lynd, for example, and of some Marxist writers) lost much of its vigour and relevance with the end of the economic depression, the outbreak of war, and the postwar reconstruction in which political debate and public policy in most Western countries came to be dominated by ideas of economic growth in the domestic sphere, and of conflict between democracy and totalitarianism in world affairs. Similarly, the postwar 'conservative' sociology (of such writers as Parsons, Lipset, Bell, Shils and Aron), which grew largely out of these changed conditions, began to lose its ability to interpret social events in a convincing manner when new cultural and political movements appeared which challenged or forsook established ways of life in many industrial countries.

The turmoil through which we have lived, at least from 1956 to 1968, makes it seem rather odd that Gouldner should write about a *coming* crisis in sociology. One way of interpreting this idea that the crisis lies in the future is to suppose that Gouldner is referring to a time when the prevailing schools of sociology will be confronted by a well-articulated alternative theory of society, based (as he suggests) upon a new 'structure of sentiments' and new 'domain assumptions'.[2] But the emergence of such a theory would be much more a resolution than a precipitation of an intellectual crisis. New ideas would then direct sociological inquiry, a new agreement about significant problems would be established, and some of the controversies which still rage— about social stability and change, about consensus and conflict— might cheerfully be forgotten or consigned to the history of the subject.

[1] In Hans Peter Dreitzel (ed.), *Recent Sociology, No. 1* (New York, 1969).

[2] 'Domain assumptions' seem to correspond closely with what Kuhn and others have called a 'paradigm'; namely, the constellation of values and beliefs shared by the members of a scientific community that determines the choice of problems which are regarded as significant and the approaches to be adopted in attempting to solve them. It is evident that 'domain assumptions' or 'paradigms', in this sense, are necessarily linked with, or include, a 'structure of sentiments'.

An essential element in Gouldner's conception of an approaching crisis is his portrayal of the present state of affairs as one in which two established schools of thought—functionalism and Marxism—continue to dominate social theory and are only just beginning to be challenged. A large part of his book is devoted to a critical examination of Talcott Parsons's theoretical system, on the grounds that American sociology can be equated with functionalism, and functionalism in turn with Parsons's theory. The attention which he gives to this theory may well seem excessive; first, because he does not really advance beyond the criticisms which have been levelled against it for some time now; and secondly, because it is very doubtful (and Gouldner does not demonstrate in any way) that functionalism, and more particularly Parsons's version of it, has enjoyed such a commanding position during the last decade even in American sociology, while in Europe it never achieved pre-eminence at all.

Marxism, as the rival sociological system, is discussed very briefly and inadequately, and its development is presented in a somewhat misleading way. Gouldner acknowledges that Marxism was, from the beginning, a major oppositional current *within* Western sociology, but he does not examine the theoretical controversies which this opposition engendered, and still engenders; instead, he reaches the conclusion that Marxism and functionalism now confront each other, geographically demarcated, on a world scale—the one embodied in Soviet sociology, the other in American sociology—in a conflict which is only mitigated by mutual borrowing and adaptation.

This may have a limited political sense. Paraphrasing Marx we might say that the ruling ideas in the world are the ideas of the ruling powers; and that the two super-powers confront each other ideologically armed with super-sociologies. But this fact is connected only in an indirect and complicated way with the state of sociological thought. In order to establish his neat contrast between Western and non-Western sociology Gouldner, having made Parsons the standard bearer of Western sociology, has to identify Marxism with Soviet Marxism, to present it as a unified, coherent and dominant theory, and to ignore the long-standing crisis in Marxist thought. Against this view it needs to be observed that Marxist *thought* has flourished principally outside the USSR, in France, Germany, Italy, Yugoslavia, and perhaps in China; that it has assumed diverse, much revised, and tentative forms; and that the intellectual debate about the nature of Marxism as a theory of society has already affected Marxism as a political creed, even in the USSR and quite evidently in other countries of Eastern Europe. Furthermore, Marxist ideas (though *not* Soviet Marxism) now have a greater influence in Western sociology than they have had for many decades. As Dreitzel notes in the introduction to his book, there has emerged '... a new readiness to utilise the Marxist point of view'; not in the sense of accepting *the* Marxist theory of society, but in the sense of using various ideas, diversely interpreted, which stem from Marxism, in order to raise new problems or to criticise other approaches.

There is another sense, however, in which a crisis may be approaching which brings into question not a particular version of sociology but sociology itself. As Robert Nisbet observed in *The Sociological Tradition* sociology was formed in the crisis of the transition to an industrial capitalist society in the European countries. Its distinctive array of problems and ideas was formed in the period from the 1830s to the end of the nineteenth century, when the urban, democratic, industrial, bureaucratic, secular societies in which we now live were being created; and it may be argued, as Nisbet does, that we continue to see the social world through the medium of these ideas. From this point of view the changes in sociological thought between the 1930s and the end of the 1950s appear as variations upon a theme. The radical sociology of the 1930s, especially in its Marxist form, was largely derivative; it made use of traditional ideas, often very crudely under Stalinist influence, and it produced no original thought such as had appeared earlier in the century, at the peak of the European revolutionary movement, in the writings of Lenin, Rosa Luxemburg, Lukács, Gramsci, and the Austro-Marxists. The conservative sociology which succeeded it was equally derivative; in one of its manifestations, the theoretical system of Talcott Parsons, it was to a large extent a summation, in a particularly arid and scholastic form, of the most conservative elements in the thought of the classical sociologists; emphasising, for example, Max Weber's 'types of social action' and his characterisation of capitalism rather than his theory of historical change, and giving prominence to Pareto's concept of social equilibrium while virtually ignoring Marx.

The rapid and profound transformation of economic and social structure which has been going on in the industrial countries since the war, and the cultural and political movements of opposition to which it has given rise, pose the question of whether we are now involved in a major change from one form of human society to another, comparable in its extent and significance with

the first transition from agrarian to industrial society. The possibility of such a fundamental change seems to underlie much of
the recent self-questioning among sociologists. Gouldner refers
to it when he writes of the changing structure of sentiments,
especially in the younger generation, and its implications; and
the same phenomenon is discussed from a different aspect by
Reinhard Bendix at several points in his recent collection of
essays.[1] Bendix accepts that the general orientation of sociology
is strongly affected by currents of thought and feeling in society
at large, and he quotes approvingly Max Weber's observation
that 'At some time the colour changes: men become uncertain
about the significance of the viewpoints which they have used
unreflectively. The path becomes lost in the dusk. The light of the
great problems of culture has passed on. Then science also
prepares to change its standpoint and its conceptual apparatus
in order to look down from the heights of thought upon the current of events.'

Unlike Weber, however, Bendix fears that it is science itself,
the embodiment of reason in modern societies, which is now being
rejected. That the fear has some justification is indicated by the
marked hostility to technology which has developed in some
social groups in the industrial countries, and by some of the new
attitudes within sociology itself which instead of finding virtue
in its 'scientific' character, as was usual not very long ago, now
reject its aim to become an empirical and positive science. But
the fear is also exaggerated. Romanticism itself—a new wave of
imagination and feeling—ends in thought and theories, and the
present-day cultural movements seem more likely to give a new
direction to sociology than to overthrow it altogether. To some
extent, indeed, these movements can already be comprehended
with the aid of existing sociological concepts. Max Weber foresaw
a growing 'disenchantment of the world' in the Western societies
as a consequence of the increasing rationalisation and bureaucratic regulation of social life; and the movements of revolt or
withdrawal with which we are now familiar can be seen as attempts
to recreate the 'poetry of life' by reviving, in highly organised
industrial societies, types of social relationship in which spon-
taneity, involvement and personal affection are predominant.

It is still possible, however, that some new intellectual synthesis
will prove more capable of interpreting these changes, and that

[1] Reinhard Bendix, *Embattled Reason: Essays on Social Knowledge* (New
York, 1970).

the map of knowledge will once again be redrawn. Something of the kind is suggested by W. G. Runciman's volume of essays,[1] even though it appears at first glance to be remote from any concern with a crisis, either intellectual or social, and to be mainly the product of a perfectly disinterested intellectual curiosity. Nevertheless, Runciman's desire to put sociology in its place, is affected, I think, by two external influences. One, which he discusses briefly, is the present confused state of the subject, in which he can find neither a distinctive method nor a distinctive content. The other, it seems to me, is the fact that sociology, in spite of this internal diversity and discord, has acquired in recent years a greatly enhanced intellectual importance, not least as one of the principal sources of social criticism. In some respects sociology appears now to occupy the place which was held earlier by political economy, as the social science to which the crucial issues of the age need to be referred for analysis and interpretation.

Runciman's argument against the autonomous existence of sociology as a science of society runs as follows: sociology, like history and anthropology, is not capable of producing general laws, and this incapacity arises from the fact that 'there are not and cannot be laws of social systems as such'. The genuine science of man upon which sociology depends is psychology, and sociology can most appropriately be regarded (as Freud also argued) as applied psychology, though Runciman adds that it is psychology *plus* social history. The specialised social sciences such as economics, demography and political science, on the other hand, although they too depend upon psychology, can produce laws in a 'loose' sense (because they deal with a more restricted range of phenomena), and thus they occupy an intermediate position, between psychology and sociology, in the hierarchy of the social sciences.

In considering this argument we have first of all to put aside the very general question of whether any kind of causal explanation of human action is possible or adequate, for if it is not—if some other sort of knowledge and explanation is required—then the inability of sociology to produce general laws will not distinguish it from any other of the human sciences. But without entering upon this problem it may be pointed out that psychology which, according to Runciman, is to provide the foundation of

[1] W. G. Runciman, *Sociology in its Place and Other Essays* (Cambridge, 1970).

the whole explanatory edifice, has itself (as he concedes) produced few, if any, significant general laws. In this situation we can scarcely be confident that a recourse to psychology is going to lead to more rigorous and satisfying explanations of social behaviour; and we may decide, in the words of Alfred Marshall when he was considering the possible incorporation of economics into a more general social science, that for the time being 'we must do what we can with our present resources'.

Runciman supports his contention that there can be no 'laws of social systems' by two arguments. One is to the effect that explanations of the workings of social systems are reducible to psychological explanations.

'To explain the origins and workings of social systems is to explain the thoughts and actions of men. Such explanations, to be sure, will depend to a large degree on the properties of those social systems of which the individual is a member. . . . But once again, whether the properties of social systems are taken as the dependent or the independent variable, when we are talking of the properties of social systems . . . we are talking of what individual human beings may be shown to think, say and do.'

What Runciman does not show is how this reduction might be carried out or attempted in particular cases, and of course he is not able to relate specific sociological explanations to psychological laws because the latter are not available. The difficulties which such reductions present may be indicated by some examples. Simmel, in an essay on 'the number of members as determining the sociological form of the group' discussed some properties of social systems which appear to depend strictly upon the size of these systems; and in another study, of social conflict, he formulated some general propositions about the effects of conflict upon the structure of social groups. It is hard to see how statements of this kind could be translated into psychological statements, at least without some loss of explanatory power, or in what way they are derivable from psychological 'laws'.

The second argument which Runciman deploys to show that 'laws of social systems' are unattainable is that the number of variables to be taken into account is too great. Here he follows the well-known discussion by J. S. Mill which concludes that 'the mode of production of all social phenomena is one great case of intermixture of laws'. But this judgement is more widely applicable, for we might say that one of the principal reasons for the immense difficulty which all the human sciences, including psychology, experience in formulating any worthwhile generalisations is that the number of variables with which they have to deal is so large. It is not clear that there is a fundamental difference in this respect between psychology as a science of mental systems and sociology as a science of social systems.

The inconclusiveness of Runciman's arguments can be shown in other ways. In the first place, he is not entirely consistent in his treatment of sociological theory. While he claims in the title essay that there are and can be no distinctive sociological theories, he seems to assume elsewhere that there are such theories and that some are better than others. Thus he concludes an essay on structuralism by saying that it 'should not be claimed to constitute a novel, coherent and comprehensive paradigm for sociological and anthropological theory'; and in an essay on 'Class, Status and Power' he writes: 'Whether there will ever be a general theory of stratification is of course a further question. But if there will, it follows from the validity of the three-dimensional distinction that any general theory will have to be expressible in terms of it.' Nowhere does he suggest that the quest for such a theory, or for a comprehensive paradigm, is an illegitimate or vain activity.

Secondly, his tenderness (in the title essay) toward the specialised social sciences, and his harshness toward sociology, in respect of their ability to produce laws, seems to arise partly from a misunderstanding. When he writes, for example, of 'demographers generalising about birth-rates', he can only be referring to generalisations which are in fact *sociological*; which relate birth-rates to other social phenomena (such as the social position of women, or the relative importance of the family as a productive unit) and explain them, however tentatively or inadequately, by reference to the properties of a whole social system (for example, by distinguishing between agrarian and industrial societies).

At the end of his title essay Runciman sums up his view of sociology in terms which, contrary to his own judgement of its position, can be regarded as justifying its existence as a distinctive science. After asserting again that it cannot be an autonomous subject he continues '. . . however useful the particular discoveries, descriptive generalisations or ideographic explanations which may be achieved under its name'. In the absence of significant laws produced by any of the human sciences it is just these particular discoveries and generalisations, and in a broader way its models of social structure, which have made sociology an important science and have steadily increased its influence upon the specialised social sciences over the past hundred years.

If sociology now appears to be going through a crisis this is not because it has failed to produce high-level laws but because many of its descriptive generalisations, models and interpretations no longer seem adequate; either they have exhausted their capacity to provoke new discoveries, or the social reality to which they are applied has changed so profoundly that they no longer seem relevant. At various points in his book Runciman offers interesting reflections upon the the relations between sociology, anthropology and history. Clearly he favours a *rapprochement* between them, as well as a closer link with what he calls at one point a 'more sophisticated psychological theory'; but he does not go so far as to suggest what form a new social theory built up along these lines might take, and he is not much concerned with the question of how such a theory would be related to the new social and cultural phenomena of the present time.

In this respect, however, his work is not very different from that of some other writers considered here. Gouldner devotes an exceedingly small part of his book to a discussion of the possible future development of sociology, and the 'reflexive sociology' which he sketches is not very inspiring. On one side it seems to echo faintly Karl Mannheim's sociology of the intellectuals in the 1920s, without its philosophical concerns, while on the other side it offers some moral injunctions to guide the life and work of the sociologist as a political radical. What it deliberately does not do, thus neglecting the most important matter, is to propose new subjects of study and new directing ideas. In the end it achieves the opposite of what Wright Mills advocated at the beginning of the radical revival: instead of turning personal troubles into public issues it turns public issues into personal troubles, by exhorting the sociologist to give his attention, narcissistically, to the problem of the relationship between being a sociologist and being a person, and to worry about his relation to his work. I do not believe that such preoccupations have ever inspired a critical analysis of society, or ever will. They are a symptom of intellectual malaise, not a remedy.

Bendix on the other hand, is mainly concerned with a defence of tradition—the Western tradition of reason and science— against what he sees as the waves of emotion which threaten to overwhelm it; in his view 'the question is whether under these circumstances the impulse behind inquiry, the belief in progress through knowledge, can remain vigorous enough'. He too does not seriously attempt to find a new path, to change the standpoint of social science itself, in order to take account of the new problems and sensibilities.

Only in Dreitzel's volume is there some indication of new directions. The essays collected here differ greatly in subject matter and approach from what might have been brought together a decade ago: they deal not with 'stable democracy' but with the experiences and potentialities of 'participatory democracy'; not with status and mobility but with the relations between classes and the rise of new classes as forces in political struggles; not with political institutions and voting behaviour but with the emergence of movements of social protest. As Dreitzel points out in his introduction the essays show a readiness to draw upon Marxist ideas and also a conception of sociology as a 'science of social crisis', as it undoubtedly was in its origins.

These new subjects are still very far from having been integrated in a general view of the present social transformation, and it remains an open question whether that will be accomplished. The most promising attempt so far to provide a general framework (and it is one to which Dreitzel alludes briefly, though in a critical vein) is perhaps the conception of 'post-industrial society', as it has been outlined, in one form, by Alain Touraine:[1] that is to say, the idea of an emerging form of society in which the progress of science would make possible the elimination of scarcity in the sphere of vital human needs and the transfer of industrial work increasingly from men to machines, thereby transforming the class system and altering the balance between work and leisure in social life; but in which at the same time the problems which arise from centralised and bureaucratic regulation, and from the dominance of a purely technological outlook, are exacerbated and provoke new kinds of social conflict, already foreshadowed by the rise of the student movement. If this conception can be fruitfully elaborated it may come to occupy the central place which the notion of industrial capitalism as a social system had in nineteenth-century sociology; and there may follow a genuine revival of sociological thought in its most worthwhile form, as a systematic reflection upon the trends of social development in present-day societies and upon the political choices which they pose.

[1] *The Post-Industrial Society* (New York, 1971). Some similar issues are raised in Norman Birnbaum, *The Crisis of Industrial Society* (New York, 1969). See Chapter 6 below.

POSTSCRIPT

Since this essay was first published Alvin Gouldner has replied to some of the critics of his 'reflexive sociology', but without understanding the main point of the criticism. His own position, he now says, '... is that every society is a social reality in part constituted by a kind of everyday social theory, and that therefore the critique of society and of theory are inseparable. This was exactly Marx's supposition, too, as evidenced by the fact that his critique of modern society, *Capital*, is also subtitled *A Critique of Political Economy*—which is to say, of economic *theory*.'[1] But this is not at all what Gouldner was arguing earlier, when he placed at the centre of his conception of 'reflexive sociology' the '*transformation* of the sociologist's self', and the '*relationship* ... between being a sociologist and being a person'.[2] Marx, however, far from indulging in such introspective brooding, set out to study the *objective* development of nineteenth-century capitalism, and the equally *objective* ideology of capitalist society as it revealed itself in the everyday 'fetishism of commodities' or in the more sophisticated theories of classical political economy. Marx's effort to construct a rigorous and realistic theory of modern society is at the opposite pole from Gouldner's romantic subjectivism which dismisses as unimportant both the substance and the method of any sociological theory, and leaves us with only personal 'visions'.[3]

[1] Alvin Gouldner, *For Sociology: Renewal and Critique in Sociology Today* (London, 1973), p. 84.

[2] Gouldner (1970), op. cit., p. 495.

[3] Ibid., p. 495.

Chapter 4

Capitalism, Socialism and Development

An atmosphere of gloom and uncertainty has descended upon development studies in the last few years. The end of the first United Nations 'development decade' was marked by a spate of reports,[1] which were provoked to a large extent by a widespread sense of failure. Nevertheless, most of these reports expressed a mildly optimistic view of the prospects for development in the next decade, although they were noticeably restrained and critical by comparison with the enthusiastic outlook which prevailed in the 1950s.

In the immediate postwar period, when the notion of 'under-developed' or 'developing' countries first became firmly established in the social sciences and in international politics, the problems of development were conceived for the most part in relatively simple economic terms. Two factors, especially, encouraged such an outlook. The experience of sustained economic growth in the Western industrial countries, in contrast with the prewar depression, created by the mid-1950s a belief that economic problems had been largely solved, at least in part through the adoption of Keynesian policies. This belief found expression, in due course, in such works as J. K. Galbraith's *The Affluent Society*

---

[1] Three major reports are: the Peterson Report, *U.S. Foreign Assistance in the 1970s: A New Approach*, Report to the President from the Task Force on International Development (Washington, D.C., 1970); the Jackson Report, *A Study of the Capacity of the United Nations Development System* (2 vols.), A Report to the UNDP Administration by R. G. A. Jackson (Geneva, 1969); and the Pearson Report, *Partners in Development*, Report of the World Bank Commission on International Development (New York, 1969). A much more critical report is that prepared by the Latin American countries, the *Viña del Mar Report*, Latin American Special Co-ordinating Commission (Viña del Mar, Chile, 1969). These and other reports are analysed, from quite different perspectives, in recent studies by Denis Goulet and Michael Hudson, *The Myth of Aid* (New York, 1971), pp. 13–64, and by Robert E. Hunter and John E. Rielly (eds), *Development Today* (New York, 1972), pp. 61–79.

and W. W. Rostow's *The Stages of Economic Growth.* So far as
the developing countries were concerned the implication was that
they could relatively quickly overcome their economic backward-
ness by the deliberate injection of capital and technology, facilitated by international aid.

Secondly, confidence in the efficacy of foreign aid was stimulated by the success of the Marshall Plan in achieving a rapid
reconstruction of the West European economies. But as Tibor
Mende has indicated, the Marshall Plan 'involved the rehabilita-
tion of modern and highly productive societies temporarily
damaged by war. These possessed the techniques, the organisational ability, and the human resources needed to re-establish their
prewar prosperity.'[1] Most of the developing countries were in
quite a different situation; hence the Marshall Plan became in
some measure a misleading model for the development of mainly
agrarian countries through foreign aid, and helped to concentrate
the attention of development agencies and advisers upon purely
economic questions while the social, political and cultural contexts of development were neglected.[2]

Of course, the broader aspects of development were not wholly
ignored. As Mende has noted a group of experts appointed by
the Secretary-General of the United Nations to work out in detail
the intentions of the UN Charter emphasised strongly in their
report, in 1950, the structural prerequisites of development; but
in the following two decades the quantitative, economic analysis
of development flourished, and the theme of structural and
cultural change received less and less attention, at least in government and international agencies.[3] Some individual scholars also
emphasised the wider context; for example, Gunnar Myrdal, who
drew attention to the importance of the economic and political
relationships between rich and poor nations,[4] Arthur Lewis, who
dealt at length with the social factors in development, in one of

[1] Tibor Mende, *From Aid to Recolonization: Lessons of a Failure* (New
York, 1973), p. 36.
[2] In spite of the fact that the Marshall Plan itself had a very clear political
objective; namely, to re-establish Western Europe as a strong defence against
communism in the conditions of the cold war. This political aim has continued
to play an important part in American aid policy, but it is only in recent
years that it has been adequately discussed in studies of the whole 'development' process.
[3] Mende, op. cit., pp. 32–4. The report, published by the United Nations,
was entitled *Measures for Economic Development* (1950).
[4] Gunnar Myrdal, *Economic Theory and Underdeveloped Regions* (London,
1957).

the most systematic treatments of the subject,[1] and Paul Baran who outlined what seemed at that time a rather eccentric Marxist analysis of economic growth.[2]

The qualified optimism of some recent studies, exemplified by Robert McNamara's book,[3] rests upon three considerations: first, that the poor countries did expand their total national income at a rate of about 5·2 per cent annually during 1960–68, which compares favourably with their previous performance and with the UN target for the decade; second, that foreign aid can be increased and made more effective, thereby helping to raise still higher the rate of growth; and third, that the means exist, and will be used, to overcome major problems (including rapid population growth).

But all these judgements are open to question. The average rate of growth during the decade of the 1960s conceals significant variations between countries. Of sixty countries treated by Clark[4] as 'less developed', ten had very high rates of increase of GNP, while half of them had rates below 5 per cent annually. When population growth is taken into account, only ten countries in the top group had increases in *per capita* GNP of 4 per cent or more annually, while the average for all sixty countries was 2·7 per cent. Since the GNP *per capita* of the rich countries grew during the same period at 3·8 per cent annually, the gap between rich and poor countries continued to widen.

Most of the development agencies (and notably the World Bank) claim or assume that the rate of economic growth in poor countries has been helped significantly by foreign aid, and that stepping up such aid during the 1970s would raise still further the rate of growth. But this doctrine has been subjected to increasingly sharp criticism, from opposed points of view. Radical critics see aid as a means by which the leading capitalist countries maintain the poor countries in a state of dependence, and obstruct desirable changes in their social structure and political systems, thus in effect slowing down the process of development. At the same time they ensure benefits for themselves in the acquisition of raw materials, markets, and opportunities for profitable investment, as well as consolidating or extending their political control over a large part of the globe. Thus Michael Hudson, analysing

[1] W. Arthur Lewis, *The Theory of Economic Growth* (London, 1955).

[2] Paul A. Baran, *The Political Economy of Growth* (New York, 1957).

[3] Robert S. McNamara, *One Hundred Countries, Two Billion People* (New York, 1973). This is a collection of McNamara's public statements as President of the World Bank.

[4] Paul G. Clark, *American Aid for Development* (New York, 1972), pp. 22–3.

the recommendations of the Peterson Report and the role of the World Bank, concludes that these are shaped mainly by the national self-interest of the United States, and particularly by the desire to reduce the mounting pressures on the US balance of payments: 'World Bank operations during Mr McNamara's first year in office served in large part to finance the operations of the United States military establishment which he had just left.'[1] More generally, he argues that foreign aid, in many cases, has had an adverse effect on economic growth. A study by Griffin and Enos,[2] upon which he draws, notes that in twelve Latin American countries between 1957–64 the rate of growth of GNP was *inversely* related to the ratio of foreign aid, and concludes that '. . . aid may have retarded development by leading to lower domestic savings, by distorting the composition of investment and thereby raising the capital-output ratio, by frustrating the emergence of an indigenous entrepreneurial class, and by inhibiting institutional reforms.'[3] Hudson goes on to say that one of the most adverse consequences of aid is that the political conditions attached to it prevent measures to insulate the developing economy and to mobilise domestic resources.[4]

The same point is emphasised by Tibor Mende, who suggests that there is a growing mood of revolt in the poor countries against their dependence, against being forced into the commercial strait-jacket of the rich countries.

'To break out of the vicious circle, in order to recover lost identity and self-respect, the very orientation of economic development has to be changed. Instead of looking outward, it must become inward-oriented and more preoccupied with the solution of local problems than with the confrontation of those created by contact with the industrial world. The degrading aid relationship must be liquidated. Integration into the world market, dependence on foreign capital, the whole North–South fixation of economic thinking, must come to an end. Instead, each country must find its own path to development, and there must be experimentation with indigenous methods and reliance on local means. Structural changes must prepare the ground for popular participation in constructive tasks, for greater savings efforts, and for more

[1] Goulet and Hudson, op. cit., p. 107.
[2] K. B. Griffin and J. L. Enos, 'Foreign Assistance: Objectives and Consequences', *Economic Development and Cultural Change*, 18 (April 1970).
[3] Ibid., p. 326.
[4] Goulet and Hudson, op. cit., pp. 122–3.

rational investment priorities. . . . if necessary, there must be no hesitation in accepting the price of isolation.'[1]

Mende goes on to say that such reasoning is by no means irrelevant or unrealistic:

'In the case of Latin America, for example, the only under-developed region then free of direct foreign control, three such interludes [when ties with advanced industrial countries were severed] brought acceleration in structural changes and often rapid industrialisation as well. These occasions were the two World Wars and the years of the Great Depression. The rapid expansionary phases of industrial development of Argentina, Brazil, Mexico, and even of Chile occurred during these periods, when the loosening of established investment trade ties seemed indeed to have favoured autonomous industrialisation and faster economic growth. . . . Similar situations, bringing freedom from foreign interference, providing protection to infant industries, and offering incentives to experiment, to take risks, and to alter established policies were created by the voluntary isolation first of Japan and later of Russia and China. Though purely economic purposes may not have been their dominant motivations, none-theless the economic results have certainly been impressive.'[2]

The radical critics thus emphasise the social and political aspects of development on a world scale, in opposition to what might be called the 'official' doctrine of development agencies and of many centres of development studies, which still concen-trates largely upon the analysis of economic and technological factors.[3] The importance of the political element is obvious when the provision of foreign aid is closely examined. In the first place much of the aid has a military, or general strategic, character. Military aid accounts for more than half of American foreign assistance; and as Michael Hudson observes, this 'security assistance' has not, on balance, fostered the recipient countries'

[1] Mende, op. cit., pp. 203–4.
[2] Ibid., pp. 204–5.
[3] As Michael Hudson comments: 'McNamara has been curiously silent about all aspects of socio-economic transformation save those of birth control and the "technological revolution"' (Goulet and Hudson, op. cit., p. 124). As might be expected this is also a feature of the World Bank reports; see, for example, *Economic Growth of Colombia: Problems and Prospects* (Balti-more, 1972). This does not mean that the official views are politically neutral; merely that they assume the persistence of the *status quo*.

economic development, 'but has imposed on them an expensive and socially destructive military overhead'.[1]

Secondly, even in the case of more strictly economic aid, political considerations have a major influence. Teresa Hayter has argued convincingly that the policies of the international development agencies (the International Monetary Fund, the World Bank, the United States Agency for International Development, the Inter-American Development Bank) 'are based on the acceptance and upholding of the existing international and national framework of the capitalist world ... there is a strong emphasis in the agencies' policies and demands on the principles of free enterprise, or reliance on market mechanisms, and on the respect of private property, domestic and especially foreign.'[2] The recent tragic history of Chile illustrates very well how these agencies operate. The Popular Unity Government of President Allende faced many difficulties throughout its period of office—the massive external debt inherited from the previous Government, the falling world price of its major export, copper—and doubtless it made some mistakes in economic policy. But its difficulties were enormously and deliberately increased by the actions of the American Government, the World Bank, the Inter-American Development Bank, and a number of private banks, in cutting off foreign credit. During the same period, however, the USA continued to provide military aid, no doubt regarding this as a worthwhile investment; as it proved to be, at least in the short run, when a group of subversive military leaders destroyed the legal government and seized power in September 1973. Following the coup, which has ended the democratic political system of Chile for the time being, the development agencies, private banks, and some governments (notably the American Government), began with indecent haste to revise their policies and to look more favourably again upon the provision of aid.

Criticism of foreign aid has come from the right as well as the left. One form of the conservative argument against foreign aid is presented in a recent collection of essays by P. T. Bauer.[3] This 550-page political tract is directed less to the problems of the poor countries as such than against what Bauer takes to be the

---

[1] Goulet and Hudson, op. cit., p. 78. Among the ten countries listed by Clark (op. cit.) as having the highest rate of increase of GNP, six (Taiwan, Greece, Korea, Israel, Panama, and Thailand) have obviously benefited, if that is the word, from massive strategic aid.

[2] Teresa Hayter, *Aid as Imperialism* (Harmondsworth, 1971), pp. 151–2.

[3] P. T. Bauer, *Dissent on Development* (Cambridge, Mass., 1972).

attempt by liberal or radical social scientists to promote comprehensive economic planning under cover of the provision of foreign aid and the diffusion of a particular doctrine about how development can be most effectively carried through. This doctrine he believes, rests upon the thesis of a 'vicious circle of poverty', from which the poor countries cannot extricate themselves by their own efforts, and upon the derived view that there is a widening gap between rich and poor countries. But the 'vicious circle' thesis, Bauer argues, is invalid, because the present industrial countries obviously did escape from their initial poverty without appreciable outside help, and some of the developing countries have made rapid economic progress in recent decades, again largely through their own efforts.

If the 'vicious circle' thesis is invalid then there is no necessary 'general trend' towards a widening gap between rich and poor countries, and Bauer then goes on to examine this question in more detail. There is not, he argues, a sharp division between rich and poor countries, but a continuum of levels of GNP. Furthermore, there are in any case great difficulties in making precise comparisons between levels of living in different nations. Finally, it is impossible to demonstrate any general trend of increasing inequality, and the problem of the 'gap' needs to be studied over definite time periods.[1]

But Bauer's own propositions and arguments are unconvincing. The 'vicious circle' thesis, as I understand it, does not propound some kind of *iron law*; it merely describes a tendency in the present day world.[2] The thesis cannot be invalidated by referring to the development of the present industrial countries from the sixteenth century onwards, which occurred in entirely different circumstances;[3] nor by pointing to the exceptional instances of poor countries which have been able to develop very rapidly.[4] All that it asserts is that most of the poor nations, in a world

[1] Bauer, op. cit., pp. 49–68.

[2] The tendency can be found also in particular regions *within* industrial countries, as Gunnar Myrdal pointed out. That is why there have been policies to deal with 'special development areas' in Britain, and why the European Community has policies and funds for regional development. In some respects foreign aid for development can be seen (ideally) as an extension of such policies to the world as a whole, treated as a single community.

[3] It should be noted, too, that this development did not take place entirely without external assistance. The profits from colonial domination (a form of *imposed* foreign aid) played some part in the process, and in the view of some writers (e.g. Baran, op. cit.) a large part.

[4] In some cases this has resulted, as I have indicated, from massive military aid, which brings in its wake other problems, of the distortion of the economy

which is economically organised and dominated by the industrial countries—and above all by the Western capitalist countries— face exceptional difficulties in trying to break out of their long-standing poverty, and hence that there is a strong tendency for such poverty to reproduce itself.

Bauer's observations on the 'widening gap' are equally mis-leading. There *is* a sharp distinction to be made between the small group of rich countries (with a GNP *per capita* of $2500 or above) and the large number of poor countries (with a GNP *per capita* between $80–$300); and the existence of some countries with a GNP in the intermediate range does not change the basic picture. It does not change it any more than the existence of middle strata within capitalist societies changes the picture of the division between wealthy property owners and the working class; only when the middle strata become very large is it necessary to consider whether a different representation of the whole structure is called for, and this is evidently not yet the case in the inter-national economy.

Bauer then introduces another element into his argument by distinguishing between 'income' and 'welfare', and suggesting that even considerable inequalities in the former do not imply in-equalities in the latter. This harks back to the familiar doctrine of conservative economists about the impossibility of making interpersonal comparisons of utility or satisfaction. The doctrine was commonly used at one time to oppose social welfare policies in the capitalist industrial societies themselves, but we have not heard very much of it lately until its sudden resurrection in this new guise as part of an argument which purports to show that there is really no need to worry too much after all about redis-tributing resources between rich and poor countries.[1]

---

and the emergence of vast inequalities within the society. In other instances chance has been overwhelmingly important. The rapidly rising GNP of the oil-producing countries of the Middle East results simply from the possession of a natural resource for which there is a high and increasing demand. Here too, a particular type of economic growth poses new problems, of establishing a more balanced economy which will maintain prosperity over the long term, and removing gross inequalities. It should also be noted that the rising price of oil, while it benefits one group of developing countries, greatly increases the difficulties of others, such as India, which depend upon large imports of oil for their economic growth.

[1] Bauer expresses this idea at an earlier point in the book by observing that material progress does not necessarily bring happiness, dignity, sensi-bility or harmony (p. 26). This comment should surely be addressed rather to the affluent and prodigal nations than to the impoverished ones.

Having formulated his criticisms at some length Bauer expounds more briefly his own conception of what is important in development; economic achievement, he says, 'depends primarily on people's abilities and attitudes and also on their social and political institutions' (p. 75). Superficially, this resembles the views of radical critics of official development policies. But what Bauer understands by appropriate abilities and attitudes, and suitable institutions, is something quite distinctive. He has in mind the emergence of individualistic, competitive entrepreneurs, and the growth of a commercial market; in the case studies of West Africa included in his book he emphasises the importance of the development of trade, and criticises the restrictions which have been placed upon free enterprise trading activities. He is far from thinking of the release of new energies and abilities, or the reshaping of institutions, by a nationalist or revolutionary movement that would embark upon a planned development of national resources. On the contrary, comprehensive economic planning, along with foreign aid, is one of the principal targets of his attack: '... comprehensive planning neither augments resources nor modernises the minds of peoples, but merely enlarges and centralises power. Such a policy is neither a condition, nor an agent of material progress. Indeed, it is likely to retard it, especially in poor countries, because it goes counter to that liberation of the individual from subjection to authority which encourages the qualities behind material success' (p. 512). This is obviously untrue. The USSR, and more recently China (which Bauer scarcely mentions), achieved rapid economic growth, partly at least because of the initial liberating effects of their revolutions.[1] Elsewhere in the book Bauer discounts the value of any kind of state intervention, criticises Gunnar Myrdal for assuming that 'economic progress is largely a matter of government policy', and goes on to say that 'it is not clear what sort of intervention by efficient independent governments would have accelerated development in eighteenth- or nineteenth-century Africa and Asia' (p. 456). The case of Japan, however, shows very well the kind of intervention that did achieve this result.

The underlying political intention of Bauer's essays is to assist the reproduction of a capitalist economy and capitalist social

---

[1] After the early period of industrialisation there are certainly problems arising from highly *centralised* planning of the supply of consumer goods and services, but it may well be possible to overcome many of the problems by decentralisation within an overall plan. These questions are very thoroughly discussed in W. Brus, *The Economics and Politics of Socialism* (London, 1973).

relations in the developing areas of the world. Some other conservative critics of development and aid, however, emphasise more strongly the need to maintain or extend the present dominance of Western, especially American, capitalism. Samuel Huntington, for example, who is well known for his contributions to American strategic thinking in Vietnam and elsewhere, has argued recently that: 'Current aid programmes need to be disaggregated in terms of their purposes and new programmes inaugurated to reflect emerging US interests in global maintenance.'[1] Another critic of American aid policies argues that the neglect of Third World countries (indicated by the low and declining level of US aid) is harmful to American economic interests, and that a new policy of more active co-operation is needed which would ensure access to markets and better opportunities for overseas investment, in order to help resolve balance of payments difficulties and generally put the USA in a stronger position for economic competition with Western Europe and Japan.[2]

One specific aspect of development which Bauer dismisses peremptorily, though many other writers treat it as having an outstanding importance, is the rapid growth of population. From one aspect, of course, this growth is an *indicator* of development; it results from the decline in mortality, itself brought about by more adequate nutrition and improved health services. On the other side, the very large population increases reduce substantially the growth of *per capita* GNP,[3] and they affect the general rate of growth by diverting resources from investment in agriculture and industry to the provision of additional schools, housing, etc. In consequence, the control of population growth itself becomes an objective to which foreign aid may be applied. This is the approach taken, for example, by Robert McNamara; in his view, 'the greatest single obstacle to the economic and social advancement of the majority of the peoples in the underdeveloped world is rampant population growth' (op. cit., p. 31), though he adds that the solution of this problem is in no way a substitute for other forms of assistance, such as aid for agriculture, industrialisation and technological advance. The developed nations should, therefore, give every possible measure of support to those countries that have already established family-planning pro-

[1] Samuel P. Huntington, 'Foreign Aid: For What and For Whom?', in Hunter and Rielly, op. cit., p. 59.
[2] C. Fred Bergsten, 'The Threat from the Third World', *Foreign Affairs*, 11 (Summer 1973), pp. 102–24.
[3] See Clark, op. cit., pp. 22–3.

grammes; they should intensify research into the biological and social aspects of population control; and they should attempt to develop a sense of urgency about the population problem (pp. 44–45).

Other writers attach a similar importance to population growth. Gunnar Myrdal devotes a long section of his massive study of South Asia to the subject, and notes that it is now commonly recognised that 'the prospects for successful economic development are crucially related to population trends'.[1] Similarly Tibor Mende singles out as one of the two major problems in the disequilibrium between the industrial powers and the developing countries the complex ramifications of the demographic explosion (op. cit., pp. 265–71). By the end of this century the world's population will have doubled (to 7 billion) in the short space of thirty-five years; in another thirty-five years it may have reached 15 billion. Behind these figures lie frightening problems of the supply of food and other resources, deterioration of the environment, and acute conflict over the unequal access to resources.

Some radical writers have criticised this concern with the control of population growth as neo-Malthusianism, in the strict sense of the term which implies that the poverty of the poor countries is the result of their own irresponsible reproductive habits. Michael Hudson, for example, formulates this kind of objection,[2] but he qualifies it by saying that it is only when demographic control is conceived as a *substitute* for institutional reform that its advocacy takes on this ideological character. In fact, very few, if any, writers on development have sought to explain the poverty of the developing countries historically in terms of population growth. They have been concerned with two quite different issues: first, given the poverty of the developing countries today (however it may have been produced) what are the consequences of the present demographic explosion for the efforts to overcome this poverty through rapid economic growth; and second, what are the implications for the world as a whole—in the use of resources, the protection of the natural environment, the quality of social life—of this unprecedented population growth?

The demographic explosion, which may appear initially as a separate, self-contained problem, a solution to which can best be sought through technical measures, does in fact raise major

---

[1] Gunnar Myrdal, *Asian Drama* (3 vols., New York, 1968), Vol. II, pp. 1389–1390.

[2] Goulet and Hudson, op. cit., pp. 125–9.

political issues that are implicit in any comprehensive conception of development. Where the rapid increase of population is a direct obstacle to economic growth, as it is in many of the poor countries, the control of population should obviously have a high priority, though it would still be only one element in the general planning of development, and the difficulties which face any kind of population policy should not be underestimated.[1] But population growth is not simply a problem of the poor countries. A major reason for concern about the demographic explosion is its consequences for the environment and for the use of the earth's resources, and from this aspect the poor countries are by no means the only source of the problem. Population is also increasing (though more slowly) in the wealthy industrial countries; but more important is the fact that these countries consume a disproportionate amount of the world's resources (the USA alone accounting for one-third of world consumption). The pressure on resources does not come only from the growth of population and the rising GNP in the poor countries, but from the continued rapid growth of the industrial countries; and any serious analysis of development on a world scale must consider means of limiting their extravagantly wasteful use of resources and eventually slowing down their rate of growth, at least in some directions.[2]

These remarks on the population question indicate, from a

[1] If extreme coercive measures, such as compulsory sterilisation, are excluded, as being likely to inflict more harm on society than does the condition they set out to cure, then a decline in the birth rate can only be effected by rational persuasion and incentives. This presupposes, to some extent, a rational society whose members respond in an enlightened way to social indicators, and that state of affairs is still far distant. There is also a two-way relation between population and development; development may affect population growth, by changing people's aspirations and ways of life, just as much as it is affected by it. So it may be argued that the best population policy is simply to press ahead with development (economic growth, urbanisation, increased social mobility) which will itself reduce the birth rate; but I think this exaggerates the effectiveness of such influences and underestimates the urgency of the population problem at the present time. Finally, there is a more obvious political issue in the fact that population size is an element in national power, and the will to control, or not to control, population growth is strongly affected by international rivalries.

[2] Such considerations still seem to be neglected by the development agencies. A paper published by the United Nations in April 1973, 'Brief Outline of the United Nations Study on the Impact of Prospective Environmental Issues and Problems on the International Development Strategy', although it refers to the problems of a *world economy*, confines its attention almost entirely to the difficulties which arise from the economic development of the *poor* countries.

particular aspect, the need for a broader and more systematic framework of inquiry. The development of both 'developing' countries and industrial countries takes place within a world system of economic and political relationships under particular historical conditions. The very emergence of a sphere of inquiry called 'development studies'—which is at the same time a field of political action—depended upon the dissolution of colonial empires and upon specific postwar circumstances such as I sketched briefly at the beginning of this chapter. An analysis of development problems and policies, including foreign aid, has to take account, in the first place, of this context. In a world which is largely dominated by a capitalist economy the process of development may actually increase underdevelopment in some countries,[1] or produce, in other cases, distortions of the economy as a result of the pursuit of strategic interests, military aid, or the activities of multi-national corporations. From the point of view of the major capitalist countries relations with the poor nations may be conceived largely in terms of maintaining their own economic and political dominance, or in terms of ensuring that the industrialisation of the rest of the world occurs in a capitalistic form.

An alternative to development along these lines seems to be provided by the policies of the Communist industrial countries, but these raise other questions. In the first place, it is not so easy in this case, because of the lack of information, to determine what the policies are or how they are carried out.[2] However, it is clear at least that the Communist countries have participated very little in the international development agencies and in multilateral aid, so that their general influence upon the course of events is limited. It is also evident that in the case of the Communist countries, as in the case of the Western capitalist countries, relations with the developing nations have been strongly influenced by the political conflict between the USSR and the USA, so that strategic aims and military aid play an important part. Finally, it has to be considered how far the development policies of the Communist countries could in any case constitute a real alternative, in the sense of a socialist alternative, to the expansion of capitalism; and a judgement on this issue must depend upon

[1] As A. G. Frank has argued in *Capitalism and Underdevelopment in Latin America* (rev. edn New York, 1969). See also the essays in James D. Cockcroft, André Gunder Frank and Dale L. Johnson (eds), *Dependence and Underdevelopment: Latin America's Political Economy* (New York, 1972).

[2] See the brief discussion in Mende, op. cit., Appendix I.

how one assesses the socialist potential of societies in which public ownership of the principal means of production and a degree of socialist planning is associated with an authoritarian, and often repressive, political system.

This question, of alternative courses of global development, raises an issue which is crucial in any conception of development; namely, what is the purpose of development, or more broadly still, what kind of world are development policies intended to create? Most liberal and radical writers on the subject either take for granted or argue that development means something more than the mere growth, in any form whatsoever, of GNP. It involves a real improvement in the general level of living, by the provision of adequate food, housing, health care, education, etc. to the mass of the population; the reduction of gross inequalities in the distribution of wealth and income; the expansion of opportunities, especially for the most deprived sections of the population. From this point it is not difficult to go on to the formulation of a distinctive socialist policy for development, the ultimate aim of which would be to establish a fundamental equality of condition on a world scale—to abolish, within and between societies, the distinction of rich and poor.

This kind of policy involves the extension, to the social system of the world regarded as a whole, of the socialist aim of creating a classless society. Obviously, the difficulties are immense. Even within particular nations, democratic socialist movements have encountered formidable obstacles in their attempts to redistribute wealth and income, to provide a greater range of public services, and to plan economic and social development. On an international scale the problems would be compounded by the fierce opposition, inspired by deep-rooted national and cultural loyalties, to any significant redistribution of wealth between nations (which *must* include some control of the rate of industrial growth in the rich countries); by the difficulty of establishing effective international agencies to implement such policies; and by the threat of an extremely authoritarian form of political and bureaucratic domination inherent in the project of planning and regulating a world economy. Even a beginning can scarcely be made until there are democratic socialist regimes well established in a number of the advanced industrial countries; and if this were the case, the process of socialist development would still, in my view, be slow— perhaps frighteningly slow in face of the terrible danger of murderous wars fought for the control of increasingly scarce resources.

But it is quite utopian to suppose that we can be saved by a sudden revolutionary transformation. Only an accumulation of reforms, directed nevertheless toward a fundamental change in the social system, is likely to be successful. Such reforms might well begin with changes in the terms of world trade to benefit the poor countries; with an increase in the proportion of grants as against loans in foreign aid, and the lowering of rates of interest on loans; with the supply of new loans and grants to help reduce the staggering burden of debt which the poor countries have already incurred as a result of previous aid; and with a sharp increase in the provision of aid in the form of scientific and technical knowledge.[1]

An analysis of the global context of development should not, however, neglect the other aspect of the question. The poor countries, although they exist in a world which is dominated by the industrial countries (both capitalist and communist), have nevertheless the power to determine, within limits, the course of their development, and to affect, more or less strongly, the international distribution of wealth. One option which is open to them is to adopt a policy of autarky, restricting imports and foreign investment by means of tariffs and other controls, and reducing as much as possible their dependence on foreign aid, especially the more burdensome types of aid. There are certainly historical precedents for the success of such a policy—China being a good example—so long as there exist forces in the society which are strongly committed to economic development and the reshaping of social institutions. But autarky will not be the most effective policy in all cases, and it need not be adopted as a permanent policy. Albert Hirschman has put forward the interesting idea that 'in order to maximise growth the developing countries could need an appropriate alternation of contact and insulation, of openness to the trade and capital of the developed countries, to be followed by a period of nationalism and withdrawnness'.[2]

---

[1] The supply of knowledge is probably one of the most useful kinds of aid, but it needs to be given in an appropriate way. It does not seem to me to make very good sense, for instance, that so many of the centres for studying development are located in the rich countries, where those engaged in such studies have only intermittent (and sometimes brief) contacts with the social situations and problems they are analysing; and it might be better to devote some of the resources to assisting and extending the work of those institutes which have been established in the developing countries, and to creating new ones.

[2] Albert O. Hirschman, *A Bias for Hope: Essays on Development and Latin America* (New Haven, 1971), pp. 25–6.

Another means by which the poor countries could strengthen their position is the formation of regional or other associations among themselves, in order to control foreign capital investment and the exploitation of their resources, to improve the terms of trade with the industrial countries, and to influence more effectively the policies of the international development agencies. One successful association of this kind is the Organisation of Petroleum Exporting Countries (OPEC), but this obviously enjoys a privileged position through its control of a particularly scarce resource. The Andean Pact (of which Bolivia, Chile, Columbia, Ecuador, Peru and Venezuela are members) is another recent attempt to establish a common defence against the economic power of the industrial countries, particularly the USA, and at the same time a means of regional co-operation in development; but its effectiveness will certainly be diminished following the overthrow of the Popular Unity government in Chile. There have also been continuing attempts to bring together the countries of the Third World as a whole, in order to formulate some very general guidelines for development policies as seen from the standpoint of the poor countries themselves, notably in relation to the terms of world trade.[1]

All these efforts from the side of the poor countries are analogous in certain respects to the activities of the labour movement within the industrial societies, and they are an essential element in the struggle for a redistribution of world resources. But there are also important differences, and it is quite unrealistic to conceive the development process simply in terms of a conflict between 'bourgeois' and 'proletarian' nations. For one thing, there are contradictory features in the policies of many developing countries, which formulate claims for greater equality between nations while tolerating, or even promoting, vast inequalities within their own societies. Furthermore, there are such profound differences between countries and regions of the Third World— differences of history, culture and social structure—and such great diversity in the problems which they face, that it seems to me unlikely that any general theory, prescribing the 'one best way' to develop, can be formulated with any great degree of plausibility. There are many roads to development, as there are many roads to socialism.

---

[1] Thus, in the meetings of the United Nations Conference on Trade and Development (UNCTAD) the developing countries have pressed for preferences for their manufactures in the markets of the industrial countries, but so far without much success.

What appears to me the most universal feature is the strength of the drive toward equality, which has now spread from its source in the nineteenth-century capitalist societies to involve the whole of mankind. The uncertainty and disillusionment to which I referred at the beginning of this chapter has arisen not merely from a recognition of the difficulties and complexities of development, but from a realisation that the whole process was misconceived. During the 1950s the debate about capitalism and socialism was muted and a new sociological theory of world history, in terms of the transition from pre-industrial to industrial society, came into fashion. The object of our intellectual and political strivings, it was claimed, should be to understand more fully and promote more effectively this particular transition.[1] It is now evident that this theory expressed the conservative mood of the time—subsequently dissipated by the radical movements of the 1960s—and the confidence in a world-wide diffusion of affluence through sustained economic growth. Present doubts about the development process result from the collapse of the theory, and the absence so far of any well articulated intellectual and practical alternative. Behind the concern about development and the relations between rich and poor nations there lies, as I have tried to show, the fundamental issue of human equality; and it is only insofar as this issue is debated in all its ramifications, and political choices formulated with reference to it, that practical and effective policies for global development will become feasible.

[1] This view is very forcefully argued by Ernest Gellner, *Thought and Change* (London, 1964). Raymond Aron, who did much to develop the notion of 'industrial society', drew attention to one feature of the new outlook when he observed that sociologists, in their conceptions of social change, had gone back from Marx to Saint-Simon.

Chapter 5

Karl Marx:
Sociologist or Marxist?[1]

The question posed in the title of this chapter is not intended to exhaust all the aspects from which Marx's work may be regarded; nor is it meant to prejudge the issue as to whether a thinker—and Marx in particular—may be *both* a sociologist *and* a Marxist. But there are advantages in putting just this question. First, the consideration of Marx's thought as one of the early systems of sociology, that is, as an attempt to formulate new concepts for depicting the structure of whole societies and for explaining massive social changes, brings into prominence the most distinctive and, I would say, the most interesting of his ideas. This has become clearer with the growth of sociological studies in the past few decades and with the accompanying re-assessment of the history of modern social thought. It is evident that the marked revival of interest in Marxism as a theoretical scheme (which is in contrast with its declining intellectual appeal as a comprehensive political creed) owes much to the recent work of sociologists; but even at an earlier time, at the end of the nineteenth century and in the first decade of the twentieth century, the most fruitful discussions of Marx's thought seem to me to have been those which arose from sociological or philosophical concerns—in the writings of Max Weber, Croce, Sorel and Pareto, for example—rather than those which originated in strictly economic or political criticisms.[2]

[1] Reprinted, with minor revisions, from *Science and Society* (Winter 1966). The essay is based upon a paper read on 30 August 1965 in the plenary session, 'A Re-evaluation of Karl Marx', at the 60th Annual Meeting of the American Sociological Association held in Chicago. A criticism of some of my arguments here was published in the same issue of *Science and Society*: Henry F. Mins, 'Marxists and Non-Marxists'.

[2] I have examined some of these early contributions more fully in an article on Marxist sociology in the *International Encyclopaedia of the Social Sciences* (New York, 1968); and in a short book, *Marxist Sociology* (London, 1974).

One important reason for the present revival of interest is the fact that Marx's theory stands in direct opposition on every major point to the functionalist theory which has so strongly influenced sociology and anthropology for the past twenty or thirty years, but which has been found increasingly unsatisfactory. Where functionalism emphasises social harmony, Marxism emphasises social conflict; where functionalism directs attention to the stability and persistence of social forms, Marxism is radically historical in its outlook and emphasises the changing structure of society; where functionalism concentrates upon the regulation of social life by general values and norms, Marxism stresses the divergence of interests and values within each society and the role of force in maintaining, over a longer or shorter period of time, a given social order. The contrast between 'equilibrium' and 'conflict' models of society, which was stated forcefully by Dahrendorf in 1958,[1] has now become a commonplace; and Marx's theories are regularly invoked in opposition to those of Durkheim, Pareto and Malinowski, the principal architects of the functionalist theory.

This is not to claim that Marxism stands alone as a theory which gives due weight to social conflict, and to the historical and mutable nature of human societies; nor that a mere delineation of the 'equilibrium' and 'conflict' models, as alternative constructions which may be useful in different contexts, appears to most sociologists as the final step which can be taken. Other scholars after Marx, and notably Simmel and Max Weber, contributed new elements to a theory of social conflict and of social change, and they brought corrections, amplifications or refutations of some of Marx's own propositions. It is true, nonetheless, that their work can only be fully understood when it is seen as *following* that of Marx.

The possibility of alternative models of society raises difficult problems which have been with sociologists since the beginning of their discipline. In a sense, modern sociologists are grappling anew with the old question of the reconciliation between 'order' and 'progress' which was one of the main themes of Comte's sociology. This intellectual affinity stems in part from the similarity in social conditions. Like Comte, we live in the aftermath of great revolutions, and in the midst of new revolutionary outbreaks and violent transformations of society. In consequence,

[1] Ralf Dahrendorf, 'Out of Utopia: Toward a Reorientation of Sociological Analysis', *American Journal of Sociology*, Vol. LXIV, No. 2 (1958).

the most important tasks of sociology now appear to be the comprehension of what is happening in the creation of new states, the accelerating growth of science and technology, the spread of industrialism throughout the world, and the revolutions in class structure, in the family, and in political systems. Unlike Comte, however, we are more concerned with finding a satisfactory theory than with expounding a new social philosophy; and we are more aware of the need to provide an explanation of social change, whereas Comte, who was confronted by the numerous theories of progress of his age, was more anxious to discover principles of 'order' and stability.

In Marx's theory, the main emphasis is put upon the conflicts within society and the structural changes which result from these conflicts; and there is an underlying scheme of the progressive development of mankind. At the same time, the theory does include some partial accounts of social solidarity and of the persistence of social forms. Marx deals at length, for instance, with the conditions in which class solidarity is generated and maintained; and at the level of a total society he explains the persistence of a particular structure by the relations between classes, the position of a ruling class, and the influence of 'ruling ideas'. Further, Marx predicts the advent of a type of society in which social conflict will be eliminated while social solidarity and harmony will be complete. In other words, we may see in Marx's theory a juxtaposition of 'conflict' and 'equilibrium' models of society in two different ways: first, that conflict predominates in the social relations within the total society, while solidarity and consensus prevail in many of the sub-groups (especially social classes) in society; and secondly, that total societies may be arranged in a historical order such that in one historical period, the only one we have experienced up to now, conflict is predominant, and in another, located in the future, solidarity, peaceful co-operation and consensus will prevail.

Nevertheless, this theory does not provide an adequate reconciliation of the two models, quite apart from the errors which it may contain in the actual description and explanation of societal conflict or class solidarity. It does not, for example, allow for the possibility that conflict itself may engender or maintain social solidarity (a possibility which Simmel explored more systematically). Moreover, it eliminates conflict entirely in the hypothetical classless society of the futute, and it seems also to postulate an original condition of human society, before the extension of the division of labour and the accumulation of private wealth, which was free from conflict. This view depends upon a historical conception which is at odds with the idea of a positive science which seems generally to inspire Marx's mature work. We may attribute greater or lesser importance to the Hegelianism or the positivism of Marx's theory, but it is impossible to reconcile them. Isaiah Berlin, for instance, has argued that:

'The framework of [Marx's] theory is undeviatingly Hegelian. It recognises that the history of humanity is a single, non-repetitive process, which obeys discoverable laws. These laws are different from the laws of physics or of chemistry, which being unhistorical, record unvarying conjunctions and successions of interconnected phenomena, whenever or wherever these may repeat themselves; they are similar rather to those of geology or botany, which embody the principles in accordance with which a process of continuous change takes place.'[1]

On the other hand, it may be claimed that many of Marx's propositions have the form at least of statements of universal laws. Thus, the famous phrase: 'The history of all hitherto existing society is the history of class struggles' may be interpreted, not as a historical principle, but as a universal law of conflict in human society. Similarly, the assertion that the form of social institutions and of ideas is determined by the economic structure of society has to be regarded either as the expression of a universal law, or as a rule of method. Even where Marx says he is formulating a law of change—for example, 'the law of motion of modern capitalist society'—this may be seen as a special law applicable to a particular type of society (capitalist or industrial), and in principle derivable from some more general law which refers to change in *all* societies. Thus, laws of social change do not have to be historical laws or principles; they may be universal, and applicable to all instances whenever or wherever they occur.

In Marx's own theory these two conceptions—the historical interpretation of a unique sequence of events, and the framing of universal laws covering repeatable events—co-exist, and later Marxists have in the main opted for one or the other view: the positivist or scientific school being represented to some extent by Engels, and most fully by Max Adler; the Hegelianising school by Lukács, Korsch, Marcuse, and a number of recent opponents of positivism, particularly in France. My own contention is that the general inclination of Marx's work, when it is traced from his

[1] Isaiah Berlin, *Karl Marx* (3rd edn) (London, 1963), p. 124.

earlier to his later writings, is clearly away from the philosophy of history and towards a scientific theory of society, in the precise sense of a body of general laws and detailed empirical statements. I recognise, of course, that it is not along this path that the main development of Marxism has occurred. Indeed, it is striking that the major contributions of Marxist research have been in the historical field, though even here they have been confined to a narrow range of problems, and that empirical investigations in the sociological domain have been rare.

A recent essay by Hobsbawm[1] restates the point about the influence of Marxism upon economic and social history with great clarity. Introducing the first English translation of Marx's only extended analysis of pre-capitalist societies,[2] Hobsbawm argues that Marx formulates here a theory of historical *progress* rather than a scheme of social evolution, and that it is these terms (i.e. from the standpoint of a historian) that his distinctions between different types of society should be considered. What Marxist historians have actually done Hobsbawm examines later, and he concludes that the recent contributions are in some ways unsatisfactory inasmuch as they have neglected certain types of society—notably the 'Asiatic society—and have greatly expanded the notion of 'feudal society' to fill up the gaps. The preoccupation of Marxist historians with just those questions which Marx himself examined most fully—the rise of the *bourgeoisie* within feudal society, the transition from feudalism to capitalism, and the early stages of capitalist society—does, indeed, seem excessive; and aside from the neglect of other types of social structure, it has also meant that the Marxist contribution to modern social history has been less substantial than might have been expected. In the main, it is not the Marxists who have studied closely the development of modern social classes and elites, of ideologies, or of political parties, or who have attempted to analyse revolutionary movements. This domain, which is closest to sociology, has unquestionably been much influenced, if not actually created by Marx's ideas, but most of the important studies have been made by scholars who were not Marxists—from Sombart, Max Weber and Michels to Geiger and Karl Mannheim, from Veblen to C. Wright Mills.

[1] E. J. Hobsbawm, 'Introduction' to Karl Marx, *Pre-capitalist Economic Formations* (New York, 1965).

[2] In the manuscript dating from 1857–58, which was an early draft of *Capital* and which was first published in Moscow (1939–41) under the title *Grundrisse der Kritik der politischen Ökonomie* (*Rohentwurf*).

In the main line of sociological inquiry no Marxist scholar has emerged to equal the achievement of Max Weber in using Marx's very general propositions about the relation between ideologies and social structure as the starting point for a vast and fruitful investigation of the role of particular religious ideas and beliefs in social change and of their connections with various social classes. Those Marxists who, like Max Adler, wanted to present Marx's theory as a system of scientific sociology have generally confined themselves to methodological discussions,[1] while those of the Hegelian school have either wandered into the happily imprecise and imaginative field of literary criticism (Lukács) or have, like the positivists, turned to methodological reflections (Sartre).

The contrast between the accomplishments of the more orthodox schools of Marxism and of those scholars who were simply stimulated by Marx's ideas to embark upon fresh research of their own, reflects no discredit upon Marx himself. Marx was always passionately interested in factual social inquiries—from the investigations of Quételet and Buret to the reports of the English factory inspectors and his own projected '*enquête ouvrière*' —and he undertook in *Capital* an empirical study of vast scope which is still unsurpassed in the literature of the social sciences. His whole work, which combines the construction of theoretical models of society with the elaboration of methods of inquiry, and with the imaginative use of these models and methods in the analysis of a type of social system and its transformations, is by any reckoning one of the great contributions to the formation of modern sociology; and when we consider how, outside the confines of the various Marxist orthodoxies, it has provoked new sociological investigations, new reflections upon problems of theory and method, and repeated reassessments (such as we are engaged upon today), then it may justifiably be regarded as the greatest single contribution—*the* decisive intellectual advance— which established our subject in a recognisable form. If Marx sometimes contradicted himself, made mistakes, moved ambiguously from a Hegelian idiom to the language of modern natural science, and back again, left some of his concepts in a logically untidy form, sometimes used essentialist definitions though he was in the main a nominalist, exaggerated social conflict in his theoretical model, this seems to me excusable in a pioneer thinker whose ideas had the power to create a new branch of knowledge

[1] But other works of the Austro-Marxists, including Karl Renner's study of law in *The Institutions of Private Law and Their Social Functions* (London, 1949), provide notable exceptions.

which, in its own development, would produce the means of correcting and refining these early formulations.

The inexcusable would be that Marx had deliberately sacrificed positive science to metaphysics, that he had sought only that evidence which supported a vision of the world and of history created by a poetic and philosophic imagination and never afterwards questioned; in short, that he was pre-eminently a Marxist, the expounder of a creed. Marx, of course, *said* that he was not a Marxist, and there is little reason to doubt that he was extremely critical of the exposition of his ideas by self-styled disciples during his lifetime. Was it that he considered these expositions inadequate, or did he object to the presentation of his ideas as a political creed? Did he see his theory chiefly as an engine of discovery, and as one which required a great deal more hard intellectual work before it would be really adequate for its purpose? We must, in any case, make a distinction between the 'Marxism' of Marx and that of the Marxists. For Marx, his own system of thought could not possibly be something established or given, a simple framework for the expression of a social or political aim. It was his own creation, worked out laboriously over a long period of time, incessantly revised and admittedly incomplete. The record of his intellectual labours, which has been set out admirably by Maximilien Rubel,[1] shows the manner in which Marx arrived at his principal ideas—the anatomy of 'civil society', the class system, ideologies, and revolutionary change—and the plans which he formed in his youth to investigate in detail these various aspects of modern society, but which he was never able to realise. On many occasions he declared that he had now, at last, completed his work on the economic system and would be able to turn to the problems of class, political regimes, ideologies, but he continued to write new drafts of his economic analysis, published a preliminary account of his discoveries in 1859, the initial volume of *Capital* in 1867, and then in the last twelve years of his life was unable even to finish the remaining parts of his economic analysis, let alone embark upon new studies in the other spheres of society which he had repeatedly distinguished as vitally important for the full development of his theoretical system. The relative sterility of Marx's later years may be explained in various ways—by his discouragement in the face of scholarly indifference to his work, by his disillusionment with the labour movement after the demise

[1] Maximilien Rubel, *Karl Marx: Essai de biographie intellectuelle* (Paris, revised edn, 1971).

of the International, by his failure to solve major problems in the economic analysis of capitalism, by illness and domestic anxieties—but it can certainly not be explained as a consequence of his self-satisfied contemplation of the completed edifice of Marxist theory, which needed henceforth only to be expounded. Marx was only too keenly aware of the incompleteness of his work, and he returned intermittently to a reconsideration of some of his fundamental conceptions; for example, the classification of pre-capitalist societies, and especially the nature of the Asiatic type of society.

In this sense, then, of considering himself the possessor of a complete and finished theory of society, Marx was not a Marxist. In another sense, which is still more important in relation to the political history of the twentieth century, Marx was also not a Marxist: he did not regard himself as the originator of a political creed which must be adopted as the unique doctrine of the working-class movement. From his earliest to his latest writings Marx takes a consistent view: in a letter to Ruge of September 1843 he writes

'... I am not at all in favour of raising our own dogmatic banner. Quite the contrary.... We do not confront the world in doctrinaire fashion with a new principle, saying: Here is the truth, bow down before it! We develop new principles for the world out of its own existing principles.... We may sum up the outlook of our Journal[1] in a single phrase: the self-knowledge (critical philosophy) of the age about its struggles and aims. This is a task for the world and for ourselves.'

And in 1880, Marx prefaces his 'enquête ouvrière' with an appeal to the French workers to reply to the questionnaire, since only they can describe 'with full knowledge the evils which they endure', and 'only they, not any providential saviours, can energetically administer the remedies for the social ills from which they suffer'.

I do not claim that Marx never deviated from this view, or that he was never tempted to impose his own conception of the aims and the appropriate tactics of the working-class movement. But the recent publication of the records of the First International[2] has shown how little authoritarian Marx was in his political

[1] The proposed *Deutsch-Französische Jahrbücher* of which one double issue was published in 1844.
[2] *Documents of the First International*, Vol. I 1864–66, Vol. II 1866–68 (Moscow, 1964).

activities, and this is confirmed entirely by his attitude to the Paris Commune and its failure. In his relations with other socialists Marx sometimes gives an impression of dogmatism, but I believe that it was rather the irritation of a great and creative thinker in his encounters with men who were not only much less able, but who lacked Marx's dedication to scientific inquiry. Proudhon, for instance, was a purely speculative thinker, Bakunin a passionate and woolly-minded revolutionary. Neither of them ever conceived or carried out a rigorous social investigation, and, hence, they were treated by Marx with a contempt which is perhaps distasteful to us, but which is not without justification.

There runs unmistakably through all Marx's work (even in his youthful writings when he is still struggling out of the toils of the Hegelian philosophy) a profound commitment to the investigation of *social facts*; a commitment which again finds expression in his preface to the *'enquête ouvrière'*, where he appeals to those who, '. . . desiring social reform, must also desire *exact* and *positive* knowledge of the conditions in which the working class, the class to which the future belongs, lives and works'. The 'Marxism' in Marx's own thought, and in that of his followers, has frequently been seen as the subordination of theoretical ideas and social investigations to a preconceived social ideal and a rigorously determined means of attaining it. I have already suggested that this view is mistaken with respect to Marx himself, inasmuch as it was his declared intention to make clear to his age *its own* strivings, and more particularly to display to the working class its real situation in capitalist society, the implications of its revolt against that situation, and the probable outcome of the working-class movement.

It will be profitable, however, to consider more closely the relations between theoretical judgements, judgements of fact, and judgements of value in Marx's work. The first point to note is that in Marx's life socialism and social science were closely interwoven. He became, at an early age, and probably through the influence of Saint-Simonian doctrines, a sympathiser with the working-class movement; and this commitment to socialism certainly preceded the full elaboration of his sociological theories. Nevertheless, from the beginning he was equally impressed by the new 'science of society' prefigured in Saint-Simon's writings (and subsequently in Lorenz von Stein's book on the social movement in France); and his later reading of the historians of the French Revolution and of the political economists was sufficient to persuade him both that there was growing up a new field and a new method in the study of man's social life, and that the development of capitalism and the rise of the labour movement formed the essential subject matter of this study. From that time, about the middle of the 1840s, Marx's participation in the socialist movement and his efforts to advance the theoretical science of society proceeded together, and fructified each other. This, after all, is not surprising, nor uncommon. The greatest social scientists have been passionately concerned about some social problem, and usually extremely partisan (I think of Max Weber, Durkheim, and Pareto) and this may account for the significance and the intellectual excitement of their work. The question is whether this partisanship manifests itself too strongly, not simply in the selection of subjects for inquiry, but in the formation of concepts and models, which become ideal-types of too ideal a kind, and in the conduct and presentation of their investigations, which become too selective, too well insulated against the possible discovery of counter-instances.

In Marx's case (but also in some of the others, and notably in Durkheim's) there is also a more profound problem. Does the theory, or the broader scheme of thought, contain within itself a theory of knowledge which eliminates the distinction between fact and value? There are several features of Marx's thought which need to be considered here. The idea of the social determination of thought appears to destroy the autonomy of moral judgements; but in the same manner it destroys the autonomy of all judgements (including those judgements which constitute Marx's own theory, so that there is no longer any point in asking whether it is true or false). But this is not a problem in Marx's theory alone: it is a problem for any deterministic theory, and in a broad sense of any scientific theory, in psychology or sociology. It may, indeed, be argued, on the other side, that one of the virtues of Marx's social theory is that it makes a much greater allowance for the creative work of human reason in the fashioning of social institutions.[1]

A more specific problem appears in Marx's theory of ideologies, which, while it excludes science from the realm of socially determined ideas, makes moral notions wholly ideological in the sense of reflecting the interests of social classes. This makes moral ideas relative, yet Marx also expresses what appear to be absolute moral

[1] Marcuse, in *Reason and Revolution* (New York, 1941), presents the case for Marx's 'critical philosophy' and against Comte's sociological positivism in these terms; and more recently Sartre, in his *Question de méthode* (Paris, 1960), has argued in a similar fashion.

judgements. If this is, indeed, the case there is a contradiction in his thought. The controversy over this question has recently come to be expressed in somewhat different terms as a result of the interest in Marx's early writings. Is there, for Marx, a permanent, unchanging essence of man, which is alienated in certain forms of society, but which in others can find its full expression, and which can thus be treated as a moral ideal in some version of a morality of self-realisation? Or is the essence of man a purely historical phenomenon, so that no universal ideal or criterion of morality can be formulated at all? I shall not attempt to resolve this problem here. Marx did not attempt to do so, and to say the least his thought is obscure on this subject, while the later Marxist contributions, such as Kautsky's *Ethics and the Materialist Conception of History*, fall far below the level of a genuine philosophical discussion. I will only say that I consider possible and plausible an interpretation of Marx's ethical conceptions as being both rationalist and historical; that is, as recognising some basic and permanent human needs which ought to be satisfied, and which can be expressed in some coherent moral ideal, and yet seeing these needs as assuming different forms in different historical states of society.

A view of this kind would allow us to resolve another problem in the theory of ideology, namely, that although it appears as thoroughly relativistic it does nonetheless permit, in conjunction with other parts of Marx's theory, an unbounded dogmatism. This occurs in the following way: all moral ideas are class ideas and thus relative, but the working class is the rising class in modern society (as shown by the sociological part of the theory) and so its moral ideas are superior and should prevail. Criticisms of the social and political aims of the working class, and even of the means employed to attain them, can only arise from other class positions and are to be condemned out of hand as inferior because *dépassé*. Not only is it possible, in this way, to adopt an absolutist moral stance, on the basis of a relativistic moral theory, but the theory of ideology can be used to dismiss any arguments of one's opponents, whether these are moral or theoretical arguments.

It is hardly necessary to observe that Marxists have in fact used the theory in this manner *ad nauseam*. It may be more necessary to say that Marx himself did not argue in this fashion. First, there is the element in Marx's thought mentioned earlier, which is concerned with a permanent human essence or morality. Secondly, careful scrutiny of Marx's work shows that he never dismissed any serious theoretical view merely on the ground that it expressed a non-proletarian ideology. From his criticism of Bauer in *The Jewish Question*, through *The Poverty of Philosophy*, up to the critical examination of modern political economy in *Capital* and *Theories of Surplus Value*, Marx undertakes primarily to show by theoretical argument and empirical tests that the views he is opposing are *false*, and only later, if at all, does he refer to their ideological sources. There is a good example in one of the lesser known sections of *The German Ideology*, where Marx criticises utilitarianism on the ground that its reduction of all human relationships to a single relation of utility results in a false conception both of human nature and of social life. Only in conjunction with this theoretical examination of the doctrine does he propose a sociological account of it as an ideology which faithfully reflects the kind of social relations that modern capitalism actually tends to produce. In this instance, I think both the theoretical and the sociological analyses are extraordinarily fruitful, and the latter could be pursued much further, as it was, for example, by Simmel in his *Philosophy of Money*, where the influence of Marx's ideas is extremely strong.

However, I do not wish to single out Marx's own scientific rectitude as the only restraint upon his ideological enthusiasms, even though it does form a striking contrast with the attitude of some of his followers. There is also the fact that in Marx's lifetime his theoretical analysis and his allegiance to the labour movement were congruent and, in a sense, mutually supporting. The labour movement developed spontaneously, and Marx could easily justify his claim to be analysing and explaining a real process of social change. The gulf between classes was widening, class consciousness was growing, the relations between classes did form the core of the social problem, and the new doctrines of working-class organisations did foreshadow the classless society which Marx predicted. Thus, Marx's theory could find empirical confirmation, and its empirical testing provided at the same time a degree of rational and factual support for Marx's moral convictions. How closely these two aspects were associated is shown especially well in the projected '*enquête ouvrière*' of 1880, which is first of all in the tradition of a long series of empirical surveys of working-class conditions, but which, secondly, goes beyond these in attempting to establish the principle of an investigation of working-class conditions by the working class itself, and which does so in order to combine in a single effort of research both a factual inquiry and a heightening of class consciousness.

Here Marx's two aims are in perfect concord. We may ask whether the combination is legitimate, and I would answer with a qualified affirmative. If sociology is to have any application to actual social life, then one of its most important applications should be the wide diffusion of knowledge about the nature of social relationships in a given society in order to increase men's conscious self-regulation of their social life. And in societies where whole classes of men are excluded from any significant part in the regulation of public affairs, it is proper to concentrate upon awakening and fostering in those particular classes a consciousness of their place in society, of their material and intellectual poverty, their lack of rights, their exclusion from power. But as the knowledge of society increases, as the position of classes changes, so must sociological thought follow these movements, revise its initial propositions, and conceive new empirical inquiries. It is here that Marx and the Marxists diverge. To take only one example: I do not think that there has been a single important contribution to the study of modern social classes from the side of orthodox Marxism. Yet, Marx's influence has been immense, and two recent works—one theoretical, S. Ossowski's *Class Structure in the Social Consciousness*, the other historical, E. P. Thompson's *The Making of the English Working Class*—show how fruitful that influence may be, so long as one is not an orthodox Marxist.

In this paper I have been concerned with a reassessment of Marx's sociology in relation to his 'Marxism'. I have not said anything, except by implication, about the validity or usefulness of his theories at the present day. Does Marx's thought belong simply to the history of sociology, or does some part of it survive today as a significant element in the general body of accepted sociological theory? I believe that the latter is true—that Marx's 'conflict' model, and especially the theory of classes, his account of ideologies, his theory of revolution, must find a place in sociological theory—but also that both are important. For sociology is not quite like a natural science where theory advances in linear fashion and the history of the subject is simply its history, inessential to the comprehension of theoretical principles; it is also somewhat like philosophy, in which perennial problems are examined from different standpoints, and where knowledge of these diverse approaches and their successive appearances constitutes the theoretical grasp of the subject. In this sense I do not think that we shall ever be quite finished with the re-evaluation of Karl Marx.

PART II

Classes and Elites

Chapter 6

In Search of a Proletariat[1]

According to Alain Touraine: 'A new type of society is now being formed. These new societies can be labelled post-industrial to stress how different they are from the industrial societies that preceded them. . . . They may also be called technocratic because of the power that dominates them. Or one can call them program-med societies to define them according to the nature of their production methods and economic organisation.'[2]

This description does not differ widely from those which have been formulated by a number of other writers. Brzezinski, for example, has observed that 'America is in the midst of a transition that is both unique and baffling . . . ceasing to be an industrial society, it is being shaped to an ever increasing extent by techno-logy and electronics, and thus becoming the first *technetronic society*';[3] while Daniel Bell, in his 'Notes on the Post-Industrial Society',[4] emphasises the central importance of theoretical know-ledge in the system of production, and the shift from a manu-facturing economy to a service economy.

But if the initial descriptions of the new society are similar, the interpretations of its historical character and potentialities are not. Brzezinski and Bell conceive it as a society in which major social divisions have been largely overcome,[5] the domination

[1] Reprinted, with minor revisions, from the *New York Review of Books*, XVIII (6) (6 April 1972).

[2] *The Post-Industrial Society* (New York, 1971), p. 3.

[3] Zbigniew Brzezinski, 'The American Transition', *New Republic* 157 (23 December 1967), pp. 18–21; reprinted in *Information Technology in a Democracy*, edited by Alan F. Westin (Cambridge, Mass., 1971), pp. 161–7.

[4] *The Public Interest* 6 and 7 (Winter 1967 and Spring 1967), pp. 24–35 and 102–18.

[5] The same idea is expressed by Raymond Aron in several of his writings on modern industrial society, especially in *Progress and Disillusion* (New York, 1968), p. 15, '. . . experience in most of the developed countries suggests that semi-peaceful competition among social groupings is gradually taking the place of the so-called deadly struggle in which one class was assumed to eliminate the other.' Daniel Bell raised some objections to my formulation of his views and an exchange of letters took place between us in the *New York Review of Books*, XVIII (11) (15 June 1973), p. 38.

of technically competent elites is more or less widely accepted, and the general course of social development is determined by a relatively harmonious process of economic growth. In such a society, it is claimed, there will be no basis for widespread dissent:

'. . . it seems unlikely that a unifying ideology of political action, capable of mobilising large-scale loyalty, can emerge in the manner that Marxism arose in response to the industrial era. . . . The largely humanist-oriented, occasionally ideologically minded intellectual dissenter, who saw his role largely in terms of proffering social critiques, is rapidly being displaced either by experts and specialists, who become involved in special governmental undertakings, or by the generalists–integrators, who become in effect house ideologues for those in power, providing overall intellectual integration for disparate actions.'[1]

Touraine's view is entirely different. The social conflict between capital and labour, he suggests, is losing its central importance in the capitalist societies of the late twentieth century, but new forms of domination (which are to be seen also in the state socialist societies) are giving rise to new social conflicts—between those who control the institutions of economic and political decision-making and those who have been reduced to a condition of 'dependent participation'.[2] The new dominant class is no longer defined by property ownership, but by 'knowledge and a certain level of education'. The revolt against it arises from the will of the dependent class to break away from its dependence and to embark upon an autonomous development. Touraine supports this idea of the changing nature of social conflict by referring to the growth of new social movements, especially those that took a prominent part in the revolt of May 1968, in France:

'One of the significant aspects of the May Movement is that it demonstrated that sensibility to the new themes of social conflict was not most pronounced in the most highly organised sectors of the working class. The railroad workers, dockers, and miners

---

[1] Brzezinski, op. cit.
[2] 'Dependent participation', or alienation, exists when 'a man's only relationship to the social and cultural directions of his society is the one the ruling class accords him as compatible with the maintenance of its own domination. . . . Ours is a society of alienation, not because it reduces people to misery or because it imposes police restriction, but because it seduces, manipulates and enforces conformism' (p. 9).

were not the ones who most clearly grasped its most radical objectives. The most radical and creative movements appeared in the economically advanced groups, the research agencies, the technicians with skills but no authority, and, of course, in the university community' (p. 18).

This is not a reversion, he observes, 'to meaningless themes like the end of the working class'. It is plain that 'no socio–political movement of any strength can develop unless it includes the labouring class, which contains the greatest number of dependent workers'. The question is a different one: whether the working class can be conceived any longer, in Marxist terms, as the principal animator of social conflicts and the privileged agent of historical change. Touraine, basing his analysis mainly upon the social movements and conflicts of the 1960s, argues that it cannot:

'In modern societies a class movement manifests itself by direct political struggle and by the rejection of alienation: by revolt against a system of integration and manipulation. What is essential is the greater emphasis on political and cultural rather than economic action. This is the great difference from the labour movement, formed in opposition to liberal capitalism. Such movements are scarcely yet beginning but they always talk about power rather than about salaries, employment or property' (p. 74).

Touraine associates with the emergence of these new social conflicts the development of an intellectual confrontation between two kinds of sociology. On one side the 'sociology of decision' is concerned with the management of social tensions, adaptation, and the reconciliation of dissenting groups. It is the sociology practised by Brzezinski's 'experts' and 'house ideologues', who serve the new rulers of society. On the other side is the 'sociology of opposition', which seeks to interpret the significance, the tendencies and aims, of those social movements which are in conflict with the existing society. Touraine emphasises that these are two *sociologies*, which must 'struggle for an explanation of the facts', not confine themselves 'within self-righteousness and the repetition of ideology'. A sociology of opposition only becomes possible when there are facts to be explained, when society begins to react to its own changes, defines new objectives, and experiences 'the social and cultural conflicts through which the direction of the changes and the form of the new society may be debated'.

This attempt—made in the particular context of French society

—to discern the social basis of the new radicalism, to furnish it with a theory of society, and to define its relationship with the labour movement and with Marxism, has its counterparts elsewhere: in Germany, in what is known as 'critical theory', and in the English-speaking world, rather less incisively, in various prolegomena to a 'critical sociology'. Albrecht Wellmer's book[1] provides a useful, though not easy, introduction to 'critical theory'. His exposition takes in three interwoven themes: first, the development of ideas within the Frankfurt school of sociology, from the writings of Horkheimer in the 1930s to those of Habermas in the late 1960s; secondly, the connection between this development and the changes in the socio–economic structure of Western capitalist societies; thirdly, the differentiation of 'critical theory' from the hermeneutic interpretation of social events on one side and from Marxism on the other.

Some of the leading ideas of the Frankfurt school were expounded by Horkheimer in a series of articles published in the mid-1930s[2] upon which Wellmer draws for much of his discussion. The Frankfurt sociologists and philosophers regarded their theoretical work as part of the revolutionary struggle which was being waged by the proletariat against capitalism. Because of the circumstances of the time—the economic breakdown of capitalism and the pre-eminent role of the working-class movement (notwithstanding its defeat in Germany and the extent of the internal divisions between communists, social democrats, and anarchists) in the opposition to fascism—the main object of their theoretical criticism was, as for Marx himself, political economy. That is to say, they were engaged in an analysis of the economic contradictions of capitalism which would have made possible a revolutionary struggle for socialism.

Even at this time, however, Horkheimer introduced another element into critical theory. Although only the proletariat *could* discover in critical theory the self-consciousness of its political struggle, it would not necessarily do so; the situation of the proletariat is no 'guarantee of true knowledge'. The revolution will only be brought about by the conscious will of the masses if there is a successful 'process of anticipation of a rational society', both in thought and in the organisation of the working-class movement.

[1] Albrecht Wellmer, *Critical Theory of Society* (New York, 1971).
[2] They appeared originally in the *Zeitschrift für Sozialforschung* and have now been collected in Max Horkheimer, *Kritische Theorie* (2 vols, Frankfurt, 1968).

This idea, that the attainment of socialism depends upon the formation of an intention to create a liberated, rational society—an intention which has to take practical shape in mass organisations—became increasingly important in critical theory when the work of the Frankfurt school was renewed after 1945, and it led to a displacement of attention from the 'economic contradictions' to the political and cultural apparatus of modern capitalism. This re-orientation was in part a reaction against the Stalinist version of Marxism, in which socialism was reduced to an expression designating the form of society whch emerged more or less mechanically from an economic transformation accomplished under the leadership of a communist party; but it was also a response to the changed social position of the working class as it experienced 'the benefits of a regenerated, state-interventionist capitalism'.

Wellmer gives particular attention to the first of these influences, in a chapter on the 'latent positivism of Marx's philosophy of history'. This 'positivism' he discovers in Marx's conception of a 'natural science' of human history, in which human activity, the self-creation of man, is comprehended only as *labour*, as the production of objects. The succession of different systems of production, including the transition to a classless society, is seen as a necessary, determined process. Although Marx also expressed (especially in his early writings) a different notion of activity, as human interaction or *praxis*,[1] the positivist conception, according to Wellmer, predominates in Marx's own thought and in later Marxism. It can be formulated as the assumption that 'the irresistible advance of technical progress, which starts with the capitalist mode of production, has to be interpreted as the irresistible advance towards the commonwealth of freedom' (p. 73). This, Wellmer argues, 'provides the starting point for an erroneously technocratic interpretation of history, which was to become a practical reality in the hands of the omniscient administrators of historical necessity' (p. 69).

The extent to which critical theory has now diverged from Marxism can be seen from Wellmer's conclusion:

'Since history itself has thoroughly discredited all hopes of an economically grounded 'mechanism' of emancipation, it is not only necessary for a theoretical analysis to take into account

[1] See the discussion in Jürgen Habermas, *Knowledge and Interests* (London, 1971).

entirely new constellations of "bases" and "superstructures"; in fact, the criticism and alteration of the "superstructure" have a new and decisive importance for the movements of liberation. In order to reformulate Marx's supposition about the prerequisites for a successful revolution in the case of the capitalist countries, it would be necessary to include socialist democracy, socialist justice, socialist ethics and a "socialist consciousness" among the components of a socialist society to be "incubated" within the womb of a capitalist order' (pp. 121–2).

He goes on to argue, finally, that Marx's concept of class has largely lost its utility as an instrument of analysis, and that because science has become the 'form of life' of industrial societies, enlightenment is only possible as an enlightenment of those who participate directly or indirectly in science. Thus the opposition between 'critical' and 'traditional' thought can no longer be interpreted in purely political terms as the expression of a class conflict, but must be settled on the ground of science itself—or in other words, mainly in the universities.

This latest form of critical theory seems to resolve the struggle for a new society into a purely intellectual contest. It is very unlike Touraine's theory, which, although it begins from similar ideas about the role of science in production and the diminishing importance of the conflict between bourgeoisie and proletariat, conceives the antagonisms in the post-industrial societies as political struggles between new social classes. Touraine emphasises the historical continuity in social movements and ideologies, and recognises that the working class is still, despite its changed conditions of life, a vital element in any radical movement.

But critical theory, in Wellmer's version of it, appears to make a clear break with the past and to separate itself as completely as possible from the traditional labour movement. The dangers inherent in such an outlook are obvious. Critical theory may become confined within a narrow intellectual milieu as a defiant, arrogant, but despairing criticism of a world in which the very desire for liberation is being extinguished, and which the critic is powerless to change. Indeed, this is the character that it assumed in Marcuse's *One-Dimensional Man*. As Wellmer himself notes, critical theory, in its later development by Adorno, Horkheimer, and Marcuse, 'conceives itself as a protest, but as a protest impotent in practice'.

Only the growth of a radical student movement overcame for a time the tendency toward pessimism and withdrawal in Marcuse's work; but this movement itself has proved too limited, too uncertain, to provide the nucleus of a force that could really change society. Wellmer, who is unwilling to accept the sterile opposition between the enlightened critic and a benighted world, tries to resolve the problem by assigning to critical social theory the task of showing 'the contradiction between society as it is, and what it could be and must be in terms of its technical possibilities and of the interpretations of the "good life" acknowledged within it'. The eventual test of the theory, then, would be that large numbers of people came to see this contradiction and entered upon a struggle to achieve the 'good life' as they understood it, in opposition to what now exists.

This is reminiscent of Marx's declaration (in 1843) that 'we develop new principles for the world out of its existing principles ... we show the true nature of its struggles ... and explain its own actions'. What is lacking is any equivalent of Marx's subsequent discovery of the proletariat; that is to say, the identification of actual social groups, already engaged in diverse conflicts, whose actions can plausibly be interpreted as developing into a general rejection of the existing form of society and an attempt to create a new social order. From this point of view, the philosophical discussion pursued by Wellmer is inconclusive, and even misleading in so far as it turns the whole question into a matter of scientific debate, and it needs to be extended into the kind of sociological inquiry that Touraine undertakes.

What is common to the work of Wellmer and Touraine is the effort to construct a post-Marxist theory of post-industrial society. Norman Birnbaum, in his volume of essays[1] (as in his earlier book *The Crisis of Industrial Society*), undertakes in a more tentative fashion an analysis of the changes in industrial societies, and a critical appraisal of the attempts to comprehend them. His general outlook is well conveyed in the essay on 'late capitalism in the United States', where he writes: 'What we face is a situation of genuine historical indeterminacy.... Our situation is ... not unlike that of the first generation of Marxists in the face of new historical forces.' In one of the best of these essays he subjects Marxism itself to a critical analysis in which its principal inadequacies are clearly set out: the difficulties with the notions of class and class conflict in the societies of the late twentieth century; the failure to analyse political power in any other way than by asserting its direct dependence upon the situation of social

[1] Norman Birnbaum, *Toward a Critical Sociology* (New York, 1971).

classes; the neglect of cultural changes and their possible consequences in political life.

Elsewhere, Birnbaum examines some of the ideas and interpretations which have been formulated either as revisions of the Marxist theory or as alternatives to it, and shows himself to be just as severe a critic of these new theoretical schemes as he is of the more orthodox and dogmatic versions of Marxism itself. Concluding a brief review of writing on the 'post-industrial revolution', he remarks that this notion 'cannot be used in serious discussion unless those utilising it are prepared to do the rigorous work of specifying precisely the social forces at work, their direction, and their consequences for the future of industrial societies' (p. 414). (This, however, is exactly what Touraine has undertaken.) Earlier in the same essay Birnbaum affirms the continuing importance of the concentration of property ownership, against the view that the industrial societies are now dominated by a technocratic elite. But at the same time he recognises that a technocratic or 'knowledge' elite which does not own property is a significant new phenomenon in these societies.

In what way, then, do these essays disclose a movement 'toward a critical sociology'? Certainly they offer a broad and often penetrating criticism of many current interpretations of the changes that are going on in the industrial countries (for example, in Birnbaum's dissection of Roszak's idea of the counterculture). They help to reveal the full extent of the disagreements and uncertainties among radical thinkers. But they do not attempt to formulate an alternative 'critical theory'. Such self-denial may have a justification. If our historical situation really has the indeterminacy that Birnbaum attributes to it, then critical thought, however much it is inspired by the aim of bringing about a liberated society, is likely to reflect, and should reflect, this state of affairs in its own tentative and exploratory character.

However, one of the intellectual disagreements in the radical movement concerns precisely the extent to which our situation *is* indeterminate, and the future indecipherable. The differences in outlook between Wellmer and Touraine on one side and Birnbaum on the other seem to arise in part from differences in the social environments in which they are active. In France and Germany the social critic forms his ideas within the socialist labour movement and an influential tradition of Marxist thought. Changes in the character of the working class (and more generally in the class structure), and the problems that arise within Marxism in attempting to comprehend these changes, may lead him to a revision of Marxism or to the elaboration of a new theory which builds upon Marxism. But this work of criticism, and the renewal of ideas, takes place in a milieu in which there are still large and active social movements engaged in a political struggle for a socialist society.

In the USA the absence of a socialist labour movement, and of any substantial body of Marxist thought, means that the social situation has been indeterminate, from the point of view of a radical thinker, for some time, and the present uncertainties repeat, in large measure, those which appeared at earlier times in this century. This characteristic is recognised, in a particularly constructive way, in a recent essay by Richard Flacks[1] based upon discussions among a group of radical social scientists. Flacks suggests that in order to stimulate the kind of intellectual work that would help to bring about a social transformation it is useful to define the objective in the following way: 'Let us imagine that an organised socialist movement or party existed in the US, what kinds of things would sociologists do who were allied to it?'

Starting from this supposition he outlines the major problems, some theoretical, but most of them empirical, which would form the subject matter of a critical sociology. The problems are broadly similar to those upon which Touraine concentrates his analysis— the potentialities of a postindustrial society seen from a socialist perspective, and the question of the possible agents of change, of the ways in which the new social groups of educated workers, technicians, administrators may develop a radical outlook and radical political action.

Thus Flacks sets out as problems for inquiry such issues as the following (which I have taken from different sections of his paper and paraphrased): To what extent could existing technology eliminate routinised human labour? What are the political, economic, cultural, and social barriers to such a development under capitalism? Is postindustrialism possible within one country; can 'post-scarcity' be achieved without imperialism? How far are Americans (and which Americans) prepared to trade certain kinds of possessions and commodities for reduced labour, improved natural and urban environments, a richer community life, education, health, and other social services? What evidence is there of a new working-class consciousness (among educated workers, for

[1] Richard Flacks, 'Towards a Socialist Sociology: Some Proposals for Work in the Coming Period', *The Insurgent Sociologist* II (2) (Spring 1972).

instance)? What are the main sources of support for and resistance to the existing movements for radical change?

The eventual test of any 'critical theory' or 'sociology of opposition' can only be the development, or failure to develop, of large-scale social movements which aim to create, and begin to create in practice, an egalitarian, noncoercive form of social life. In the meantime the theory remains hypothetical. What justifies its existence at present, and makes such theoretical inquiry worthwhile, is the potentiality that has been revealed in the labour movement and in the new social movements of the past decade for a renewed activity to transform society.

Chapter 7

Class Structure and Social Consciousness[1]

In the opening pages of *History and Class Consciousness*[2] Lukács formulates a distinctive view of Marxism: '[Marxist theory] ... is essentially nothing more than the expression in thought of the revolutionary process itself.' This fundamental idea is restated in a variety of forms throughout the book. In a later essay, for example, Lukács characterises historical materialism as 'the self-consciousness of capitalist society', and elsewhere he argues, in the course of an analysis of the theory of knowledge in bourgeois philosophy, that the problems which arise from the separation of subject and object can only be resolved when a historical being appears which is at the same time both subject and object; which expresses in thought (as subject) its own historical practice (as object). This subject–object is, of course, the proletariat in capitalist society.

[1] Reprinted from István Mészáros (ed.), *Aspects of History and Class Consciousness* (London, 1971).

[2] First published in 1923, under the title *Geschichte und Klassenbewusstsein*, the book contains eight essays, some of which had appeared previously in slightly different versions. Soon after its publication the book was condemned as 'revisionist', 'reformist' and 'idealist' by the representatives of official Marxism; notably by Bukharin and Zinoviev at the 5th Congress of the Communist International in 1924. In the early 1930s Lukács himself publicly disavowed his book, and it was not reprinted until 1968, almost fifty years after the earliest essays in it had first appeared. The new edition contains a preface, dated March 1967, in which Lukács discusses some of the vicissitudes of his work and re-examines in a critical spirit some of the ideas which he expounded in the early 1920s. I shall refer to this critical reassessment later. Notwithstanding the account which Lukács has now provided, and other discussions, it is still not entirely clear why the book should have been so strongly condemned by the official Marxists, particularly in view of the fact that Lukács expresses the idea of the dominant role of the Communist Party in a manner which is entirely consonant with Leninism and Stalinism. It would be worthwhile, now that Lukács' book is available again, to undertake a comprehensive reconsideration of the intellectual history of Marxism in the decade after the First World War, when many of its ideas were being revised in the context of the Russian Revolution and other revolutionary movements.

Lukács' version of Marxism plunges us at once into difficulties. Marxist theory, it is claimed, is the expression in thought of the revolutionary process; but it is Marxist theory itself which tells us that there is a revolutionary process, and defines its character-istics. Or to state the problem in another way: Marxism is in part a theory of class ideologies, yet at the same time it is (or may be represented as being) itself a class ideology; and its validity or worth as an ideology is held to depend in some way upon its truth as a theory. Lukács himself recognises, and discusses briefly, the difficulty which arises from the fact that historical materialism has to be applied to itself; his solution is to claim that Marxism is true in the context of a particular social form of production, namely modern capitalism, and thus to accept a qualified relativism.[1] But he does not deal fully with that aspect of the question which is most important in his own work; namely, that if Marxism is conceived essentially as class consciousness this presupposes the result at which Marxism as a theory arrives—that classes, class conflict and class consciousness exist as primary historical forces. This presupposition underlies Lukács' book and gives a particular quality to the discussion, which is through-out ideological—that is to say, concerned with how Marxism should be conceived in order to be an effective instrument of the revolutionary proletariat—rather than theoretical or em-pirical.

It is not my purpose in this essay to consider the general features of Lukács' interpretation of Marxism, but simply to examine his analysis of class consciousness.[2] Since, however, it is in *History and Class Consciousness* above all that Lukács expounds his method, and since this method is connected in a peculiarly close fashion with the idea of class consciousness, it will not be possible to avoid some general reflections upon his conception of the proper Marxist method, or what he terms 'orthodox Marxism'.

In the essay on 'Class Consciousness' Lukács traces the his-torical development of the working class in capitalist society, and notes especially the general differences between the phenomenon of class as it appears in this specific form of society and the similar

[1] Lukács, op. cit. (French trans.), p. 263.
[2] The four essays in *History and Class Consciousness* which are most relevant to my discussion are: 'What is Orthodox Marxism?' (March 1919), 'The Changing Function of Historical Materialism' (June 1919), 'Class Consciousness' (March 1920), and 'Reification and Proletarian Consciousness' (1923).

phenomena in earlier forms of society. Following indications which were given by Marx, mainly in *The Poverty of Philosophy*, but also in a section of *The German Ideology* where it is suggested that class itself, in one sense, is a creation of the bourgeoisie, Lukács emphasises two important features: first, that class manifests itself in capitalist society as a national, rather than a local, bond; and second, that the two major classes of capitalist society —bourgeoisie and proletariat—are 'pure' classes, inasmuch as their economic character and interests emerge plainly and are no longer obscured by other kinds of relationships. Lukács, again following Marx, sees these circumstances as being exceptionally favourable for the development of working-class consciousness, but it is noteworthy that he does not advance beyond what Marx had already sketched, either in considering the history of working-class movements since Marx's time, or in examining, in the light of that history, some of the obstacles to the growth of working-class consciousness in capitalist society, and some of the difficulties in interpreting its character and course.

One example of these problems, which Lukács does not explore, is to be found in the contrast between the respective social situations of the bourgeoisie and the proletariat. Marx evidently took as his model of the development of classes and class consciousness the rise of the bourgeoisie in feudal society; yet there are important differences between that process and the subsequent development of the working class. The bourgeoisie was a third class in feudal society, not the directly exploited class, and it was directly associated with a new mode of production based upon a new technology. The situation of the proletariat is more similar to that of the feudal peasantry, and like the peasantry the industrial working class is not very clearly connected with a new, more progressive form of production. It is more obviously subjected to, and determined by, an established system of production. Marx once expressed the difference between feudalism and capitalism in an aphorism: 'The hand mill gives you a society with the feudal lord, the steam mill a society with the industrial capitalist'. The problem I have raised can be put in equally simple form by asking: what kind of mill would give rise to a classless or socialist society? In order to deal with this question it is necessary either to investigate, both structurally and historically, the role of the working class in the development of whatever new technology it is that will engender a new society; or else to present the issue in quite a different way by arguing that the working class has a freedom denied to any previous class, such that it is able to engage in an autonomous, conscious struggle for a new type of society without being the bearer of new technological forces.[1]

A second example of these problems bears more immediately upon the subject of class consciousness. While it may be true that the conditions of capitalist society permit the more rapid development of classes on a national scale,[2] and also bring economic interests more clearly into prominence,[3] other elements within these same conditions may impede the formation of new classes, and obscure the character of economic relationships. Thus, geographical and social mobility, the growing complexity of the division of labour, the expansion of the middle classes, all affect the possibility that the working class will develop as a political community with a distinct consciousness of its place in society and its long-term aims. Equally, the nature of capitalist production may obscure the fact of exploitation, even though it establishes economic interests as paramount. Neither the slave, nor the serf, can be in any doubt that he works in whole or in

[1] This question is evidently linked with problems in Marx's theory of social revolution, as this is applied to the particular case of capitalism. In general the theory states that a social system experiences a revolution when new powers of production develop (represented by a particular class) which can no longer be contained within the existing system; but in the case of capitalism Marx seems to emphasise an internal breakdown, resulting from the fact that capitalism is inherently unstable. The working-class revolution will have as its basis, not the progress of technology, but the strains produced by economic crisis, the accumulation of misery, and the conscious acceptance by the proletariat of a doctrine or doctrines which formulate a new social ideal.

[2] 'The real fruit of their battle lies, not in the immediate results, but in the ever expanding union of the workers. This union is furthered by the improved means of communication which are created by modern industry, and which place the workers of different localities in contact with one another. It was just this contact that was needed to centralise the numerous local struggles, all of the same character, into one national struggle between classes. . . . And that union, to attain which the burghers of the Middle Ages, with their miserable highways, required centuries, the modern proletarians, thanks to railways, achieve in a few years.' Marx and Engels, *The Communist Manifesto*.

[3] 'It is inevitable . . . that landed property, the *root* of private property, should be drawn completely into the movement of private property and *become a commodity*; that the rule of the property owner should appear as the naked rule of private property; of capital dissociated from all political colouring; that the relation between property owner and worker should be limited to the economic relationship of exploiter and exploited; that all personal relationships between the property owner and his property should cease, and the latter become purely *material* wealth; that in place of the honourable marriage with the land there should be a marriage of interest, and the land as well as man himself sink to the level of an object of speculation.' Marx, *Economic and Philosophical Manuscripts*.

part for the benefit of another man; but the wage-earner cannot perceive in such a direct way that a part of his labour is appropriated by others. Marx's object, indeed, in *Capital*, was to pierce the veil of commodity production and exchange in order to show the real social relationships which made possible the production of surplus value. But this theoretical model, which delineates the relations between classes in the process of production, is quite distinct from the actual historical development of social consciousness in particular classes; even though it does itself influence social consciousness. It is essential therefore, to study the real development and to relate the results of this study to the original economic analysis in order to discover whether the model is adequate. Lukács fails to do this, and instead substitutes a theoretical or speculative history for real history.

There is a third set of problems—connected on one side with the different social positions of the bourgeoisie and the proletariat, and on the other side with the question of the formation of class consciousness—which concerns the relation between thought and action. The thinkers who helped to form the consciousness of the bourgeoisie, and expressed the bourgeois outlook in social doctrines and world views, were themselves bourgeois; in this case, therefore, we do not need to suppose that there is a large gap between a form of social activity and the representation of that activity in thought. But in the case of the proletariat its consciousness is partly formed and expressed—for example, in Marxism itself—by thinkers who are *not* proletarians but bourgeois; and a genuine problem presents itself about the relation between the practical life of the working class and the interpretation of that life in socialist doctrines.

One of the principal themes in *History and Class Consciousness* is the consideration of this problem. Lukács writes, in the essay on orthodox Marxism, that '. . . a knowledge of its real situation and aims is not given immediately or naturally to the proletariat as a class (and still less to each individual proletarian)'; and he then goes on, in the essay on class consciousness, to make a distinction between 'psychological class consciousness', i.e. the immediate consciousness which workers have of their situation in society (which Lukács also describes as 'false consciousness'), and a 'possible consciousness' or 'imputed consciousness'. The argument is set out in the following passage:

'The sense of the notion of class consciousness is not confined to what men have thought, felt and willed in particular historical and class situations. This is important as the *material* of historical studies. But by relating this to the *totality* we arrive at the category of *objective possibility*: that is, the thoughts and sentiments which men would have had if they had been capable of grasping perfectly their situation and interests. This imputed rational reaction is class consciousness.'

In some respects this line of thought corresponds with Marx's ideas on the development of working-class consciousness, from the stage of sporadic and isolated actions to maintain wage-levels to the stage of political organisation and political struggle on a national scale. But important differences appear if we consider the relation which is posited between the earlier and later stages, and the manner in which the transition from one to the other is conceived. Lukács, in fact, does not see the question so much in terms of a historical development of consciousness as in terms of a more or less absolute distinction between 'psychological consciousness' and 'imputed' rational consciousness. The former is the actual consciousness of the working class, which Lukács describes as the material of historical studies,[1] not as a phenomenon which has important social effects, or which provides some kind of test of social doctrines themselves. The 'imputed' rational consciousness of the working class, on the other hand, is for Lukács, Marxism itself; that is to say, a social theory already worked out and established, which is brought to the proletariat from outside. Lukács repeats this notion still more plainly in the 1967 preface, where he associates his distinction between 'psychological' and 'imputed' or 'possible' consciousness with the distinction which Lenin made between 'trade union consciousness', which is all that the working class can attain by itself, and 'socialist consciousness' which is provided by revolutionary intellectuals. In practice, the meeting place of the working class, with its undeveloped consciousness, and the intellectuals, is the *party*; but the meeting is one-sided, for the party embodies above all a correct theory of the world, and it is therefore dominated by the ideologists. Lukács expresses this view when he refers to 'the correct class consciousness of the proletariat and its organisational form, the communist party'.

It should be evident that these conceptions diverge widely from

---

[1] The sense of this phrase is not entirely clear, but it seems to mean that actual working-class consciousness in a particular historical situation is only of interest as material for comparison with what a 'rational' consciousness would have been in that situation.

the idea of class consciousness which Marx adumbrated in various writings. Marx states quite plainly that the working class will, through its own efforts and experiences, attain a fully developed consciousness of its class situation and aims. Indeed, he considered that this process had already advanced some way, in the form of the various socialist movements, before he undertook his own studies. In *The Poverty of Philosophy* he observed that:

'Economic conditions had in the first place transformed the mass of the people into workers. The domination of capital created the common situation and common interests of this class. Thus this mass is already a class in relation to capital, but not yet a class for itself. In the struggle, of which we have only indicated a few phases, this mass unites and forms itself into a class for itself. The interests which it defends become class interests.'

Again, in one of his latest writings—the introductory note to his *Enquête Ouvrière* of 1880—Marx insisted that only the workers can describe 'with full knowledge the evils which they endure', and 'only they, not any providential saviours, can energetically administer the remedies for the social ills from which they suffer'. According to Marx, then, the working class was able to become a *class for itself*, and to assume responsibility for its own destiny. What part would be played in this process by intellectuals, by political parties and movements, Marx did not examine, but it seems clear that these would in any case be subordinate to the general development of the working class. At the other extreme, Lukács subordinates the working class to the 'rational consciousness' expounded by party ideologists, and thus provides an intellectual justification for the unrestrained dictatorship of the party which has characterised all the Soviet-type societies since 1917.

The results at which Lukács arrives derive only in part from his conception of Marxist method. The most important influence in determining his approach and conclusions is the initial definition of Marxism as class consciousness, rather than as a theory which stands in a complex relationship with the social outlook of the class with which it is mainly concerned. So far as method is concerned Lukács is more inclined to depart from than to follow his own prescriptions. In his essay on orthodox Marxism he emphasises two methodological notions: the *fluidity of concepts* (which he treats very briefly along the lines of Engel's discussion in *Anti-Dühring*), and the idea of totality, by which he means 'the integration of the facts of social life (as elements in a historical development) into a totality' in which they reciprocally influence each other. It may be questioned whether these ideas are so distinctive of Marxism,[1] but for the present purpose it is more important to notice that Lukács observes his own methodological rules very imperfectly. For example, his account of the differences between classes in capitalist society and classes in other forms of society leads, in his own words, toward a 'typology of class consciousness' (obviously influenced by the ideal-types of Max Weber); that is to say, toward a relatively fixed categorisation of types of class consciousness considered *in themselves*. The working class, and working-class consciousness, are not treated at all as elements in a total historical process, and Lukács, unlike Marx, does not relate them to the continuing development of human labour and of the forms in which it is organised.

Similarly, in spite of the insistence upon the fluidity of concepts the actual tendency of Lukács' writing is to reify them, and to turn such concepts as class, class consciousness, and even Marxism itself, into fixed and absolute entities. This propensity is strikingly illustrated by Lukács' initial discussion of Marxist method, in which he makes the following claim:

'Even if one were to suppose, without accepting, that modern research had demonstrated the factual inaccuracy of all Marx's specific propositions, an orthodox Marxist could accept all these new discoveries and reject all Marx's propositions without being compelled in any way to renounce his Marxist orthodoxy. Orthodox Marxism does not mean an uncritical acceptance of the results of Marx's research ... it refers exclusively to Marx's method.'

I find this passage difficult to understand, in a number of ways, and it is surprising that Lukács should repeat it, with great approval, in his new preface of 1967. Does it mean, for instance, that someone who rejected Marx's theory of class and class conflict would still, nevertheless, be a Marxist? Or would this question be met by arguing that the idea of class forms part of Marx's *method*, and that only the details of class relations in

[1] In my view Marx's thought is distinguished by its content—its theoretical statements—rather than by its method. Lévi-Strauss has commented on one aspect of this in his criticism of Sartre in the final chapter of *The Savage Mind*: 'It is possible that the requirement of "totalisation" is a great novelty to some historians, sociologists and psychologists. It has been taken for granted by anthropologists ever since they learned it from Malinowski.'

particular situations belong to the category of propositions which Lukács would allow to be rejected? More generally, what is the sense of saying that Marxist orthodoxy consists in accepting Marx's method, if at the same time it should be the case that this method produces nothing but false propositions? The significance of these questions, and others which might be derived from them, is that they reveal the fluidity of the notions of 'method' and 'theory', and the difficulty of separating the methodological and theoretical elements in any complex body of social thought. But Lukács, far from recognising this fluidity, establishes (without specifying) an absolute distinction between theory (propositions) and method which seems to me untenable, whether one is a Marxist or not.

There is another aspect from which to consider Lukács' book, which brings out, and at the same time helps to explain, its predominantly ideological character. To a much greater extent than is the case with other expositions of Marxism, Lukács' book is *zeitgebunden*; that is to say, deeply impregnated with the ideas and concerns of a particular historical time and place. It may be said, of course, that all social thought bears the marks of the age in which it was produced, but still there are differences: some systems of thought (and some works of art) have a more or less universal character and appeal. Marx's own thought unquestionably shows the impact of early industrial capitalism and of the French Revolution, but it is evidently not bounded by the conditions of Marx's time; besides an interpretation of the contemporary world it provides universal concepts and theories which are far from having lost their value and significance today.

With Lukács' book, however, one is inclined to say that it does primarily express, through a particular conception of Marxism and of the proletariat, the character of a very specific period. These essays were written at a time when revolutionary movements were occurring throughout much of Europe. The Russian Revolution had been successful, and it was followed by revolutionary struggles in Germany and Austria, and by a short-lived revolutionary regime in Hungary, in which Lukács himself took a leading part. His book provides, through the medium of an interpretation of Marxism, an idealised portrait of the revolutionary movement and the communist party; in contrast with a critical view of the same phenomena, such as was given, for example, by Rosa Luxemburg. In the light of the fact that there were no serious revolutionary struggles in some of the most advanced capitalist countries, that elsewhere the revolutions failed, and that where they succeeded (then and later) they produced, not a socialist society, but dictatorship, it is reasonable to see a greater validity in the more critical forms of Marxist theory, and to regard Lukács' work as expressing a very limited, transient mood and orientation. In many passages of his 1967 preface Lukács himself formulates a judgement of this kind on the ideas expounded in *History and Class Consciousness*. He observes, for instance, that his theory expressed a typical attitude to the basic problems of its time, and belongs to a period when the possibility of revolution in Europe was still real; and in a still more critical vein, that the idea of revolutionary practice set out in the book is closer to the left-wing messianic utopianism of the time than it is to Marx's own doctrine.[1] Perhaps the most disillusioned judgement which he makes upon his work, however, is to be found in his reflection at the beginning of the preface, upon what he refers to as 'the prevalent uncertainty of the present time about what a man should regard as the essential and durable content of his thought, and as his enduring method'.

The enormous gulf which separates us, and Lukács, from the period 1917–23, when these essays were composed, is brought home most forcefully if we consider the question put in the title of the first essay: 'What is Orthodox Marxism?' For us, today, this question manifestly has, and can have, no intellectual sense. A hundred varieties of Marxism flourish, as the hundred flowers were once supposed to bloom, and who is to say which is orthodox, which heretical? Is any serious thinker even interested in such a question? The only meaning which we can now attach to the term 'orthodox Marxism' is a historical one; it refers to a political dogma, promulgated by party leaders and upheld with the aid of the police and the executioner, which became established in the USSR in the 1920s and endured until 1956. In this particular historical form it is best described as 'official Marxism'.

In the concluding part of this essay I propose to examine class consciousness from a different point of view, based upon a different idea of Marxism. The starting point for this study is a general methodological proposition; namely, that Marxism is to be regarded primarily as a theory of society, not as an ideology. Its function is to explain class consciousness, not to express it fully. This is not to deny that Marxism (like every other social theory) has an ideological aspect; that it develops in particular

[1] It is also close to the messianic utopianism which flourishes in some circles at the *present* time, and this no doubt accounts in some degree for the renewed interest in Lukács' book.

historical conditions, expresses preferences and commitments which originate outside any social science, prescribes forms of action directed toward valued ends. But these two aspects—the theoretical and the ideological—are separable in some degree, and should be held separate. The least valuable form of Marxism is that in which they are conflated, as in Lukács' notion of Marxism as nothing more than the developed consciousness of the proletariat; for on one side this makes impossible any testing of the theory (which is assumed to be true, at least for a given historical period), and on the other side it can be shown that there is historically no complete coincidence between the consciousness of a class and a particular social theory. This point may be illustrated, in the first place, by considering the development of bourgeois class consciousness. This was not fully and exclusively expressed in any single theory, but assumed diverse forms in different times and places; thus, it may be argued that the bourgeois ideology is to be found in the political theory of Hobbes and Locke, in the Utilitarian philosophy, in the *Encyclopédie*, in classical political economy, or in the Protestant ethic. In fact, there is a cluster of ideas—about property, work, government, human nature, etc.—not entirely harmonious and not represented in any single theory, which may be taken to constitute the bourgeois outlook; but this outlook has to be constructed as an ideal-type, which can then be compared with actual historical manifestations. The case is similar with the development of working-class consciousness. Here too a number of related ideas, about labour, exploitation, equality, co-operation, find expression in diverse social theories, which range from Marxism to anarchism; and again it is necessary to construct an ideal-type of the working-class outlook, which may be compared with the actual development of class consciousness in different societies at different times.

The point of this construction of an ideal-type and its comparison with the real phenomena of social consciousness is not, as with Lukács, to assert the existence of a gap between 'psychological class consciousness' and a 'correct class consciousness' (i.e. Marxism) which is to be closed by the ideologists, but to describe, and so far as possible to explain, the divergences between the ideal-type and reality, and if it proves necessary, to reconstruct both the ideal-types and the theory in which they are used in order to arrive at a better understanding of the phenomena. Marx's conceptions of the bourgeoisie as a ruling class, and of the proletariat as a revolutionary class, can be treated in this way.

I have discussed elsewhere[1] some of the instances in which social conditions diverge from the ideal-type of a 'ruling class', and I shall not pursue this theme on the present occasion. If we now consider the situation of the working class in capitalist society from this point of view we have to distinguish two separate questions; one concerning the diversity within and the differences between particular societies, the other concerning the historical changes which have occurred with the development of capitalism as a social system.

It is obvious that the forms of working-class organisation and consciousness vary widely from one country to another. In France and Italy a considerable part of the working class gives its support to the communist party; that is to say, to a party which is officially Marxist and revolutionary. In Britain, West Germany, and the Scandinavian countries, a still larger proportion of the working class supports the mainly reformist social democratic or labour parties. On the other hand, in the USA the working class has had no distinctive political organisation, on a mass scale, since the First World War, and has produced no widely accepted radical or socialist doctrine. Even in those countries where a majority of the working class supports a distinctively working-class party (notably in Britain, where the association between class membership and political allegiance is particularly strong) there exist, nevertheless, a variety of left-wing parties and sects, all of which receive some working-class support. Furthermore, there is in all countries a substantial part of the working class which gives its support to liberal and conservative parties.

Over a fairly long period of time, therefore, the political consciousness of the working class has assumed diverse forms of expression within each country, while the dominant type of expression has come to differ quite radically from one country to another. It is by no means easy to give a satisfactory account of these variations; but it is clear, at least, that—to use the words which Marx employed in discussing a similar problem—'we shall never succeed in understanding them if we rely upon the *passepartout* of a historical–philosophical theory whose chief quality is that of being supra-historical.'[2] There is no basis for the view

---

[1] *Elites and Society* (London, 1964), Chapter II.

[2] Unfortunately, the official Marxists, among them Lukács, have done precisely what Marx warned against; they have shown a marked reluctance to engage in detailed historical studies of these phenomena and have relied instead upon the generalities of a historical–philosophical theory. In consequence, they have made a negligible contribution to our understanding of social classes in the twentieth century.

that the differences in working-class consciousness correspond with stages in the development of capitalism in such a way that a more revolutionary consciousness appears at a more advanced stage; for it is in Britain and in the USA, which have been, in different periods, the most developed capitalist countries, that a revolutionary working-class consciousness has most obviously failed to emerge. On the contrary, it may be claimed with greater plausibility that a revolutionary consciousness has established itself most strongly in those capitalist countries which were relatively backward and had a low *per capita* income.[1]

Aside from these general factors there have clearly been particular influences at work in each society, which have helped to create what may be called a 'national style' in politics. Here I can only mention very briefly some of the possible influences, which would need to be analysed more rigorously in any worthwhile comparative sociology of the manifestation of class consciousness in political doctrines. There has been in France the influence of a long revolutionary tradition; in Germany and in the countries of the former Hapsburg Empire the strains resulting from defeat in the First World War; in Britain, the conservative sentiments engendered by a long period of imperial rule, allied with social reform at home; in the USA the obstacles to class formation presented by ethnic and geographical divisions, the legacy of Negro slavery, and the egalitarian ideology. These national traditions and peculiarities, together with the economic factors which I have mentioned, need to be put in relation to Marx's model of the formation of a revolutionary proletariat if we are to be able to assess critically his whole theory of class and class conflict.

But a critical assessment of this kind requires also that we should pay attention to the second set of questions which I posed earlier; namely, those questions concerning the development of capitalist society as a whole. For Marx's theory of class was not a completely self-contained and autonomous body of propositions; it was linked with, and partly dependent upon, an analysis of the structure of capitalism as a total social system, and of the main tendencies in the historical development of that system. A Marxist

---

[1] This is suggested by S. M. Lipset, *Political Man* (New York, 1959), pp. 61–2. More recently, Alain Touraine, in *La société post-industrielle*, pp. 26–7, has observed that 'it is only in such countries as Italy and France, where the society is characterised by uneven industrial development, and by the resistance of archaic social and cultural forces, that the working class movement still has a certain revolutionary orientation'.

account of classes at the present time, therefore, involves a study of twentieth-century capitalism along the lines of Marx's unfinished study of nineteenth-century capitalism, and a similar attempt to determine the main directions of change.[1]

One of the most significant changes which has occurred between Marx's time and our own, as a consequence of developments in technology and in the whole system of production, is the steady expansion of the middle classes, which has as its correlate the contraction of the working class. This process has gone farthest in the USA, where the numbers engaged in middle-class occupations already exceed those in working-class occupations, but it is taking place more or less rapidly in all the capitalist countries. Marx himself touched upon the possibility of such a development when he wrote of the 'continual increase in numbers of the middle classes ... [who] rest with all their weight upon the working class and at the same time increase the social security and power of the upper class'; and still more plainly in several passages of the *Grundrisse*[2] in which he analyses the effects of machinery:

'Once brought within the capitalist process of production the instrument of labour goes through various metamorphoses, the last of which is the machine, or rather, the automatic system of machines ... directed by an automaton which is a self-acting motive force ... At this stage the machine works by itself; the worker has only to supervise the machine's activity and to ensure that nothing goes wrong with it. ... The process of production has ceased to be a process of labour ... The worker appears superfluous ... and the process of production a technological application of science. ... As large-scale industry develops the creation of wealth will depend less and less upon the duration of working time and the quantity of labour used, more and more upon the force of machines. ... It is man's productive powers in general, his understanding of nature and his ability to master it, which now appear as the basis of production and wealth.'[3]

It is true that Marx sets his discussion of these phenomena

[1] It would also involve, more broadly, a study of the new forms of stratification and political power in the Soviet-type industrial countries, but I shall not discuss these questions here.

[2] *Grundrisse der Kritik der politischen Ökonomie* (Rohentwurf) is the title given to the manuscript written by Marx in 1857–58, which was first published in full in 1939–41.

[3] Ibid., pp. 584–93.

in a particular context, and that when he refers to the application of science as the new basis of wealth he is speaking mainly of a potentiality in capitalist society which will be fully realised only in some future state of society. But the process which he describes has actually occurred within capitalism; the use of science has become immensely more important than physical work, and this change has transformed the structure of occupations, which in turn has affected the class structure. What consequences this change has had, and will have, for social consciousness, is still unclear. It depends on one side upon whether the new middle classes inherit and perpetuate a middle-class ideology; or rather, one should say, which of the possible middle-class ideologies— ranging from certain forms of left-wing radicalism to Fascism— are likely to become predominant. At the present time there are contradictory movements: a part of the middle class in some countries is preoccupied with threats to its traditional position in society, and with the need to re-establish 'law and order' (i.e. to repress dissent), while another part, including students and younger members of professional and scientific occupations, appears to be developing a more radical outlook. On the other side, the new social consciousness cannot help but be affected by the decline of the traditional working class; particularly by the decline of such occupations as coal-mining which gave rise to closely-knit, class-conscious political communities which played a leading part in the socialist movement. But in this case, too, there are contradictory tendencies. It may be that, as is often asserted, the ideologies (and the political practice) of labour and social democratic parties, and even of the communist parties in Western Europe, have become gradually more reformist, to such an extent in some cases that a national political consensus between 'left-wing' and 'right-wing' parties may be said to exist. If this is so, it is reasonable to suppose that the changing ideologies reflect in some degree the declining political importance of the working class. But such ideas were more readily accepted by sociologists in the 1950s than they are today, for there has now emerged an opposite tendency; among some young workers and workers in technologically advanced industries a new radicalism has appeared which finds expression in claims for a larger share in the management of the enterprise, and in the renewed interest in general notions of 'participation', 'industrial democracy' and 'workers' control'.

The task of a Marxist sociology is to investigate these changes in class structure, placing them in the total context of changes in the system of production (including, besides those aspects which I have mentioned, such phenomena as the development of giant international corporations), and to examine in detail, along the lines which I have sketched, the consequences which the changes have in the creation of new forms of social consciousness. But in order to deal thoroughly with these questions we must also take account of a second major change in modern capitalism, the achievement, over the past twenty-five years, of sustained economic growth, uninterrupted by major economic crises, which has produced a marked and continuing improvement in the general level of living. The effects of this change upon social consciousness are twofold. First, it reinforces the tendency, produced by the movement into middle-class occupations, to establish as predominant the image of modern societies as 'middle-class societies', in which other classes appear increasingly marginal in a political and ideological sense. Second, it establishes economic growth itself as a new ideology. Political debate in the capitalist countries has been increasingly concerned with such questions as technological progress, modernisation and growth; and these issues have overshadowed earlier preoccupations with class inequalities. Of course, it may be said that the indefinite continuation of steady economic growth is far from being theoretically demonstrated. Nevertheless, the experiences of twenty-five years, together with theoretical arguments concerning the ability of a 'managed' capitalist system to avoid serious economic crises, have persuaded a large part of the population that a condition of sustained economic growth and steadily increasing prosperity is both a reasonable expectation and a pre-eminent value; while on the other side the Marxist theory of capitalist crisis, which figured so prominently in the political struggles of the 1930s, has now been tacitly, or in a few cases explicitly, abandoned.

The intellectual uncertainties of the present time, to which Lukács alludes, are revealed in the disarray which prevails within some established ideologies (notably in Marxism itself) and in the emergence of a confusing variety of new doctrines, or new styles of thought (for example, in the student movements) which seem to be only loosely connected with social classes, or indeed with any identifiable social group which could be seen as a potentially effective agent of social change. It has become increasingly difficult to be sure of having understood the influences which form political consciousness, and thus to be able to discern the main direction of events. One thing at least is plain; we have long since passed out of the era in which the real consciousness of social groups, expressed in their beliefs and actions, could be discussed as mere 'psychological', 'false' consciousness, and be contrasted with the 'rational consciousness' enshrined in the ideology of a communist party.

Chapter 8

Class and Politics in Western Europe[1]

During the 1950s many sociologists came to accept the view that the class structure in Western European countries was undergoing a profound transformation, and that the direction of change was toward a form of society in which class differences would be much less marked, the barriers between classes less formidable, the opposition and conflict between them less acute, and the consciousness of class membership itself less vivid and intense. An extreme version of this view maintained that classes had almost, if not quite, disappeared as significant social groups in the most industrially advanced countries. The principal factors bringing about this new situation were generally considered to be the rapid and continued rise in levels of living; the advance of technology and the associated changes in the organisation of production; a redistribution of wealth and income resulting in part from the extension of social services financed out of progressive taxation; a higher rate of social mobility, due in large measure to the expansion of educational opportunities; and finally, in the ideological sphere, the overshadowing of earlier social problems by the post-war concern with economic growth in the industrial countries, industrialisation in the developing countries, the population explosion, and the threat of nuclear war.

These changes were described and interpreted in diverse, but largely complementary ways, in the writings of some of the most widely read social scientists of the 1950s and early 1960s. J. K. Galbraith, in *The Affluent Society*—a book which epitomises, in many respects, the social thought of that time—argued that there had occurred a 'decline of interest in inequality as an economic issue', and that the progressive increase of aggregate output was now seen as an alternative to redistribution. In line with this argument Galbraith redefined the 'social problem' as being no

[1] Reprinted from Margaret Scotford Archer and Salvador Giner (eds), *Contemporary Europe: Class, Status and Power* (London, 1971).

longer class inequalities, but the contrast between private opulence and public squalor.

Ideas of this kind did not merely reflect American experience in the postwar period. M. M. Postan, in his *Economic History of Western Europe, 1945–64*, has observed that the ascent of the European economy after 1945 was steeper and smoother than in any other period of modern history. Between 1918–38, he calculates, productivity in Western Europe increased at a rate of 1·7 per cent per annum, whereas between 1945–63 it increased at more than twice that rate, 3·5 per cent per annum. The aggregate GNP of Western Europe (at constant prices) was 2½ times greater in 1963 than in 1938. At the same time this postwar boom was much less interrupted by recurrent crises than was the case in any earlier period. The causes of this vigorous and more or less continuous growth are not entirely clear, but two important factors, according to Postan, were the very high rate of investment (much of which was government or government-sponsored investment), and the rapid and widespread advances in technology. Postan also suggests how an 'ideology of growth' emerged, not simply as a reflection of actual growth, but also arising out of earlier preoccupations with full employment which had their source in the controversies of the 1930s. 'Full employment', he writes, 'eventually developed into a policy and an economic philosophy much wider in its implications ... into a policy of economic growth.'

It is this process of growth, and the concomitant changes in the organisation of production and in government policy, with which Galbraith has been largely concerned, without considering in any detail its effects upon social stratification.[1] Two other influential social scientists, Raymond Aron and S. M. Lipset, have examined more directly the changes in class structure, in the context of economic growth and political action. Aron's view, which is expounded most fully in *La lutte de classes* (1964) and *Progress and Disillusion* (1968), may be summarised in the following way: as a result of economic development the system of stratification in industrial societies has become much more complex and the polarisation of society between the two antagonistic classes has not occurred; the proportion of industrial or manual workers in the population has not increased, and in the most advanced societies it has begun to decrease; working hours have been reduced and real incomes have increased; the rate of

[1] In his recent writings, especially *The New Industrial State*, Galbraith has discussed some aspects of stratification, and I shall refer to these later.

social mobility has increased or is now increasing. These changes mean, according to Aron, that the essential conditions for the formation and maintenance of a class system—the cohesiveness of each class, its continuity from generation to generation, the individual's awareness of belonging to a class, and the self-consciousness of the class itself—have been greatly weakened, if not destroyed. More broadly, Aron, like Galbraith, has re-defined the 'social question' in the second half of the twentieth century, by substituting for the contrast between capitalism and socialism a contrast between industrial and non-industrial societies; and by singling out as the vital and determining fact in modern societies the application of science to production irrespective of the character of the economic regime in which it occurs.

Lipset has treated the changing class structure in much the same way, though placing a stronger emphasis upon the 'end of ideology' and expressing with fewer qualifications the conviction that the old class structure of capitalist society has largely withered away. In *Political Man* (1959) he reached the conclusion that the conjunction of affluence and political democracy had already established the 'good society' (initially in the USA), with the result that no fundamental social and political changes can be expected, or for that matter desired, in this type of society. In a later essay on the western European countries,[1] he argues that '. . . instead of European class and political relationships holding up a model of the United States' future, the social organisation of the United States has presented the image of the European future'—that is to say, of a relatively 'classless' society from which there would be absent any profound ideological oppositions or political conflicts about the basic structure of the society.

Both Lipset and Aron arrived at the conclusion that class conflict and ideological politics had diminished greatly in the advanced industrial countries and would almost certainly con-tinue to decline. Lipset asserted the existence of a constant trend toward greater equality of income and the transformation of the class struggle into a process of limited bargaining between interest groups; while Aron observed, with some reservations, that '. . . experience in most of the developed countries suggests that semi-peaceful competition among social groupings is gradually taking the place of the so-called deadly struggle in which one

[1] S.M. Lipset 'The Changing Class Structure and Contemporary European Politics' in S. R. Graubard, *A New Europe?* (Boston, Mass., 1964).

class was assumed to eliminate the other'.[1] However, the re-appearance of flux, uncertainty and more intense conflict in political life since the mid-1960s has cast doubt upon some of these interpretations and is leading to reappraisals of the ideas about class structure which were current a decade ago. Aron's remarks on the class struggle, for example, were written before the events of May 1968 in France, and that upheaval, although it was initiated by a student revolt, seemed to some observers to assume the character of a massive confrontation between classes, of a kind unknown since the 1930s. The same events, in the context of a general resurgence of radical movements, prompted Lipset to intimate a revision of his earlier ideas; in the preface to a collection of papers on comparative political sociology[2] he writes:

'The year 1968 marks a watershed in the history of democratic mass politics: the quiet years of accommodation, integration and domestication were finally over, new waves of mobilisation and counter-mobilisation brought a number of Western democracies out of equilibrium, a new generation challenged the assumptions and the rhetoric of the old. The year 1968 also marks a watershed in the history of the international discipline of political sociology: the violent eruption of new forces did not only challenge the models and the theories of the fifties and sixties, but also forced a revaluation of data-gathering techniques and analysis strategies.'

In what way do the political events of the late 1960s oblige us to reconsider the kind of analysis of class structure which was commonly made in the previous decade? Let us consider first the contrast between the effects of economic growth and of re-distribution. There can be no argument about the reality of increasing affluence in the Western European countries, or about some of its consequences. A much larger proportion of the popu-lation than ever before has attained a level of living which, in material terms, is equivalent to that which was regarded as characterising the middle class a generation or so ago. Moreover, the continuance of economic growth at present rates will ensure that increasing numbers attain this level. In this sense, at least, we may speak of the emergence of 'middle class societies'. It is

[1] *Progress and Disillusion* (New York, 1968), p. 15.
[2] S. M. Lipset and S. Rokkan, Preface to *Party Systems, Party Organiza-tions, and the Politics of New Masses* (Papers of the 3rd International Con-ference on Comparative Political Sociology, Berlin, 1968).

also plausible to argue that a few years of economic growth at postwar rates makes a greater difference to working-class levels of living than any redistribution of wealth and income could achieve.

But these facts may be regarded in a different way. It is undoubtedly the case that working-class levels of living have improved largely as a result of economic growth, because there has been little or no redistribution of wealth or income. In Britain, several recent studies suggest that while there may have been some redistribution of income in favour of the poorest sections of the working class over the whole period since the beginning of this century, there was no substantial change between the 1930s and 1950s, and after 1959 it seems probable that there was again increasing inequality.[1] Similarly, although the concentration of wealth in the hands of the top 1 per cent of the population declined between 1911 and 1960, there was still no significant redistribution, since 75 per cent of all personal wealth remained in the hands of the top 5 per cent of the population (as against 87 per cent in 1911–13) and these property owners received 92 per cent of all income from property.[2] So far as the evidence is available there seems to have been no greater redistribution in other Western European countries.

Thus, although the general level of living has risen considerably, the *relative* positions of the various classes have changed little, if at all, since before the war; and the economic bases of class differentiation—the ownership or non-ownership of property— remain much as they were. The question we have to consider is whether these class differences have the same social and political significance at the present time, in conditions of general prosperity, as they had in the earlier history of the Western European societies. One thing is clear: we can no longer contrast working class and upper class (or *bourgeoisie*) simply in terms of poverty and wealth. There is a great deal of poverty in the affluent societies, but it is not the poverty of a whole class, or of a majority of the population. It is the poverty of particular social groups— old people, ethnic groups, immigrant workers, or workers in declining industries—and its abolition involves specific social policies, not necessarily a transformation of the class system; although it may be the case that such policies have been, or would

---

[1] See, for a summary of the data, S. Pollard and D. W. Crossley, *The Wealth of Britain* (London, 1968), Chapter 9.

[2] See Pollard and Crossley, op. cit.; J. E. Meade, *Efficiency, Equality and the Ownership of Property* (London, 1964).

be, more actively promoted by working-class or left-wing parties than by right-wing parties.

More generally it may be argued that increasing prosperity changes the character of the relations between classes even though their relative positions in the hierarchy of income and wealth remain unchanged. Aron, for instance, suggests that '... even if relative inequality has not been changed appreciably, the general increase in wealth has narrowed the gap between different modes of living. If the basic needs ... are provided in an approximately similar way, what real difference is made by great fortunes or huge incomes ... ?'[1] This view took a more specific form in the idea of the *embourgeoisement* of the working class; that is to say, the assimilation of the affluent working class into the middle class in terms of economic situation, style of life, cultural values and political outlook. It was partly a misleading analogy with the social situation in the USA (which has a historically unique class system), partly the social peace of the 1950s in the Western European countries, which gave credibility to this conception of a 'new working class'; but subsequent research, as well as the revival of radical politics, have cast doubt upon the existence of a general trend toward *embourgeoisement* in the cultural and political sense. The most thorough investigation yet made of affluent workers, by Lockwood, Goldthorpe and their colleagues, shows that there has been no change in the political allegiance of these workers, and concludes that '... the understanding of contemporary working-class politics is to be found, first and foremost, in the structure of the worker's group attachments and not, as may have been suggested, in the extent of his income and possessions.'[2] In France and Italy the political loyalty of a large part of the working class to the Communist Party is undiminished, as is the attachment of workers to the Social Democratic Party in West Germany, or to socialist parties in other Western European countries. In the Scandinavian countries, as Erik Allardt has pointed out, class membership has become increasingly important in voting; as traditional class barriers have been reduced working-class voters have been more apt to vote for workers' parties than before.

Nevertheless, it may be that a change in the political outlook and aims of the working class has come about as a result of increasing prosperity and can be discerned in the changing objectives

[1] Aron (1968), op. cit., p. 11.
[2] J. H. Goldthorpe, D. Lockwood, F. Bechhofer and J. Platt, *The Affluent Worker: Political Attitudes and Behaviour* (Cambridge, 1968), p. 82.

of the traditional working-class parties themselves, which no longer seek a fundamental transformation of capitalist society, but only the enactment of reforms within it. This notion, however, also seemed more plausible in the 1950s than it does in the late 1960s, when there is a marked, though still limited, revival of radicalism in working-class politics. In my view, the future development of the class system, and hence of some important aspects of political life, will be more strongly affected by changes in the situation of the working class in the process of production than by increasing prosperity. Among the most significant changes in the economic systems of the industrial societies is the movement of labour from the agricultural and extractive industries sector to the manufacturing sector, and then from the manufacturing sector to the services sector;[1] and within manufacturing industry itself the shift of labour from manual to clerical and professional occupations. This process has gone farthest in the USA, where clerical and professional workers already form a larger proportion of the labour force than do manual workers, but it is continuing rapidly in the Western European countries. Postan notes that in the UK employment in manufacturing industries increased between 1948 and 1962 by 1·1 million workers, but that 745,000 of these were 'salaried workers', mainly clerical and technical personnel. Similar changes have occurred in the other industrial countries, and they are likely to be accelerated with the advance of automation. Thus, it may be expected that the working class—the traditional class of manual, industrial workers, which is the subject of Marxist theory and of many sociological interpretations—will continue to contract as a proportion of the population, and this will necessarily have important social and political consequences. The working class can no longer figure in the same way as the rising and expanding class which Marx, for instance, depicted. It should be noted, moreover, that certain occupations, such as coal mining, whose members played a major role in the labour movement because they formed particularly class conscious and radical communities, have experienced an exceptionally rapid decline in numbers.

There is another important influence upon the situation of the working class in some of the developed industrial countries of Western Europe, which has similar implications; namely, the influx of immigrant workers either from former colonial terri-

---

[1] In Colin Clark's terminology, from the primary to the secondary and then to the tertiary sector.

tories or from the poorer countries of Europe.[1] These immigrants go, for the most part, into the least attractive and worst paid manual jobs, and they form a distinct section of the working class. In Switzerland their numbers (about one third of the total labour force) are such that they are coming to constitute almost the whole of the manual working class, and Swiss citizens can look forward to a situation in which they themselves do not need to enter manual occupations at all. This is an exceptional case, but the numbers of immigrant workers are also quite considerable in France and Germany. The fact that these workers are citizens of another country, speak another language, and participate in a different culture, largely excludes them from political life in the countries where they work, with some important consequences for working-class political movements in those countries. The most significant features are the growing heterogeneity of the working class as a result of ethnic diversity, and the creation of a distinct, socially isolated sub-proletariat. In these respects there is some resemblance to the conditions in the USA at an earlier time when ethnic differences and the distinctive position of the Negroes impeded the development of a radical labour movement.

One of the most striking features of the changing class structure is, therefore, the onset of a decline in the size of the traditional working class. This contraction of the working class implies the expansion of the middle classes. In terms of the occupational structure, as well as in terms of levels of living, the advanced industrial countries of Western Europe may be seen as being already, or as very close to becoming, predominantly 'middle class' societies. The question we now have to consider is whether this new, expanding middle class does, in fact, continue to have the economic, cultural and political characteristics of the middle class as it existed earlier in the present century. This is a tangled issue, not least because the European middle class of the first third of the twentieth century was itself 'new', in the sense that it was composed increasingly of clerical workers and professional employees, rather than independent professional people and small businessmen, and for that reason was becoming less homogeneous. Nevertheless, the middle class as a whole was still a relatively small and privileged section of the population, more or less clearly marked off from the working class. The new middle class of post-war Europe is a much larger, more diverse, and expanding group,

[1] Since my essay first appeared a comprehensive study of this question has been published: Stephen Castles and Godula Kosack, *Immigrant Workers and Class Structure in Western Europe* (London, 1973).

whose members may be less conscious of occupying a distinctive class position.

The question as to whether there is a historical continuity between this new middle class and its predecessors, or whether its economic and social situation, and its political outlook, are now profoundly different, has been answered in three different ways. The first answer, which was most prevalent in the 1950s, emphasises the elements of continuity and foresees the advent of middle class societies in which political conflict arising from opposed class interests will have ceased, and will have been replaced by a broad consensus of opinion about general matters of economic and social policy, disturbed only by minor and transitory disagreements between more 'conservative' and more 'progressive' groups. This view includes the idea of the assimilation of the working class into middle-class society, but it is not entirely clear whether it implies the disappearance of an upper class. Some sociologists and political scientists have argued that there is no longer an upper class in the USA, at least in the sense of a class which rules society, and that upper classes in the European countries are in process of dissolution. These writers see the industrial societies as becoming wholly middle class, with many different social groups having power or influence in particular areas or on particular occasions, even if it is no more than a veto power. Other social scientists, however, while accepting the thesis that the working class is being incorporated into middle class society visualise the new society as remaining divided between the mass of the population and an upper class, an elite, or a coalition of elites. Thus, C. Wright Mills counterposed the ruling elites and the masses in American society; and Herbert Marcuse, in *One-Dimensional Man*, describes the advanced industrial societies as societies of 'total mobilisation' in which the mass of the population sacrifice liberty to comfort under the rule of the large business corporations and the political elite, cajoled and persuaded by the mass media which these groups control. There is collusion and alliance between business and organised labour; dissent and opposition no longer have a social base; but the distinction between the rulers and the ruled still remains.

The second interpretation of these changes conceives the new middle class (or at least large sections of it) as a new dominant class, which differs, however, from previous ruling groups in including a relatively large part of the population, and in being much more committed to the general welfare through its commitment to economic growth. Galbraith refers to this new class, in

The New Industrial State, using the term 'technostructure' to describe the organisation of the 'very large group of people', ranging from the most senior officials of the corporation down to those who are just above the level of routine clerical workers and manual workers, who now participate in the management of industry and more generally in the determination of social policies; and he attributes a particular importance to the rapidly growing part of this class which he calls the 'educational and scientific estate'. Dahrendorf, in an essay on changes in European class structure,[1] expounds similar ideas, though with a number of qualifications. He suggests that the ruling groups or elites (which he regards as being still quite small in numbers, but recruited increasingly from the middle class) plus what he calls the 'service class' (the bureaucrats and managers) may constitute a new ruling class in the European societies. In his view, however, these groups together form a relatively small part of the population (not more than 15 per cent of the whole); and their importance lies not in their numbers, but in the fact that their values, especially that of individual competition, have spread to all other groups. To some extent Dahrendorf's thesis supports the idea of historical continuity; the values of the new 'service class', as he presents them, do not seem very different from the values of the old 'middle class'. Nevertheless, the gradual increase in the numbers of those in the 'service class', and their infiltration of the former ruling class (as Dahrendorf sees it), may produce in the European countries a new dominant class of the kind which Galbraith describes as already existing in the USA. It is possible, however, to interpret the same phenomena in another way, as the rise to power of a new minority, comprising the technocrats and bureaucrats. This conception, which goes back at least to Veblen, and which revives the ideas expounded in the 1940s about the managerial revolution, has been put forward especially in France in recent years; first by Georges Gurvitch,[2] and lately by Alain Touraine.[3] The theme of Touraine's argument is that the major social struggles in the advanced industrial countries are no longer centred upon the ownership of property; thus, they are no longer struggles between the old social classes of capitalist society. Social conflict now takes the form of a 'directly political struggle and a rejection of alienation, a revolt against a system of integration

---

[1] Ralf Dahrendorf, 'Recent Changes in the Class Structure of European Societies', in S. R. Graubard, *A New Europe?* (Boston, Mass., 1964).

[2] Georges Gurvitch (ed.), *Industrialisation et technocratie* (1949).

[3] Alain Touraine, *La société post-industrielle: naissance d'une société* (1969).

and manipulation'; it opposes various social groups, and above all the students, to the bureaucratic and technocratic controllers of society.

The third interpretation diverges radically from those which I have so far discussed, in regarding the new middle class primarily as a variant form of the working class which is now emerging in the advanced industrial countries. It has been expounded from one aspect by Serge Mallet,[1] and from another by some of the groups in the student movement. Mallet claims that it is the technically and professionally qualified workers in the most modern industries who have been most opposed in recent years to the capitalist organisation of industry, and who have taken up most vigorously the traditional working-class struggle to transform the ownership and management of economic enterprises. Within the radical student movement the idea has been formulated that students are apprentices being trained to take their place in the technically qualified working class of the future, and it is suggested that students are coming to see themselves increasingly in this light, as potential workers rather than professional and middle-class people. This is still, in fact, the outlook of a small minority, but it has had wider influence in the radical movements of the 1960s and it may presage a significant change in the social consciousness of the 'educational and scientific estate' in the next generation. Already there are some indications of the kind of change which Mallet discusses, in the growth of white-collar and professional trade unions, and in their increasing militancy and even radicalism. During the events of May 1968 in France a number of professional groups became very radical in outlook and developed a collective orientation quite opposed to the traditional middle-class individualism, and even to the 'instrumental collectivism' which Goldthorpe and Lockwood have ascribed to the new middle class.[2]

These diverse interpretations describe tendencies, all of which are present, none of which is clearly predominant, in the Western European societies. The working class has not yet withered away, nor has it been absorbed fully into a traditional middle class; there is not yet an established technocratic-bureaucratic ruling class; the 'new middle class' does not yet conceive itself as a working class, and it remains to be seen whether the students of

[1] Serge Mallet, *La nouvelle classe ouvrière* (1963), and 'La nouvelle classe ouvrière en France', *Cahiers internationaux de sociologie*, XXXVIII (1965).

[2] John H. Goldthorpe and David Lockwood, 'Affluence and the British Class Structure', *Sociological Review*, XI (2) (July 1962).

the 1960s will actually bring about or sustain a new social awareness in their eventual professional occupations. Before these
tendencies can be more adequately assessed we have to consider
another aspect of the class structure—the situation of the upper
class—which is evoked, directly or indirectly, in the theories about
the new working class and the new middle class. Is there any
longer an identifiable upper class in the Western European
societies? Is it still the capitalist class of Marxist theory; a class
which exercises political rule because it owns the essential instruments of production? Or has the old upper class disintegrated,
and has its political power been dispersed among numerous
pressure groups or taken over by a new elite?

As I indicated earlier the upper class is far from having lost
its superiority in the possession of wealth or in the share of the
national income which it receives. But is it the same upper class
as it was half a century ago, and does its wealth still give it a
preponderant influence in determining the course of economic
and social life? So far as economic affairs are concerned, those
who consider that important changes have taken place refer generally to two phenomena: the growth of public ownership of
industry, and the separation between ownership and management
in private business. However, publicly owned industry does not
account for more than about 15 per cent of the total employment
of wage and salary earners in Britain, and less than this in most
other Western European countries. M. M. Postan concludes his
survey of the effects of nationalisation by saying that nationalised
industry has been 'a powerful but not predominant ingredient
in "mixed economies"'.[1] Alongside the gradual extension of
public ownership there has occurred an increase in governmental
regulation of the economy as a whole, closely associated with
planning for economic growth, and this too, it has been argued,
diminishes the power of the private owners of wealth. But the
association between business corporations and government can
be interpreted in different ways; as the growing control of private
interests by an elected political authority, or as the growing
control of government by private interests. It is by no means easy
to unravel these lines of influence and power running in opposite
directions, but it may be attempted by looking at the extent to
which representatives of the large corporations occupy important
political posts, and by examining the character of particular policy
decisions or of general economic and social policy over a longer

[1] Postan, op. cit.

period. The fact that there has been no substantial redistribution of wealth and income over the past half-century is one indication that the upper class has maintained its preponderant influence upon the course of events, while another indication of the same kind is provided by the tenacious and largely successful resistance to the extension of welfare services, as a result of which there are vast inequalities in the provision of housing and education, and very few attempts to increase the range and variety of goods and services provided free of charge to the whole population.

The second question which I have raised, concerning the separation between ownership and management of industry, is important insofar as those who emphasise this separation go on to argue that it has eliminated or drastically reduced the control which the owners of wealth have over the economy, and at the same time has changed the social character of the large business corporation. There is indeed a formal separation between ownership and control (between share-ownership and management functions) in modern business firms, even though many predominantly family businesses (some of them large), survive;[1] but the existence of a real social distinction between owners and managers is much more doubtful. Mills noted, in *The Power Elite*, that the categories of the 'very rich' and the 'top executives' overlap considerably in the USA, and there is little doubt that the same is true in European countries, although the European upper class has been much less thoroughly studied than has the American. Postan observes, for example, that in the Western European countries the *grande bourgeoisie* has adapted itself to the demands of the managerial age by ensuring that its members acquire the requisite education for careers as business executives. In France, this process began in the late nineteenth century when the Ecole Libre des Sciences Politiques provided members of the upper class with the skills necessary to maintain their dominant position in business and in the higher administration; and in other European countries certain kinds of university education have been directed towards the same end.

The general development towards managerial and technocratic control of business enterprises would only have a significant effect upon the social situation of the upper class of property owners if there were very considerable mobility through the educational system. In fact, however, access to higher education in the Western European countries has changed only slightly over the past thirty

[1] See Jean Meynaud, *La technocratie* (Paris, 1964), Chapter III.

years; in Britain, the proportion of university undergraduates from working-class homes was 23 per cent in the period 1928–47, and 25 per cent in 1961, while in Germany the proportion of working-class students has risen only from 5 per cent before the war to 6 per cent today, and in France there has been a similarly modest increase from 6 per cent before the war to about 8 per cent today.[1] It is not surprising, therefore, that the elite groups—business leaders, higher civil servants, a large part of the political leadership—continue to be recruited largely from the upper class and the upper levels of the middle class in these societies.[2] The upper class still perpetuates itself by passing on wealth, educational privileges, and occupational chances, and these things ensure the continuing concentration of property ownership, prestige and power in a few hands. Of course, there is some circulation of individuals and families between the upper class and other social classes, but there is no evidence to suggest that this circulation is now more extensive or more rapid than it was at any earlier time during the last hundred years.

The upper classes in the Western European countries thus remain relatively closed groups, in which the continuity of membership from generation to generation is still strongly marked. In the rest of society social mobility may have increased over the past few decades, largely as a result of the changing occupational structure,[3] but it is clear that most mobility occurs *within* classes rather than between them. A study of intra-generational occupational mobility in France, based upon an inquiry conducted by the Institut National de la Statistique et des Etudes Economiques, shows that between 1959 and 1964 about 14 per cent of manual workers changed their occupations, but two thirds of them remained in manual jobs, while one third went into non-manual jobs; among non-manual workers some 12 per cent changed their

[1] See P. Bourdieu and J. C. Passeron, *Les héritiers* (Paris, 1964).

[2] See the discussion in my *Elites and Society*, op. cit., Chapter IV; and on Germany, Wolfgang Zapf (ed.), *Beiträge zur Analyse der Deutschen Oberschicht*.

[3] The most thorough discussion of the problems involved in making historical comparisons of rates of social mobility will be found in Peter M. Blau and Otis D. Duncan, *The American Occupational Structure* (New York, 1967), Chapter 3. In order to obtain strictly comparable data it would be necessary to repeat studies of mobility (designed for comparability) at regular intervals. The first attempt along these lines, so far as I know, is the mobility study being carried out at Nuffield College, Oxford; this is intended to make possible comparisons with the data of the 1949 study reported in D. V. Glass (ed.), *Social Mobility in Britain* (London, 1954).

occupations, again with two thirds remaining in non-manual jobs while one third went into manual jobs.[1] Where there is movement (either intra-generational or inter-generational) between classes it takes place usually over short distances; for example, from the skilled working class to the lower levels of the middle class. In no Western industrial society is there any considerable amount of long-range mobility, from the working class directly into the upper class or elites.

Nevertheless, the relatively high rates of *occupational* mobility which most studies reveal may have a strong influence upon class structure, and particularly upon the character of the working class, insofar as such mobility tends to inhibit the formation of occupational communities which have a continuing membership over several generations, and which may constitute focal points around which a more general class consciousness is able to crystallise. I drew attention earlier to the possible importance of this factor in the case of coal miners, but it may well be that occupational mobility, when it rises above a certain level, has consequences similar to those which flow from the decline of an occupation in terms of its size and economic importance. If this is so, the outcome might be a general decline in the class consciousness of workers; and many observers have reached the conclusion, though often upon quite different grounds, that this has been happening.[2] Their results are contradicted however, as I have noted, by recent studies of working-class political allegiance.

The most important implication of the preceding discussion of the major social classes is that the extent and nature of changes in class structure have to be assessed in large measure by an examination of the political movements and political conflicts which take place in a society. Few social scientists would dissent from the view that class interests and class consciousness have been pre-eminent elements in the political life of all the Western European countries over the past hundred years, although they have assumed diverse forms of expression and have been more or less strongly affected by other social divisions—of religion, language or culture—in the different countries. The question of a changing class structure in these societies then resolves itself

[1] Michel Praderie, 'La mobilité professionelle en France entre 1959 et 1964', *Etudes et Conjuncture* (10) (October 1966).
[2] See especially A. Andrieux and J. Lignon, *L'ouvrier d'aujourd'hui* (1960); H. Popitz, H. P. Bahrdt, E. A. Jüres and H. Kesting, *Das Gesellschaftsbild des Arbeiters* (1957); K. Bednarik, *Der junge Arbeiter von heute: ein neuer Typ* (1953).

into a question as to whether class-based political struggles have retained their importance, or whether new forms of political activity and new political aims have emerged, and in the latter case, how these new forms and objectives are related to the undoubted changes in the occupational structure and the system of production.

In the first place we should note the extent to which class is still a major force in politics, not only because the upper class retains its character as a group of large property owners, in spite of the development of new technological and professional elites, but also because the working class still adheres strongly to its own long-established organisations, the trade unions and working-class political parties, and has its social outlook largely shaped by the historical traditions of the labour movement. The decline of union membership in the USA, which Galbraith cites in the course of his argument about the emergence of a new industrial system, has no counterpart in Western Europe, where trade union membership has generally increased since the war, and the growth of white-collar unionism has been closely correlated with the expansion of manual workers' unions.[1] Similarly, working-class support for labour and socialist parties has tended to grow rather than decline, and in the later 1960s a more radical outlook seemed to be spreading in some sections of the labour movement, as evidenced, for example, by the revival of interest in the concept and practices of workers' control.

Nevertheless, it may be said that the present time marks a turning point, when the established class parties have attained a peak in their development, while new political forces are beginning to challenge their dominance. There are four main directions, it seems to me, in which a new style of politics has become apparent. The first style is that associated with the rise of new elites, committed above all to rationality and efficiency in production and administration, and subscribing to the doctrines of technological progress and economic growth, who may be able to establish themselves and become accepted as the controllers of society for the sake of the economic benefits which they can assure. The second style is directly opposed to this; it is the radical movement, mainly among students at present, which attacks the technocratic and bureaucratic character of modern industrial society, and proposes 'participation' and 'community' as alternatives to the 'authority' and 'elitism' implied in the conception

[1] See Adolf Sturmthal (ed.), *White Collar Trade Unions* (Urbana, Illinois, 1966).

of a society directed by experts. Alone, the student movement is unlikely to accomplish very much, but its influence may grow if it finds a sympathetic response either in the working-class movement (from which, after all, its radical ideas derive), or in those middle class groups from which the students largely come by virtue of their family origins and which they subsequently enter on their own account as professionally qualified workers.

The other two styles of politics, though differing widely in some respects, are alike in having as their basis a community which is quite distinct from social classes. At one extreme are the regional or nationalist movements which have sprung up in recent years (for example, in Scotland and Wales, among the Flemish speaking people of Belgium); at the other extreme is the movement for a European community. In both types of movement there is a strong emphasis upon a cultural identity which is seen as transcending the divisions within the community, and this cultural quality, along with considerations of economic development, become the focus of political thought and action. These two styles largely exclude the distinctions based upon class differences and the political issues which are of vital importance to the traditional parties insofar as they represent particular classes; thus, in the discussions of a European Community, the question as to whether the new Europe will be capitalist or socialist is scarcely ever raised.

The future development of these styles of politics in relation to the established parties and movements can only be discussed at present in a speculative manner. Nevertheless, there are certain conditions and processes of change which can be determined more exactly and which are likely to have an important influence. The decline of the manual working class as a proportion of the population will continue, but it is unlikely to be so rapid as to undermine the militancy and radicalism of a considerable part of the trade union and labour movement. It may be that trade union militancy will become increasingly defensive, particularly in those occupations most affected by technological advance, and will play a smaller part in animating movements for radical change in society, but there is, as yet, little indication that such a state of affairs is coming about. On the other hand, radicalism may receive an accession of strength as the expansion of higher education continues at a rapid pace, if we assume that the ideological orientation of the student movement continues to be that of the late 1960s; and experience so far, in Europe, suggests that student radicalism is something more than a passing mood.

There is another circumstance of vital importance for the future development of classes and political movements which is extremely difficult to evaluate; namely, the probability that economic growth will continue in the same rapid and uninterrupted fashion as during the past two decades. The difficulty arises from the lack of an adequate theory of a 'mixed', but predominantly capitalist and market economy. The Marxist theory of capitalist crisis is obviously no longer satisfactory; but on the other side the expectation of continued prosperity and growth seems to rest upon purely empirical and short-term observations, without any theory which would explain what changes have occurred in the capitalist economy which now eliminate the possibility of crises. There is no certainty, therefore, about the future development of the economy, and thus about some important aspects of the class structure— the radicalism of the working class, the expansion of the middle class, and the rise of new elites.

In spite of the imponderable elements, and the diversity of interpretations, to which I have drawn attention throughout this essay, I think a tentative conclusion is possible, at least in a negative form. There is, as yet, no sign that in the western European countries the egalitarian impulse which came to life with the rise of the labour movement has lost its force. Indeed, the struggle for equality, arising out of the relationship between social classes in a capitalist society, may have been reinforced by the more directly political conflicts which now take place in various spheres over questions of authority and participation in decision making.[1] Insofar as classes have been, and largely remain, the principal embodiment of inequality in modern societies their political significance is undiminished.

[1] See especially the discussion in Touraine, op. cit., p. 68 et seq.

Chapter 9

The Administrative Elite[1]

In all complex societies high government officials form an important part of the 'governing elite' or 'political class'—the minority which, at any time, effectively rules a society.[2] The position of higher civil servants in modern industrial societies is especially influential, as a result of the great extension of state activities, the growing technical complexity of public administration, and the organisation of the civil service as a professional career based upon educational diplomas and training. Indeed, Max Weber, whose writings on bureaucracy form the starting point for all modern discussion of the subject, asserted that 'the power position of a fully developed bureaucracy is always very strong, and under normal conditions, supreme. The "political master" finds himself in the position of the "dilettante" in the face of the "expert" when he confronts the trained official established as manager of the administration.' This remains true, Weber suggested, whether the political master is the whole people (armed with the rights of 'initiative', 'referendum', and the recall of officials) or an elected parliament.[3] Weber's judgement of the magnitude of bureaucratic power was clearly influenced by his experience of bureaucracy in Germany, but also by his general opposition to socialism, which he saw as the culmination of bureaucratic rule. One of the principal doctrines which he was attacking throughout his writings on this subject was that of the

[1] Reprinted, with minor revisions, from Irving L. Horowitz (ed.), *The New Sociology: Essays in Social Science and Social Theory in Honor of C. Wright Mills* (New York, 1964).

[2] The term 'governing elite' was used by Pareto and the term 'political class' by G. Mosca. Both writers emphasised, in opposition to the Marxist notion of a ruling class based upon economic power and represented in the political sphere by various and changing groups, the idea of an 'elite' comprising those individuals who actually wielded political power at a given time and the inescapable necessity of such an elite. I have examined some aspects of their doctrines in my *Elites and Society* (London, 1964).

[3] Max Weber, *Wirtschaft und Gesellschaft*, Chap. VI, 'Bureaucracy' (English trans. in H. H. Gerth and C. Wright Mills, *From Max Weber*, London, 1947).

Marxists, who maintained that bureaucratic power was merely one aspect of the rule of the bourgeoisie in capitalist society, that it would diminish in a socialist society, and would eventually 'wither away' along with the state itself. Lenin, in *The State and Revolution*, elaborated Marx's analysis of the Paris Commune in his argument that during the transition from capitalism to socialism the power of public officials would be reduced by making them elected and subject to recall at any time, and by paying them at 'workmen's wages'. In fact, the experiences of present-day Communist societies reveal that high officials, both in the dominant party and in the state (and the two spheres are closely interrelated), are able to attain a privileged position in respect of power, prestige, and real income; in other words, to become a vital part, if not the whole, of the governing elite. Nevertheless, recent events also show that bureaucratic power is not unopposed or unrestrained even there; and it cannot be inferred from these particular experiences that Weber's assertions about the connection between all forms of socialism and bureaucracy hold true.

Modern sociological studies of elites have dealt principally with the Western industrial societies, and they have emphasised particularly two features of the social hierarchy in such societies: first, the plurality of elites, and secondly, the problematic nature of the relationships between the different elites and between elites and social classes. G. D. H. Cole, for example, defined elites as 'groups which emerge to positions of leadership and influence at every social level—that is to say, as leaders of classes or of other important elements in the social structure'; and he went on to observe: 'Not all elites rest on a class basis, or are to be regarded as class representatives, but some do and are, and a special importance attaches, in modern societies and especially in the older societies which have been developing from aristocracy towards some form of democracy, to the relations between classes and elites and to the differences that emerge with the increasing complexities of class structure.'[1] Raymond Aron has likewise drawn attention to the shifting relationships between elites and social classes, in a study of the connections between class structure and political power in which he distinguishes five elite groups which are important elements in the 'political class': political leaders, government administrators, economic directors, leaders of the masses, and military chiefs.[2]

[1] G. D. H. Cole, *Studies in Class Structure* (London, 1955).
[2] Raymond Aron, 'Social Structure and the Ruling Class', *British Journal of Sociology*, I (March 1950).

The principal attempt to show, in one society, that the major elites may be regularly associated and in agreement about the ends of policy, over a period of time, as well as being recruited mainly from a particular social class, is C. Wright Mills' study of the 'power elite' in the United States.[1] Nevertheless, Mills criticises and rejects the Marxist conception of a ruling class based upon economic interest, and he introduces many qualifications into his thesis concerning the unity of the power elite, which is finally expressed as 'the often uneasy coincidence of economic, military and political power'.[2] His main propositions are rather: first, that changes in technology and in social institutions have produced an unprecedented concentration of power, and have widened the gulf between elites and masses (a thesis which has many points of connection with Weber's theory of the extension of bureaucracy); and, second, that the character and policies of an elite cannot be assessed merely by looking at the social origins of its members (although this is an important fact), but must also be considered in relation to the formation of the members' outlook by their training and experience, and to the historical and institutional framework in which they act.

What is the character of the administrative elite? What is the nature and extent of its power? What significance does the mode of recruitment to this elite have in the system of power and stratification as a whole? It will help our inquiry if, before turning to empirical materials, we first consider these questions in general terms.

The character of the administrative elite may be delineated initially by comparing it with other types of elites. It differs from other social elites principally in being relatively small, well-defined, homogeneous (as a result of training and the practice of the occupation), and cohesive. Furthermore, it is directly involved in the exercise of political power, and this distinguishes it from a number of other groups which may have high social prestige but lack power. The elite of political leaders, which is even more directly concerned with power, differs from the administrative elite especially in being less easily circumscribed, and less unitary in the sense that in most modern societies there are competing or conflicting sub-groups (rival political parties or factions within one major party). The intellectual elite may be still more difficult to define, and it is evidently less organised, less

[1] C. Wright Mills, *The Power Elite* (New York, 1956).
[2] Ibid., p. 278.

cohesive, and in the strict sense less powerful than most other elites. Only the military elite has many similarities with the administrative elite, but in Western societies it has ordinarily been excluded from the direct exercise of political power. When we try to go beyond such a comparative analysis to measure more directly the distinctiveness and cohesiveness of an elite, many difficulties appear. Nevertheless, it is possible to indicate some relevant conditions which are in principle measurable, such as the control by the group over its own recruitment, the similarity of the members in respect of social and cultural background, the extent of interaction among members within and beyond the specific sphere of activity of the group, supplementary bonds (e.g. kinship) between the members; and also criteria by which the solidarity of a group may be judged—the degree of similarity in members' conceptions of the group and in their evaluations of public events which concern the group, overt manifestations of *esprit de corps*, and so on. Judged in these terms the administrative elite will be shown to be a very cohesive social group.

The second question, concerning the nature and extent of the power[1] wielded by the administrative elite, leads us into some intricate problems of analysis and some difficulties of empirical verification. It is clear that the individual members of the elite may be influential in society at large in much the same way as other individuals whose occupations have high prestige. Moreover, since high officials have regular contacts with political leaders they can perhaps more easily bring their personal influence to bear upon particular decisions. But what power does the administrative elite, as a group, have in its everyday and continuing activities? It is usually argued that this power is closely circumscribed in democratic societies, where higher civil servants act under the authority of a political executive which is itself responsible to parliament and to the electorate. The officials, according to this view, execute decisions which have been made by others, in terms of interests and values which lie outside their sphere of influence. However, in practice the higher civil servants may have

[1] By 'power', I shall mean throughout this essay the ability of an individual or a group to attain its end in a course of action even against the opposition of others who are involved in that course of action (see Max Weber, 'Class, Status, Parties', in *Wirtschaft und Gesellschaft*); by 'influence', I shall mean the ability of an individual or group to change by persuasion, on particular occasions, the course of anyone who wields power. Evidently, there may be cases in which it is difficult to discriminate precisely between 'power' and 'influence'.

a good deal of autonomy, and they may have formed their own corporate view of what are 'wise', or 'sensible', or 'practicable' policies. At the stage where a policy is being implemented they may have the power to obstruct, delay, or modify its working. Equally, at an earlier stage, when a policy is being formulated, they may have, by virtue of long experience and expert knowledge of the departments which they administer, a considerable influence upon the ideas and decisions of the minister who is nominally their chief. Their power will be all the greater where the political executive changes frequently, and where ministers have little experience of government in general or of the particular departments for which they are responsible. The growing technical complexity of modern government, as has been noted, also enhances the power of the permanent officials. In some cases, the policy-making powers of important officials are explicitly recognised, in the rules or conventions by which certain appointments in the public service are treated as 'political appointments', and are made not by ordinary promotion but by nomination in accordance with the wishes of the political executive.

These considerations lead to further questions concerning the sources of, and the restraints upon, bureaucratic power. As we have seen, Max Weber was inclined to regard the growth of bureaucratic power in modern societies as inexorable; the various grounds for this view included the congruence of bureaucratic administration with the general rationalisation of social life, the indispensability of the technically expert administrators, and the permanence and continuity of the administration in contrast with the impermanence and changeability of the political executive. Weber added that the bureaucracy was able to strengthen its position vis à vis the political executive by enveloping its activities in the strictest secrecy. In considering the possible restraints upon bureaucratic power Weber went no further than to suggest that the adherence of high officials to general legal rules in accordance with which they would execute impartially and effectively the decisions of every legitimate political ruler, and the degree of stability of the political order as a whole, might have a certain influence. It seems likely that these factors have a greater importance than Weber, in his preoccupation with German circumstances, was prepared to recognise. One significant restraint upon the power of an administrative elite is the development, within the elite itself, of a professional ethic which upholds the ideal of the political neutrality of officials. On the other side, it is probable that the power of an administrative elite will be increased (whether deliberately, in a striving for power, or otherwise) in conditions where the legitimacy of the political regime itself is unsettled.

The development of a professional ethic in the civil service can in fact be traced in most modern societies, although there are great variations in the degree to which it is genuinely accepted and made effective. In Britain, the political neutrality of the civil service has been strongly emphasised in the professional code, and a postwar Socialist Prime Minister expressed his confidence in its effectiveness. Lord Attlee wrote: 'There were certainly some people in the Labour Party who doubted whether the civil servants would give fair play to a socialist government but all doubts disappeared with experience.'[1]

The circumstances have been different in France, where the prevailing view since the early nineteenth century has been that civil servants, and particularly the higher civil servants, owed political loyalty to the regime of the day. C. Chavanon has referred to Napoleon's demand for 'complete loyalty from all civil servants, and even from all who occupied equivalent positions'[2] to his own regime; and later political rulers made the same claim. The political influences within the civil service probably attained their highest point during the difficult years of the Third Republic after the Dreyfus case, but they have continued down to the present time. In an essay on the postwar situation, R. Catherine claims that the 'politicalisation' of the civil service has proceeded rapidly again since 1945;[3] and R. Grégoire concludes a discussion of the whole question with the observation that the idea of the political neutrality of civil servants is still less generally accepted and less influential in France than in Britain.[4]

The traditional lack of confidence in the political neutrality of high officials is illustrated by an institution which has no counterpart in the British administrative system: the *cabinet ministériel*.[5] Every minister, on taking up office, appoints a personal staff of trusted collaborators who act as intermediaries between him and the permanent officials of his department. Some members of these *cabinets* are themselves higher civil servants, frequently

---

[1] Clement R. Attlee, 'Civil Servants, Ministers, Parliament and the Public', *The Political Quarterly* (Oct.–Dec. 1954), p. 308.

[2] C. Chavanon, *Les Fonctionnaires et la fonction publique* (Paris, 1951).

[3] R. Catherine, 'Les fonctionnaires', in M. Duverger (ed.), *Partis politiques et classes sociales en France* (Paris, 1955).

[4] R. Grégoire, *La Fonction publique* (Paris, 1954), pp. 331–5.

[5] For a comprehensive account of the *cabinet ministériel*, see J. L. Suerin, 'Les cabinets ministériels', *Revue du droit publique et de la science politique* (Nov.–Dec. 1956), pp. 1207–94.

drawn from one or another of the *grands corps* and especially from the *Conseil d'État* and the *Inspection des Finances*; others come from outside the civil service. The existence of the *cabinets*, and particularly the growth in the number of their personnel, reflects, as Grégoire has noted, the doubts that ministers feel about the loyalty and reliability of the higher permanent officials in their departments.[1]

The case of France also lends support to the proposition that the independent power of a bureaucracy is most likely to be established where the political order is unstable. In France, the insistence upon loyalty to a particular regime (and even to party governments) encouraged the formation of political attitudes among the higher civil servants, while the instability of political regimes led them to assume (or to be disposed to assume) an independent political role. This phenomenon has been frequently noted, and sometimes exaggerated, by observers of French politics. Thus, Karl Marx wrote in *The Eighteenth Brumaire of Louis Bonaparte* that the 'enormous bureaucratic and military organisa-tion ... this appalling parasitic body which enmeshes the body of French society like a net and chokes all its pores' seemed to have made itself completely independent of civil society. More than a century later, H. Lüthy writes of the *grands corps* and especially the *Conseil d'État* and the *Inspection des Finances*:

'They constitute a supreme and sovereign self-recruiting body, immune from political intervention, responsible to no-one outside their own hierarchy, a rock against which all political storms beat ineffectively and in vain; a completely closed mandarin system, even in the social choice it exercises in reproducing itself; its *esprit de corps*, the sense of belonging to a chosen elite fostered from childhood in the great boarding schools which prepare pupils for *la carrière*.'[2]

An eminent French political scientist, André Siegfried, expressed a very similar view of the political role of higher civil servants, but he went further in relating it to more general theories of the 'managerial revolution'. He argued that

'... two groups of experts are tending to assume a leading position in the state as in the economy. The elite of the administration is recruited essentially among the *Inspecteurs des finances* and

[1] Grégoire, op. cit., p. 333.
[2] Herbert Lüthy, *The State of France* (London, 1955).

the members of the *Conseil d'État*; it is a general staff which radiates everywhere. Since these administrators frequently transfer to the private sector, they are to be found in the banks and in large scale industrial and commercial enterprises. The second source is the *polytechniciens*, who form the elite of the technical departments of state, but are also increasingly the managers of large scale industry.'[1]

While the preceding considerations show that the administrative elite occupies a position which may be presumed to be powerful, it is more difficult to marshal empirical evidence for the actual exercise of power in specific circumstances. This is, however, a general difficulty which bedevils most studies of power as an empirical—not simply a constitutional—phenomenon; and it is likely to be particularly acute where the group to be studied has reason to conceal as much as possible the power or influence which it wields. Nevertheless, if we are not to rest content with the view (which is at least as difficult to support) that there are no power groups at all in society but only an intricate web of innumerable influences and counter-influences whose outcome resembles fate—or else to accept that the relations of power are entirely inscrutable—then we must try, so far as possible, to test our assertions about power groups by an examination of actual instances in which important social issues are decided. The power of economic interest groups, and the influence (to rate it at its lowest) of pressure groups of various kinds, have been demonstrated in a number of cases;[2] and studies along similar lines might produce evidence of the exercise of power by high officials in certain situations. It has often been asserted, for instance, that the policies of the Popular Front government of Léon Blum (1936–38) were obstructed by the higher civil servants. My own investigation of this period indicates that some legislative projects may have been obstructed, notably the bill for reforming the civil service itself, which, after being approved by a large majority in the Chamber in 1936, was passed from committee to committee through the intervention of officials until it finally expired with the fall of Blum's government in 1938.

So far I have considered two social facts which may affect, in opposite senses, the power position of an administrative elite:

---

[1] André Siegfried, *De la IIIème à la IVème République* (Paris, 1957), p. 246.
[2] The introduction of commercial television in Britain provides a good example: see H. H. Wilson, *Pressure Group: The Campaign for Commercial Television* (London, 1961).

the development of a professional code of political neutrality and the instability of the political regime. Another important element is suggested by the third question posed above, concerning the relation between the administrative elite and the class structure of society. For it may be held that the administrative elite is only one section of the dominant class in society, and that its independent power, at one extreme, and its political neutrality, at the other, are modified and curtailed by the interests and aims of the class which it represents. Weber paid little attention to this problem; and in fact he eliminated it by two arguments which are crucial in his whole account of the development of bureaucracy. The first is that bureaucracy, in the sense of rational and impersonal administration based upon technical competence and educational diplomas, proceeds along with 'democratisation' and the levelling of social differences, with the result that social classes cease to have great political importance; and the second, that the officials—the managers of the administration—are the most obvious successors to the owners of the means of production as the rulers of society. These arguments were later developed in Burnham's theory of the 'managerial revolution',[1] and they have attracted renewed attention through the criticisms of bureaucracy in the post-Stalinist Communist societies.[2]

Whatever may be the case in the last-named societies, it can scarcely be claimed that the process of social levelling has gone so far in the Western capitalist societies that elites, including the administrative elite, no longer have any connection with social classes. As H. J. Laski observed, in the absence of a democratic educational system, the effective public service will be 'confined to the comfortable classes of the community'; and he added that this implied: 'First, the experience upon which its members will draw is not representative of the community as a whole; and even the new facts they encounter will be envisaged in terms of that special experience. Secondly, the advice they will offer to the political executive will be fairly narrow in range, unless they contain among them what is, in any case, rare, men of great imaginative insight.'[3] Lord Attlee's observation upon the relations between Socialist ministers and higher civil servants, quoted earlier, also expresses the fear of class opposition to social reforms; and his statement that such fears were groundless has to be seen in the context of the postwar situation in Britain, where the reforms

---

[1] James Burnham, *The Managerial Revolution* (London, 1943).
[2] See especially, Milovan Djilas, *The New Class* (London, 1957).
[3] H. J. Laski, *A Grammar of Politics* (4th ed., London, 1941), p. 399.

undertaken by the Labour Government continued, in many respects, policies already widely accepted during the war, without introducing any new measures of a radical kind; and where the social composition of the higher civil service had already undergone some changes as a result of wartime recruitment.

The significance of the relationship between the administrative elite and the class structure has been shown in another way by historical studies. J. D. Kingsley, in a study of the British higher civil service,[1] advanced the thesis that the administrative system in Britain worked smoothly and effectively because the members of the political executive and the heads of the civil service were drawn from the same social class and thus had similar views on important issues of public policy. And in his account of how this situation had come about, he suggested that the growing strength and influence of a particular social class in economic and social life had determined the greater participation of that class in the exercise of both political and administrative power. The agitation for civil service reform in the mid-nineteenth century had the same origins and significance as the agitation for the Reform Bill of 1832. It expressed the resentments and aspirations of the industrial capitalist class. John Bright's description of the Foreign Office as 'the outdoor relief department of the aristocracy', and the embittered remark of an anonymous author that no one could obtain a position under the government who lacked family influence or had not been born in lawful wedlock, manifested such class sentiments. A historical interpretation of this kind, which links changes in the composition of the administrative elite with changes in the situation of social classes, may also be helpful in understanding more recent events. In so far as the opportunities for individuals of working-class origin to enter the higher civil service have increased, the fact may be explained by the greater strength of the working class in society as a whole; and the actual extent of such opportunities in any society, measured over a period of time, may prove a useful index of the changes in its class structure.

The recruitment of elites has a special importance in the modern industrial societies, which have been developing toward a democratic form of society which comprehends not only equal political rights and competition for political power, but also greater economic and social equality, at least in the sense of equality of opportunity. It may be argued, as Weber did, that some

[1] J. Donald Kingsley, *Representative Bureaucracy* (Yellow Springs, 1944).

equalisation of social conditions was an important prerequisite for the growth of bureaucracy, since the recruitment of officials strictly on the basis of ability and qualifications could only be established when public office became accessible in principle to all citizens, instead of being reserved for members of a particular social stratum. In fact, the doctrine of the *carrière ouverte aux talents* was a corollary of the principles of *liberté, égalité, fraternité*. Weber went further in asserting that the spread of bureaucracy would itself bring about a further growth of equality; but, while we should recognise the influence which the ideas of ability and merit, in the context of the scientific and technical complexity of modern societies, have had in breaking down earlier social privileges, it is necessary to qualify Weber's prognosis. Recruitment to public offices by competitive examination, or on the basis of educational qualifications, only brings about a real equality of opportunity if those of equal ability have equal chances of preparing themselves for the public service, by obtaining the necessary diplomas or the necessary training for the entrance examinations. In practice, therefore, the selection of individuals for the higher civil service, as well as for many other high status occupations, takes place, for the most part, at the point where individuals are selected for higher education. And the history of institutions of higher education shows that they have been largely reserved for individuals from the upper strata of society. Indeed, they have had a pre-eminent role in perpetuating class differences which could no longer be maintained by inequalities in civil and political rights.

A study of recruitment to the higher civil service will throw light upon the processes of social mobility in a society. It will show how far there is equality of opportunity in one important sphere of society, and if it covers a period of time it may reveal the extent and trend of change. A study of recruitment to a single elite group may add useful information to that obtained from general studies of social mobility in a whole population; for the latter will ordinarily present the total outcome of different kinds of mobility (between adjacent social strata as between social strata which are far apart), while a study of elite recruitment will reveal the amount of long-range mobility. The opportunities to rise directly from the lowest to the highest social positions have a particular importance, for they play a large part in forming the individual's judgement of the open or closed nature of the class system, and thus in determining the character and intensity of class consciousness.

The amount of mobility may also have important effects upon the administrative elite itself. If changes in the recruitment of the elite result in its members being drawn in substantial numbers from several social classes and strata, the social bonds which unite the members cannot any longer arise merely from the similarities of social origin, but are likely to be formed principally by the occupation itself and by the the educational experience which leads up to it. In this case the higher civil servants may become more conscious of themselves as an occupational elite, rather than as members of a traditional social class; and this may lead, in the circumstances of a particular society, either to a strengthening of the idea of 'political neutrality' (the occupation being conceived in terms of technical competence rather than in terms of power), or to a more rapid development of the administrative elite as a new power group and even, in association with other groups, as a new class. This last possibility is the theme of much recent discussion of the 'rule of the experts'—the technocrats and bureaucrats—and it was, of course, the underlying concern in Weber's analysis of social trends in the modern industrial societies.

Chapter 10

Cohesion and Division in Indian Elites[1]

The elite groups in Indian society have not as yet been closely studied. The composition and recruitment of elites, the relations between them, their prestige and influence, the extent to which they are separated from the mass of the people, the degree of their internal unity, are all subjects upon which the available information is both scattered and incomplete. This essay is, therefore, exploratory in nature. I shall attempt to distinguish some of the important elements which make for cohesion or divison in Indian elites, and to assemble what pertinent knowledge can be gleaned from recent studies.[2]

It is interesting, first of all, to observe some broad differences between elites in India and in the industrial societies. In the latter, according to one well-known study,[3] five elite groups may be distinguished: political leaders, government administrators, economic directors (businessmen and managers), leaders of the masses (principally trade-union leaders), and military chiefs. Not all of these groups have the same importance in India. Thus, for reasons which B. B. Misra has elucidated in his book *The Indian Middle Classes*, no real bourgeoisie has developed in India, and although individual businessmen and specific interest groups may have some political influence, there does not seem to be, at present, a business elite exerting the kind of pervasive social and political influence which is apparent in the Western societies. Similarly, the trade-union leaders, because of the slow growth of unions and

[1] Reprinted from Philip Mason (ed.), *India and Ceylon: Unity and Diversity* (London, 1967).

[2] I have discussed the general characteristics of elites and their role in the developing countries in my *Elites and Society* (London, 1964); and the case of India more particularly in 'Modern Elites in India', Chapter IX of *Towards a Sociology of Culture in India* (edited by T. K. N. Unnithan, Indra Deva and Yogendra Singh, New Delhi, 1965).

[3] R. Aron, 'Social Structure and the Ruling Class', *British Journal of Sociology*, Vol. I, Nos. 1 and 2 (March–June 1950).

the predominantly agricultural and rural character of Indian society, do not yet form an important elite. The position of the military chiefs is less clear. Until a few years ago most observers would have said that in India, unlike many other developing countries, the political role of military leaders was unimportant; but the border conflicts with China and Pakistan and increasing military expenditure have changed the situation, and the place of the military elite in Indian society now needs to be re-examined.

The two elite groups which are unquestionably important are the political leaders and the high government officials. These groups have borne the major responsibility for India's economic and social development thus far, and they are likely to bear it in the foreseeable future. It is with their position in Indian society that I shall be mainly concerned. There is, however, one other group which deserves attention: the intellectuals. In all literate societies, at least, intellectuals have an important place, whether as scribes, as experts, or as ideologists; and in the modern industrial societies they have become more influential both as experts in the fields of science, technology, and economic management, and as ideologists responsible for expressing and forming social doctrines and ideas in democratic regimes. Their role may well be of outstanding importance in the developing countries, where they are the rare possessors of scientific and technical knowledge, and where also, as ideologists, they may inspire radical movements for social change.

This discussion so far may suggest that since there are, in India, fewer elite groups at the national level—the major ones being the political leaders and government officials—there is probably less competition between elites than is the case in the Western industrial societies. A like conclusion may be drawn from the sphere of political leadership itself. India is not a 'one-party state', but it is a 'one-dominant-party system',[1] without any effective rival to the governing Congress Party. In these conditions, it is possible that divisions will emerge *within* the elites themselves, and this is made easier where there are already major social differences— such as those of caste and language—which provide a foundation. There have not been lacking scholars who have seen, in present-day India, the signs of profound disunity in the national elites. Two of the divisions which they discern are that between traditionalists and modernists, and that between regions; and I shall begin with a discussion of these issues.

[1] The phrase is used by W. H. Morris-Jones, *The Government and Politics of India* (London, 1964).

The distinction between tradition and modernity is frequently made with reference to the developing countries, but it is not easy to set it forth in precise terms. It would hardly be illuminating if it meant only the contrast between a previously established form of society and the present conditions of change; that is, a simple chronological opposition. Generally, the distinction formulates the experience of the West European countries in passing from feudalism to modern capitalism, from the *ancien régime* to the *régime moderne*. On one side of this divide is a form of society in which religious thought is pre-eminent, technological and economic change is slow, the movement between social strata is limited, and the strata themselves are very clearly separated; on the other side is a type of society in which thought is mainly secular, and science and technology assume great importance, economic change is rapid, and there is considerable mobility between the various social strata. In these terms, a contrast may be drawn between the traditional system of Indian society, especially of Hindu society, and the new system which is being established through industrialisation and political democracy. The question then is: are there now any influential traditionalist elites? Here the observation made by D. P. Mukerji seems to me just: 'Everywhere the old elite-groups have disappeared; here too they are going; and no new ones, barring the professional politician and the bureaucrat, are to be seen. To keep Brahminism as a going social concern in this universe is an old maid's dream. . . . Ten presidents can wash the feet of ten thousand Brahmins but the Brahmin's prestige in this field cannot be restored.'[1] There have been no significant Brahmin social and political movements, and even the more traditionalist religious groups have turned their attention increasingly to social welfare activities of a modern kind.

The absence of distinctive traditionalist elites—even the 'communal' political parties, where they have any strength, are not wholly traditional—means that the opposition between traditionalism and modernism, so far as it occurs, finds expression within the dominant elites. This opposition can be easily discerned, but not so easily evaluated, in political life. In the Congress Party, it was expressed in some measure by the differences between Gandhi and Nehru—but Gandhi was not simply a traditionalist, and Nehru was not simply a modernist. It is expressed at the present time by the coexistence of different 'styles' or 'idioms'

[1] D. P. Mukerji, *Diversities* (New Delhi, 1958), p. 73.

of politics: the modern, the traditional, and the saintly, to use the terms which W. H. Morris-Jones has employed.[1] The modern style is represented by the system of parliamentary democracy, by the courts and the higher administration. The traditional element is to be found largely in village politics, where caste, kinship, and factions have an important role. Finally, saintly politics has its basis in ancient religious ideals; it was one element in Gandhi's political thought, and it is expressed most fully today by Vinoba Bhave and J. P. Narayan.

This differentiation of political 'styles' refers primarily to the existence of levels or areas of politics which are in some degree self-contained and separate from each other. A study of Orissa, by F. G. Bailey,[2] illustrates this point and brings out some additional features. The author distinguishes between an 'elite arena' of politics, which is that of the state government, and a 'village arena'. The former is modern, the latter traditional. But there is also an intermediate region, that of constituency politics, where the two extremes meet and have to accommodate themselves to each other. In this process, Bailey suggests, the political activities of the state and the constituencies tend to absorb and transform (that is, modernise) those of the village. The elite itself appears to be more or less united—both socially and politically—and Bailey poses the question whether it could not be conceived as a middle class which is 'set in opposition to the peasants or the landless labourers or the industrial workers of Orissa'.[3] This idea is rejected mainly on the grounds that there is no corporate group of peasants and workers—and thus no clearly defined rival elite within the state—and also that the unity of the elite is, in fact, mainly displayed in its relations with external groups, with the elites of other states and with the Delhi Government.

A recent study of political leadership in Uttar Pradesh shows the Congress Party much more distinctly as a middle-class elite whose power is based upon property ownership:

'In all four rural districts studied, the leadership and the major sources of support for the local Congress organisations have been drawn from the high caste ex-tenants of the *zamindars* and *talukdars* and from the petty and middle ex-*zamindars*. Power in the countryside rests upon control of the land. The power of the Congress rests upon its network of relationships—established

[1] Morris-Jones, op. cit., p. 52.
[2] F. G. Bailey, *Politics and Social Change: Orissa in 1959* (Berkeley, 1963).
[3] Ibid., p. 228.

through its leadership and through its control of local government and co-operative institutions—with the locally influential communities in the villages, with those who control the land.'[1]

The unity of this leadership is continually threatened by factional conflicts, which are a traditional feature of Indian society, and which have their source in patron–client relationships such as those between landowner and tenant, lawyer and client, leader and local community (the latter involving caste loyalties, but extending beyond a single caste). Factions have been able to flourish in Uttar Pradesh in part because the political supremacy of Congress in the state has not been seriously challenged. When there is a challenge, as in one district from the Swatantra Party, the ruling group closes its ranks and factionalism declines.

On the national level the political elite, and especially the governing Congress Party, also has to deal with the traditional politics of the village on one side and with the saintly politics of the *Bhūdan* movement on the other. But here, too, just as in the case of Orissa or Uttar Pradesh, the influence of modern politics as practised by the elite seems to be preponderant, while within the elite itself there is equally little evidence of any profound division between modernists and traditionalists. No doubt some Congress leaders are more deeply concerned about cow protection or the prohibition of alcoholic drinks, others about the development of the steel industry or the provision of military equipment, but such differences have not produced any major rifts. If any single issue could be pointed to as a source of disunity at the present time, it would probably be the differences of opinion about the desirable scope of public as against private enterprise in India, or, more broadly, the respective merits of socialism and capitalism as forms of society—and this is a thoroughly modern question.

Among the high officials and military chiefs the problem of tradition versus modernity scarcely arises, for both groups are entirely modern in their education, their activities, and their professional outlook. The case of the intellectuals is different and more complex. In most modern societies intellectuals have formed a rather vaguely defined social category, within which diverse groups have emerged and have coexisted or contended with each other. From the eighteenth century up to the present time one prominent line of division, in the Western societies,

---

[1] P. R. Brass, *Factional Politics in an Indian State: The Congress Party in Uttar Pradesh* (Berkeley, 1965), p. 229.

has been that between conservative and radical intellectuals. More recently, the opposition has been complemented, or as some would argue, supplanted, by a distinction between 'scientists' · and 'humanists'. It is possible to trace some divisions of this kind in modern India; to see, for example, in Ram Mohan Roy a progenitor of a radical intellectual class which reached maturity in the independence struggle, or to observe the formation of a modern intellectual class through the introduction of Western science and the establishment of Western universities in India. But these developments in Indian culture have not produced such a rigorous opposition of doctrines, on such an extensive scale, as occurred in many of the Western countries. There has been no 'battle of the books', no influential group of *philosophes*, no general conflict between science and religion. In part this must be explained by the fact that Western thought was introduced into India by a colonial ruling power, and was diffused in a foreign language; with the consequence that the struggle for independence could be seen as demanding a reaffirmation of the traditional culture, perhaps interpreted in new ways and incorporating some elements borrowed from the West, but still fundamentally Indian. This contest between the indigenous and the foreign still continues, in discussions of the use of the English language, although it has lost the sharpness which it had for earlier generations, for Tagore or Nehru. Its outcome is well expressed by I. P. Desai when he writes: 'What we may have is a Western-influenced, Indian-oriented ideology and the large mass of the new intellectuals probably belongs to this category. Ideologically, we do not have genuine Westernisation.'[1]

On the other side, Brahminism, which established the cultural unity of the traditional society, is incompatible, in many respects, with the conditions of life in a developing industrial society, and it has lost much of its vitality. Yet its influence is still considerable, and as M. N. Srinivas has observed on numerous occasions,[2] the processes of Westernisation and Sanskritisation are going on together in modern India. Thus, while some members of higher castes become Westernised—and this may be a very imperfect Westernisation—members of lower castes are being drawn more

[1] I. P. Desai, 'The New Elite', in *Towards a Sociology of Culture in India*, op. cit., p. 154.

[2] See, for example, his *Caste in Modern India, and Other Essays* (Bombay, 1965), Chapter 2, 'A Note on Sanskritisation and Westernisation'; and also 'Changing Institutions and Values in Modern India', in *Towards a Sociology of Culture in India* (op. cit.).

fully into the traditional type of society by the adoption of Brahmin doctrines and practices. The result is a mixture of modern and traditional ideas, rather than a confrontation between them.

This is especially striking in a field where the pre-eminence of modern ideas might be expected to be uncontested, in the social sciences. It is often suggested that the sociologist or anthropologist, and even the economist, working in India needs to have a peculiarly intimate acquaintance with the traditional society, regardless of the matter which he is studying. D. P. Mukerji claimed, for instance, that

'. . . the study of Indian traditions . . . is the first and immediate duty of the Indian sociologist', and further '. . . it is not enough for the Indian sociologist to be a sociologist. He must be an Indian first, that is, he is to share in the folk-ways, *mores*, customs, and traditions for the purpose of understanding his social system and what lies beneath it and beyond it. He should be steeped in the Indian lore, both high and low. For the high ones Sanskrit is essential . . .'[1]

This kind of obligation was not laid upon the early political economists and sociologists in European countries; it was not suggested, nor did they consider, that they should steep themselves in the culture of feudal Europe before proceeding to investigate the problems set by emergent capitalism. The difference marks the extent to which traditional ideas affect Indian social thought and produce a compound which is neither traditional nor modern.

It would be necessary to study much more closely than has yet been done[2] the development of intellectual occupations and of modern culture in India before judging how enduring this compromise between traditional and modern thought is likely to be. For the present, it undoubtedly exists, and the intellectual community is not rent by a struggle between modernists and traditionalists. Much more apparent is the diversity of regional cultures, and it is the diverse effects of regionalism which have now to be examined. The dangers of a 'balkanisation' of India have been presented most forcefully in a recent book by Selig Harrison.[3] His argument runs as follows: India comprises diverse

[1] Mukerji, op. cit., pp. 232-3.
[2] The most comprehensive attempt to date is E. Shils, *The Intellectual Between Tradition and Modernity: The Indian Situation* (The Hague, 1961).
[3] S. S. Harrison, *India: The Most Dangerous Decades* (Princeton, N.J., 1960), especially Ch. III, 'The New Regional Elites'.

cultural regions which in the past were held together by the dominance of Sanskrit and of a national Brahmin elite, and subsequently by the dominance of English and of a British (or British-educated) political and administrative elite. Since Independence, English no longer serves as a national language, and the claims of Hindi to replace it are challenged and opposed; at the same time there has been a tremendous upsurge of the regional languages and cultures. These developments are likely to create insurmountable barriers between the linguistic regions, to impede mobility on a national scale, to intensify local loyalties, and to provoke demands for greater regional automomy; in the end, they may give rise to separatist movements.

The strength of linguistic loyalties is undeniable, as is the vitality of the regional cultures. The first has been demonstrated by the mass insistence upon establishing states based upon major linguistic areas, which resulted in the creation of Andhra, the partition of Bombay State between Gujarat and Maharashtra, and most recently the division of Panjab into Panjabi- and Hindi-speaking states. The second may be indicated by the fact that while no one has ever spoken of an Indian renaissance, the Bengali renaissance in the early part of the century has been universally recognised, and that the revival of literature, music, and dance at the present time is primarily a regional phenomenon. Nevertheless, the conclusions of Selig Harrison's study, and in particular the analogy which he suggests between the situation in India and that in Eastern Europe when the Balkan states were created after World War I, are open to objection. In the first place the cultural unity of India is much more ancient and profound than was that of the Hapsburg Empire, and if its religious basis has become weaker in recent times it is still not negligible. On the other hand, it is a mistake to exaggerate the degree of unity in the past, and to overlook the new unifying factors which have appeared more recently. The cultural unity of India before the British period was not, for long periods, reinforced by a political and administrative authority which was securely established over the whole territory. It is in modern times that an effective central government and administration has been established and it has grown stronger in the last two decades by being founded upon popular consent.

Secondly, it should be remembered that India is, by intention, a federal, not a unitary state. In such a political system it is natural that the rights of the component states should be strongly asserted, and it is by no means evident that the Indian states are more intransigent, or more frequently in conflict with the federal government than are, for example, the states in the USA or the provinces in Canada.

Thirdly, it is misleading to suggest that the linguistic loyalties which are manifest in India are exceptional, or to be compared only with those in Eastern Europe half a century ago. Within the last few years there have been violent conflicts in Belgium between the two linguistic groups; there has been in Britain a remarkable growth of Welsh nationalism; and in Canada a linguistic minority concentrated in the province of Quebec has engendered a strong nationalist movement, which includes an active separatist wing. The Canadian example provides an instructive contrast with the situation in India. The cultural backgrounds of the French–Canadian and the English–Canadian communities are in most respects more diverse than those of the regional groups in India; for one community is Latin, the other Anglo-Saxon, one is Catholic, the other mainly Protestant in religion. Against this must be set the fact that there are only two major linguistic groups, and that a policy of bilingualism and biculturalism is conceivable, if optimistic. In India there are fourteen major linguistic groups, and the only solution of the language problem seems to be to establish one national language alongside the regional languages. Whether this is more or less difficult to achieve than bilingualism remains to be seen.

There can be no doubt that the existence of distinct cultural regions, which are also, within limits, separate political entities, affects the composition and the activities of elite groups. But how divisive its effects may be is a question that needs careful examination. Consider, first, the implications for intellectual life. It is true that in some aspects—in literature and music, for example, or even in the writing of history—the influence of the regional culture may be all-important. Even so, there is an element of unity in so far as the different cultures draw upon a common stock of themes derived from Hinduism. And if the Hindu religion itself should decline rapidly with the disintegration of the caste system, as some scholars believe is likely, there is still no reason to suppose that the accumulated cultural traditions which Hinduism animated will suddenly vanish, any more than the culture inspired by Christianity has disappeared in the predominantly secular modern Western nations. Furthermore, there are large and growing areas of intellectual life which are not influenced in any important way by a regional culture; the natural sciences do not have a 'national', let alone a 'regional', character, and even the social sciences, in spite of the attempts to connect them with specifically Indian traditions, are most likely to develop along lines which will make them part of a universal body of knowledge.

In this sphere, then, there seems to be no obstacle to the free movement of intellectuals throughout India. This would be facilitated by general use of a national language in higher education; and the spread of Hindi as a second language in non-Hindi-speaking areas, together with the continued use of English, suggests that the difficulties, although considerable, are not insuperable. Literary culture and art are bound to be closely dependent upon the regional language; the sciences, technology, management, and administration are not. In order to establish precisely the extent of regional divisions in the intellectual elite it would be essential to examine the degree of geographical mobility, and whether it is increasing or decreasing, among such groups as university teachers, scientists, and journalists. M. N. Srinivas has pointed out that in earlier times religious pilgrimages helped to unify Indian society: 'Linguistic barriers, and differences in customs and usage, do not seem to frighten pilgrims: on the other hand, they seem to enjoy the diversity of India.'[1] It may be that this unifying element in modern India will be supplied in part by the mobility of intellectuals; and it is worthy of note that university teachers, for example, have generally been hostile to the undue emphasis upon regional culture and in particular to the idea of an exclusive use of the regional language in higher education.

In the political sphere, it has already been shown, there are regional elites. But these elites are deeply involved in the national political system. The major political parties are all national parties, and even where their strength is mainly concentrated for the time being in particular regions—the Swatantra Party in Gujarat, the Communist Party in Kerala—they still contend for power on an all-India basis. Thus the political leaders are inescapably caught up in national politics, and many of those in the regional elites aspire to become national leaders. The politicians in the state governments are, of course, very much concerned with the development of their particular region, and they are frequently in conflict with the Delhi government, especially with regard to the location of projects under the Five-Year Plans. But there is little in the activities or pronouncements of the regional elites which diverges from the ordinary representation of local interests in other federal systems. The state politicians in India

[1] *Caste in Modern India, and Other Essays*, op. cit., pp. 105–6.

do not insist more strongly upon their claims to a share in development projects than do, for example, the provincial governments in Canada when the allocation of federal funds in highway construction, electric power, or higher education is under discussion. Again, it is necessary to ensure, in the national government and in governmental agencies, that the various regions are adequately represented, and in particular that a balance between north and south India is maintained. But is the distinction between north and south any greater than in the USA, or the question of representation more delicate? The answer is by no means obvious.

The evidence at the present time seems to me to indicate a growing division in Indian politics, not between traditionalists and modernists, nor between regions, but between ideological groups of a modern kind. To some extent the development of ideologies has been obscured, and hindered, by the dominance of the Congress Party, which encompasses a considerable variety of social and political views; but in the last few years there has been a more vigorous conflict of doctrines, following the growth of the Swatantra Party on one side and of the Communist Party on the other. The themes which dominate political discussion, as India's fourth general election approaches, are not those of traditional culture versus industrialism, nor of regional versus national development; they are the problems of economic growth, of the distribution of wealth and income, of planning and free enterprise. The effect of the growth of opposition parties is likely to be a greater unity of the elite in the Congress Party, and a development in India of competition between political elites which are much more clearly defined by their social and political aims.

An observer once remarked about the French Chamber of Deputies in the 1930s that there was a good deal less difference between two deputies, one of whom was a Communist and the other was not, than between two Communists, one of whom was a deputy and the other was not. A similar observation might be made about the Lok Sabha, with reference to the differences of region or caste among its members. It would certainly be true of the high officials in the Indian Administrative Service (IAS). Their social background is diverse in terms of regional origins (although some regions are over-represented), and in terms of caste (although the higher castes predominate, largely because of their advantages in secondary and university education, and in spite of the reservation of places for members of scheduled castes).[1] But any divisive consequences of such diversity are greatly diminished by the prevalence of common elements: the large proportion who have been educated in 'public schools', and still more, the intensive training given to probationers at the national Academy of Administration, and the ethos of a small elite group which has very strong traditions. The members of the IAS are allocated to state cadres, but this does not divide the service on regional lines, partly because at least half the cadre in each state has to come from outside the state, and partly because officials are deputed for periods of service in the central administration. The IAS, although it has something of a federal character, is, like the *grands corps de l'Etat* in France, or the Administrative Class of the Civil Service in Britain, a very distinct, cohesive, and powerful elite.[2]

So far in this essay I have said little about the divisive influence of caste. The significance of caste, and the changes which it is undergoing in modern India, are questions of great difficulty and complexity, and in the present context I can only set out very briefly some suggestions as to the bearing of caste membership upon the formation and the stability of elites. It is necessary, first, to distinguish between the traditional castes (*jati*), which are local and small-scale groups, and the modern caste associations which endeavour to widen caste loyalties and to bring together in a single group '. . . those castes (*jati*) which form a category by virtue of a common name, a common traditional occupation, and a roughly common status position in their respective caste systems . . .'[3] The caste associations usually extend over a linguistic region or state, and in some cases they attempt to cover the whole of India. Their degree of organisation and influence varies considerably in different parts of India, from the well-organised and powerful Nair Service Society in Kerala to the association of the Orissa Oilmen-Vaisyas, which, according to F. G. Bailey, is still in the formative stage and has little political influence.

The influence which a caste association may have on a national

[1] There is more information on the administrative elite than on most others. Sources include R. K. Trivedi and D. N. Rao, 'Regular Recruits to the I.A.S.—A Study', *Journal of the National Academy of Administration*, Mussourie, Vol. V, No. 3; a forthcoming study by V. Subramaniam; and Morris-Jones, op. cit., pp. 121–3.

[2] Similar observations could be made about the Indian Foreign Service.

[3] Bailey, op. cit., p. 130. Bailey describes very clearly the differences between castes and caste associations, on pp. 122–35.

scale is revealed by M. S. A. Rao's account of the Yadavas,[1] who comprise a number of allied castes—Ahirs, Gopals, Gollas, and others—engaged chiefly in the occupations of cowherd and milk-seller in different parts of India; but who also claim to include a number of earlier ruling dynasties among their members. The All-India Yadav Maha Sabha, which was formed in 1924, has been especially active in pressing for the formation of a Yadav regiment in the Indian Army, and M. S. A. Rao suggests that the Yadav members of the Lok Sabha act together to sponsor the activities of the caste association.

Another national association which is active and influential is that of the Marwaris, the All-India Marwari Federation. Selig Harrison, in his account of the 'new caste lobbies',[2] discusses among other groups both the Marwaris and the Ahirs. Of the latter he observes that in Uttar Pradesh they have allied themselves with the Jats and some other castes to form an influential coalition; but this view has been questioned by Paul Brass, who notes that in the Meerut district of UP, where the political influence of caste is strong, nevertheless all factions '. . . are multicaste in composition', and the diversity of castes '. . . makes it impossible for a faction seriously interested in obtaining power to restrict its membership to particular groups'.[3] A series of nine studies on the third General Elections published in the *Economic Weekly* between July and September 1962[4] shows that the influence of caste affiliation upon voting varies greatly from place to place; that it is never the sole influence, but has to contend with economic interest, ideological commitment, attachment to individual leaders, and other factors; and that it is not usually pre-eminent.

Caste loyalties are undoubtedly strong in many regions, but they are probably most effective in village communities and become weaker in the larger caste associations which are active in state and national politics. Only detailed studies of the caste associations themselves and of their relations with the political elites in the states or at the centre—studies which, rather surprisingly, have not yet been undertaken—would make it possible to decide this point. Although some students of Indian politics foresee an increasingly important role for the caste associations

[1] M. S. A. Rao, 'Caste and the Indian Army', *Economic Weekly*, Vol. XVI, No. 35 (29 August 1964), pp. 1439–43.

[2] Harrison, op. cit., Ch. IV.

[3] P. Brass, op. cit., p. 148.

[4] Reprinted as a pamphlet under the title *The Third General Elections: Studies in Voting Behaviour*, Bombay, *Economic Weekly*.

in the near future, it does not appear that at present they play a major part in the selection of political leaders or in the creation of political divisions. To some extent, perhaps, they reinforce regional distinctions, but not all caste associations are organised on a regional basis, and some of them—the Marwari Federation, for example—have been opposed to regionalism.

The caste associations, so far as they are politically active, take part in state and national politics, and they may in this way affect the composition and the policies of the political elite. The *jati*, on the other hand, are mainly engaged in village politics, and so they are of less interest in the present context. It is worth noting, however, that even in village politics, where the sway of the traditional social organisation is strongest, it is far from clear that caste loyalties always have a predominant influence. A. H. Somjee has edited a series of village studies in Gujarat which show that although there is in some cases a major conflict between Patidars and Barias, this is overshadowed elsewhere by the opposition between kin groups or generations within one of the castes, or by the formation of alliances between castes on the basis of economic interests;[1] and André Béteille has concluded from a study of a Tanjore village that political power has to some extent detached itself from caste, that the balance of power is unstable, and that 'factors other than caste play an important part in maintaining it and changing it from day to day'.[2]

If the importance of caste in the political sphere is thus doubtful then it is even more so with regard to the other elite groups—the administrators, the military chiefs, and the intellectuals—for these groups are recruited on the basis of individual merit and achievement; they are not bound, as political leaders are, to the representation of various communities and interests in the society. In fact, caste distinctions do seem to play a small part in these elites. Among the high officials and the intellectuals the most apparent differences are those of region and language, but they are overcome, as I have suggested, by a substantial amount of geographical mobility, and by the influence of the standards which are established by the professional group itself. Caste loyalties, which may or may not be strong initially among those who enter the higher administration or the intellectual elite, seem to be overshadowed, if not extinguished, by a commitment to the more universal aims

[1] A. H. Somjee (ed.), *Politics of a Periurban Community in India* (Bombay, 1964).

[2] A. Béteille, *Caste, Class and Power: Changing Patterns of Stratification in a Tanjore Village* (Berkeley, 1965), p. 200.

of these elite groups; and this process is helped by the fact that the functions of administrators and of intellectuals (at least, of those in the universities) are modern and 'Western', hence incompatible with the traditionalism of caste. In the case of the military it has been suggested that caste differences are more significant, in part as a legacy of British rule, with its concept of 'martial races';[1] but even if this is true at the regimental level, it is questionable whether it affects the upper levels of the military hierarchy. The military chiefs, like the high officials, are trained on Western lines and they probably have much more in common with each other than with other members of their respective castes.

The cohesion of these elites—political, intellectual, military, and administrative—is facilitated by the fact that entry to them depends in large measure upon property ownership, or educational qualifications, or both. Their members come predominantly from similar middle-class environments, have similar educational experiences, and deal with each other as middle-class, professional people. These common elements may well outweigh any differences of caste or language; and such evidence as there is, principally on the high officials, suggests that they do.

The elements which make for unity or disunity in the elites may now be summarised. Unity is fostered by the middle-class origins of elite members, by their similar educational experiences, by the particular training which they undergo and the traditions of their profession in the case of administrators, military chiefs, and intellectuals. In the case of political leaders, educational background is less important, and it is above all the ideology and organisation of the Congress Party, the patronage which it dispenses, and the memories of its part in the independence movement, which serve to maintain unity. The divisive factors are those of region, language, kin group, faction, caste, and ideology. In the administrative and military elites all of these seem to be relatively unimportant at the present time. Among the intellectuals there are divisions arising from regional differences, and from the divergence between traditionalists and modernists, but these divisions are still not acute.

The political leaders are divided along many different lines—those of caste, of region, of kin group, of faction, of social doctrine (traditional versus modern, conservative versus radical)—but the fact that the Congress Party has governed India for two

---

[1] See the article by M. S. A. Rao mentioned earlier.

difficult decades, and has suffered only minor reverses, is an indication that the forces of unity have so far prevailed. It is partly,
indeed, the existence of so many different lines of division, cutting
across each other, which explains the cohesion of the political
elite. A member of the elite may ally himself on one occasion
with his caste fellows, on another with those from his region, on
yet another with a particular faction, or with a group of those
whose social philosophy is akin to his own; and this variability
of alliances and groupings diminishes the likelihood of any major,
irreparable division. There is still another factor which now
promotes unity in the political elite; namely, the emergence of
stronger opposition parties on an all-India scale. Many studies
have shown how the Congress Party is able to overcome factional
disputes when it is seriously challenged by rival political elites,
and in the fourth General Elections it will have to confront, on
a much more extensive scale, the opposition of the Swatantra
Party and the Communist Party.

It is very likely that in the next decade the conflicts within
Indian society will assume a more ideological character, and will
come to resemble more closely those in other modern nations.
The divisions of caste and region will add to the complexity of
these conflicts, but I do not think they will be decisive in themselves. Probably the most important question is going to be which
of the various elites, or combination of them—the political parties,
the officials, the military chiefs, the intellectuals, or others which
may emerge—can establish itself as the 'governing class'; and
this depends above all upon the ability of an elite to assure India's
economic development and to represent adequately the aspirations
of the mass of the people. In this situation the Congress Party
has still a decided advantage, because it has inspired and directed
the economic progress of the last two decades, and through the
scheme of *panchayati raj* has initiated a genuine extension of
democratic government which has brought it more closely into
contact with the people.

PART III

Social Movements and Political Action

Chapter 11

Conflict and Social Change[1]

We are very far from possessing a sociological theory of conflict at the present time. A number of writers indeed have pointed to a marked decline of interest in the subject from the beginning of this century until the last decade or so. Lewis Coser, for example, in his introduction to *The Functions of Social Conflict*[2] observes that while the early American sociologists (particularly Small and Cooley) recognised the importance of social conflict, and even assigned a positive value to it, the sociologists of the 1950s showed little concern with the subject, and when they treated it at all it was to dismiss it briefly as a purely disruptive phenomenon. This was in line with the prevailing functionalist conception of the nature of human societies. Another writer, Alastair Buchan, has remarked, with reference to international conflicts, that '... until very recently ... the study of war and peace attracted nothing like the degree of intellectual attention that has been devoted for three or four generations to economic analysis ... and, whatever the reasons, there is no generally acknowledged corpus of theory ...'[3]

This is not to say, of course, that there was no interest at all in the phenomena of social conflict after the period in which the founders of sociology and the classical nineteenth-century writers made their studies. Marxism, which has been the pre-eminent social theory of the last hundred years, treats conflict, especially class conflict, as a fundamental characteristic of society. Even in this case, however, it is true to say that the underlying interest in social conflict did not produce much in the way of new reflection upon, or empirical investigation of, the class struggles and the international wars of the twentieth century. It is chiefly since the mid-1950s that social scientists have rediscovered the significance of conflict—a belated awakening to the character of this century,

---

[1] Reprinted from John C. McKinney and Edward A. Tiryakian (eds), *Theoretical Sociology* (New York, 1970).

[2] (New York, 1956.)

[3] *War in Modern Society: An Introduction* (London, 1966), p. xii.

with its two world wars, its ideological confrontations, its dictatorships, its revolutionary movements and wars of national liberation, and finally its possession of the means of mass destruction through nuclear war. From a somewhat unreal view of societies as harmoniously integrated wholes, disturbed only by minor and transitory 'deviations', we seem now to have moved toward a conception of the co-existence of integrating and disruptive forces in the actual historical life of particular societies and in the system of relations between societies, a conception close to that which was set forth more than half a century ago by Simmel: '... there probably exists no social unit in which convergent and divergent currents among its members are not inseparably interwoven. An absolutely centripetal and harmonious group, a pure "unification", not only is unreal, it could show no real life process. ... Society, too, in order to attain a determinate shape, needs some quantitative ratio of harmony and disharmony, of association and competition, of favourable and unfavourable tendencies.'[1]

Yet this recognition of the social significance of conflict is scarcely even the beginning of wisdom. Any man, let alone a social scientist, living in the world of the 1960s, must be remarkably insensitive if the daily experience—either direct or through the mass media—of armed struggles in Asia, Africa, and Latin America, of Negro revolts in American cities, of student rebellions in many countries, does not awaken in his mind some notion of the ubiquity of conflict and its importance in shaping human affairs. From the social scientist, however, we expect more than this simple acknowledgement of a fact. What is it that the sociologist, in particular, may be expected to provide? The list is long, and encompasses the main problems of a sociological theory of conflict. The diverse forms of conflict should be enumerated; the incidence and extent of conflict more precisely stated and their fluctuations noted; the varying balance between division and conflict on one side, integration and harmony on the other, more carefully described; the causes of conflict investigated (and so far as is necessary, or possible, traced from the social to the

[1] From Georg Simmel's essay *Der Streit*, first published as Chapter 4 of his *Soziologie* (Leipzig, 1908). I quote here and in subsequent references from the English translation by Kurt H. Wolff published under the title *Conflict* (New York, 1955). There was an earlier translation by Albion Small of a different version of the essay in the *American Journal of Sociology*, Vol. 9 (1904). Small was profoundly interested in the problem of conflict and drew for his own theories upon Marx, Gumplowicz, and Simmel.

psychological and biological spheres); the effects of conflict examined.

TYPES OF CONFLICT

Many of these questions were considered by sociologists in the nineteenth century, and have been taken up again in recent years. Let us see, first of all, what the earlier writers contributed toward a body of useable theory. Not all of them attempted to distinguish in a formal way between types of conflict; nevertheless, a simple distinction was made implicitly between international conflict (wars between nations, or empires, or tribal groups), and internal conflict (revolutionary struggles, civil war). The relative importance of these two types of conflict was variously estimated. Comte and Spencer were chiefly concerned with international conflict (and with a historical contrast between militant and industrial types of society); so, later on, were Gumplowicz and Oppenheimer. Marx, on the other hand, regarded internal conflict (the struggle between classes) as the most significant form, and his social theory has little to say about international conflict. Later, there were attempts to develop, within Marxism, a theory of imperialism and war (by Lenin, Hilferding and Rosa Luxemburg among others) but this still assumed as its starting point the fundamental conflict between classes.

This simple distinction between internal and international conflict, though important,[1] is clearly not adequate. There are variations in the intensity of conflict, and in the extent to which the use or threat of force is involved; there may also be qualitative distinctions to be made. Simmel, for instance, distinguished between conflict and competition, treating the latter as an indirect form of conflict: 'linguistic usage reserves the term only for conflicts which consist in parallel efforts by both parties concerning the same prize'.[2] He went on to examine some specific features of competition, namely, that its outcome itself does not constitute the goal, that each competitor aims at the goal without using his strength on the adversary, and that it does not begin from hostility. Within the forms of direct conflict, both internal and international, there is a range of means employed, from intellectual persuasion, the influence of prestige or propaganda, economic or political

---

[1] It can be generalised to refer to all social groups: and we may then refer to internal and external conflict, or intragroup and intergroup conflict. The latter terms are employed by Coser, op. cit.

[2] In the second chapter of *Conflict*, pp. 57–86.

pressure, up to the use of overt violence. One of the characteristic forms of conflict in modern societies, industrial conflict, displays several of these features. In the early stages of industrialisation in the Western countries, industrial conflict was sporadic and often violent (notably so in the United States); in the advanced industrial societies today such conflict is continuous, regulated, and generally nonviolent. Yet it is still not confined entirely or permanently to purely industrial issues or to the sole use of argument, influence, and economic pressure in disputes. Marx's theory envisaged an extension of industrial conflict into the political sphere and the eventual formation of a revolutionary working class; and although the actual course of events has not conformed in detail with these predictions (particularly in respect to the growth of a revolutionary movement), it has been close enough to leave open the question as to the scope and character which industrial conflict may assume. It is evident, in any case, that even in the most peaceful times the threat of force is never far distant from any major industrial dispute.

Such attempts to classify the forms of social conflict have been intended to make the problem more amenable to investigation. They do not presuppose the absence of more general characteristics which are perhaps to be found in all the diverse forms of conflict, or which link these forms together. Conflict may have its source in some universal element of human nature, as Simmel suggested when he wrote that 'it seems impossible to deny an *a priori* fighting instinct',[1] and as a number of recent writers, whose work I shall review later, have indicated. Or it may be that there are universal features of social structure which necessarily generate conflict. These are questions to which I shall return.

MEASUREMENT OF CONFLICT

The rudimentary classification discussed so far at least makes it easier to move on to a further stage of theoretical construction, namely, the search for regularities in the emergence, extent, and duration of social conflicts. This requires an accumulation of quantitative historical information concerning different types of conflict; and the work in this field, which in any case presents great difficulty, has so far been fragmentary. The two kinds of conflict which have been most fully examined from this point of

---

[1] Simmel, op. cit., p. 29.

view are war and industrial conflict. Among the early sociologists, Comte and Spencer both discussed the prevalence of warfare, but their conclusions on the tendency of warfare to diminish in an industrial state of society were not based upon any quantitative comparisons. Similar objections may be raised against most of the sociological discussions of war until quite recently. The earliest attempt to deal comprehensively with the incidence and scale of warfare in different periods was probably that of Pitirim Sorokin in the third volume of *Social and Cultural Dynamics*,[1] but the measures which he used were fairly crude and some of the inferences drawn from the material are invalid. A few years later an exhaustive historical examination of warfare was published by Quincy Wright under the title *A Study of War*,[2] and this too assembled much quantitative information. The most thorough and reliable quantitative inquiry to date is that of L. F. Richardson in his *Statistics of Deadly Quarrels*,[3] which brings together a large volume of data—though covering a relatively short period (roughly from 1820 to 1949)—and attempts to discover the correlates of war, that is, other social events which are associated with the occurrence of war. Richardson's study did not yield any very significant positive correlations, but it did dispose of some facile generalisations about the causes of war and the conditions of peace, while at the same time suggesting that there had been a tendency for the incidence of warfare to decline in relation to population size in the twentieth century. There remains the possibility that an extension of such investigations to other historical periods would reveal long-term fluctuations in warlike activity.

The studies of industrial conflict have also been somewhat disappointing from the point of view of rigorous quantitative comparisons, even though many countries now publish statistics of some kind on the incidence, extent, and duration of industrial disputes. The most thorough statistical study is K. G. J. C. Knowles's *Strikes: A Study in Industrial Conflict*[4] which deals with the United Kingdom in the period 1911–45 and attempts to correlate strike activity with other social phenomena. There is no work of similar scope on other industrial countries, and there have been few attempts to make comparisons between countries or between historical periods. Two short studies in this field—

[1] (Cincinnati, 1937.)
[2] (Chicago, 1942), 2nd edn, 1965.
[3] (Pittsburgh, 1960.)
[4] (New York, 1952.)

Clark Kerr and Abraham Siegel, 'The Interindustry Propensity to Strike: An International Comparison',[1] and Arthur M. Ross and Paul T. Hartman, *Changing Patterns of Industrial Conflict*[2]— do bring together data for international comparisons. The first suggests reasons for a greater strike-proneness in certain industries, which Knowles also discussed, while the second distinguishes varying patterns of strike activity as between different groups of countries, and also examines long-term trends. The authors discern a decline in strike activity—a 'withering away' of the strike, as they call it—and also a change in the character of strikes, from major instruments of bargaining to sporadic protests; but it is possible that these are actually short-term fluctuations.

When we consider the difficulties which arise in measuring with any precision such phenomena as wars and strikes (although they appear to be relatively easy to isolate and define), and note how little work has yet been devoted to these problems, it is not surprising that other types of social conflict should have presented seemingly unmanageable difficulties for sociological analysis. How are we to measure the extent of class conflict in a society? How are we to determine the degree of competition, or its fluctuations over time? How then can we determine the balance between the forces of harmony and conflict, integration and division, within given societies; how can we make comparisons between societies in this respect; and how can we relate the phenomena to other social events? There is no obvious answer to these questions, except to say that in many cases it will be necessary to use a variety of indirect measures, and to employ such imprecise numerical terms as 'more' and 'less'. For example, in the study of class conflict it is relevant to consider the formation of trade unions and employers' associations, the occurrence of conflict in various forms and especially the incidence of violence, the expression of attitudes in manifestoes, journals, and other media, the emergence of political movements, and the elaboration of conflicting social doctrines. Some of these phenomena can be measured fairly precisely, while in other cases the magnitude has to be estimated very roughly in a mainly descriptive account. Notwithstanding these difficulties, which are additional to the conceptual difficulties encountered in dealing with such social entities as class or ideology, I think that some tentative historical

[1] In Arthur Kornhauser, Robert Dubin, and Arthur M. Ross, *Industrial Conflict* (New York, 1954), pp. 189–212.
[2] (New York, 1960.)

and intersocietal comparisons could be formulated, when all the relevant criteria are brought together. If not, we should be obliged to conclude that conflict theories are as untestable as are functionalist (or, if you like, organismic) theories.

CAUSES OF CONFLICT

The inability as yet to demonstrate any significant patterns in the occurrence of major forms of social conflict has not prevented the appearance of theories which claim to provide causal explanations of conflict, and especially of war, by correlating it with other phenomena; in the case of war, for example, with imperialism, with overpopulation, or with national characteristics. These claims must be regarded, for the present, as vain. This does not mean that any kind of causal explanation is ruled out. Leaving aside, for the moment, a more systematic inquiry into possible regularities and fluctuations in conflict, there are two other approaches, mentioned earlier, which may be considered.

One of these is to look for the causes of conflict in human nature, and to posit, as did Simmel, a 'fighting instinct'. In an exchange of letters with Einstein on the prevention of war, Freud asserted the existence of a destructive or aggressive instinct in human beings which cannot be suppressed, though it is always countered by another instinct, of sympathy or love.[1] Recent biological and anthropological studies have generally supported the notion that there is an aggressive instinct, resulting from natural selection, which is widely distributed among the vertebrates and is to be found among the primates, including man. Washburn suggests that men 'inherit the biology of aggression that was adaptive in the past', and that it is nurtured by many customs, although it is no longer adaptive: 'for the modern, crowded, scientific world, the human actor, particularly the male, is too dominance-seeking and too aggressive'.[2] Similarly, Konrad

---

[1] Freud's letter was originally published in 1933 by the League of Nations International Institute of Intellectual Co-operation. It is reprinted in Sigmund Freud, *Collected Papers*, Vol. 5 (New York, 1959), and also in *War: Studies from Psychology, Sociology, Anthropology*, Leon Bramson and George W. Goethals (eds) (New York, 1964). This latter book very usefully assembles some of the major writings on war by de Tocqueville, William James, Sumner, Park, Spencer, Malinowski, Freud, and Raymond Aron, among others.

[2] S. L. Washburn, 'Conflict in Primate Society', in Anthony de Reuck and Julie Knight (eds), *Conflict in Society* (London, 1966), pp. 11–12.

Lorenz in his book *On Aggression*[1] examines aggression as 'the fighting instinct in beast and man which is directed *against* members of the same species', and which has as its chief positive functions the apportionment of territory, sexual selection, defence of the young, and the establishment of social ranking.

It is clear, however, that an explanation of actual conflicts along these lines cannot be complete. Neither individuals nor groups are perpetually engaged in conflict, and a theory which depends upon a permanent and constant aggressive instinct cannot explain the cycle of conflict and absence of conflict. What it does is to draw attention to an underlying propensity to engage in aggressive behaviour, and to show the biological basis of such a propensity. In order to explain actual conflicts we have to determine, in addition to this general condition, more specific causes. This may be done by adopting a theory of *interests*. Conflict occurs when territory is invaded, when young are threatened, when social ranking is disturbed or challenged. (This last case fits quite closely the Marxist theory of class conflict.) In human societies, biologically determined interests become culturally elaborated, and Lorenz recognises this by the use of the term 'militant enthusiasm' to describe the human version of biological aggressiveness in relation to interests.

These considerations lead back to the sociological aspects of the problem. Assuming the existence of an aggressive propensity, can we explain actual conflicts by means of a theory of interests and of the clash of interests, broadly along Marxist lines? Marx's theory is, in a formal sense, genuinely explanatory. His conception of the universality of class conflict provides only a general model; the important part of the theory is that which deals with classes in capitalist society, and which asserts that the increasing divergence of interests between bourgeoisie and proletariat (together with a growing awareness of the divergence) will result in increasing conflict. Let us suppose that Marx's assertions have been falsified, that class conflict has in fact diminished in the advanced industrial societies—a view which many sociologists appear to hold strongly, even in the absence of rigorous measures of the extent of class conflict. If this is so, then we have now to explain the diminution of class conflict by arguing that divergence of interests is not so closely correlated with conflict, or that the divergence of interests between the classes has decreased, or that

[1] (Vienna, 1963; translation, New York, 1966.) There is a good criticism of 'instinctivist' theories, especially those of Freud and Lorenz, in Erich Fromm, *The Anatomy of Human Destructiveness* (New York, 1973), Chapter 1.

some other factor has affected the degree of conflict. For example, we may refer, as I myself have done in a descriptive way, to the influence of nationalism in moderating internal conflict.[1] Another argument against the Marxist theory has been presented by Ralf Dahrendorf,[2] who suggests that the intensity of class conflict in the nineteenth-century capitalist societies was due to the super-imposition of political conflict upon industrial conflict: 'The opponents of industry—capital and labour—met again, as *bourgeoisie* and proletariat, in the political arena ...'[3] Dahrendorf argues that industrial and political conflicts have been dissociated in what he calls 'postcapitalist societies'; there are now criss-crossing lines of conflict in place of a fundamental cleavage in society.[4] From this criticism of Marx, Dahrendorf proceeds to outline a more general theory of conflict, which is, very briefly summarised, that conflict is a necessary element in all imperatively co-ordinated associations.[5] If then it can be shown that impera-tively co-ordinated associations are a universally necessary feature of human society, it follows that conflict is also universally neces-sary. This theoretical model, which does not of course encompass intersocietal conflict, resembles the biological theory of aggression in accounting for the occurrence of internal conflict in general, while not explaining the periodicity, scale, or intensity of conflict. To deal with the latter questions we need not only the kind of sociographic and statistical studies which I have mentioned in the previous section, but also an investigation of possible varia-tions in the structure of social groups (and in a wider context, of the international system of relations between total societies) which favour or discourage conflict.

Some reflections upon these structural differences are to be found in Simmel's essay, and they have been extended and system-atised by a number of recent writers, among them Coser and van Doorn.[6] Simmel observed that conflict might become particularly

[1] In *Classes in Modern Society* (New York, 1966; and London, 1965). This argument itself follows Simmel's analysis of the effects of external conflict upon the internal cohesion of a social group.

[2] See *Class and Class Conflict in Industrial Societies* (Stanford, 1959).

[3] Ibid., p. 268.

[4] This applies, in a particular context, an observation of Simmel's which has been elaborated by Coser in *The Functions of Social Conflict*; namely, that the crisscrossing of conflicts prevents the disintegration of a social group along one primary line of cleavage.

[5] '... the distribution of authority in associations is the ultimate "cause" of the formation of conflict groups.' Dahrendorf, op. cit., p. 172.

[6] Coser, op. cit.; J. A. A. van Doorn, 'Conflict in Formal Organisations' in *Conflict in Society*, op. cit., pp. 111–32.

bitter in groups based upon very intimate relations (such as kin groups or sects), or between groups which represented causes rather than interests (for example, classes since the time of Marx); but his remarks provide clues rather than conclusions. Coser sets out in a more formal way the propositions implicit in Simmel's essay, but his treatment is analytical, and does not attempt to establish generalisations about the actual occurrence of conflict under varying conditions of group structure and goals. Similarly van Doorn, following Simmel, distinguishes between a coalition type of organisation and a sect type of organisation, and he suggests that tensions in the latter tend to produce extremely radical and ruthless internal conflict. The empirical evidence to support such assertions is admittedly slight. Do we know, in fact, that the intensity of conflict varies significantly with the structural difference between coalition and sect, between groups based upon intimate or impersonal bonds, between interest groups and ideological groups? Is it possible to establish that variations in conflict are correlated with the degree to which organisations are imperatively co-ordinated (or is there no sense in speaking of *degrees* of imperative co-ordination)? These questions can hardly be resolved, perhaps not even properly formulated, without a much more satisfactory natural history of conflict than we yet possess.

THE EFFECTS OF CONFLICT

It has proved easier to study the effects of social conflict than its causes, although similar difficulties and inadequacies appear in both lines of inquiry. Lewis Coser's summary of his work on the functions of social conflict probably represents well the main direction of sociological interest: '... we have examined a series of propositions which call atention to various conditions under which social conflict may contribute to the maintenance, adjustment or adaptation of social relationships and social structures.'[1] These 'positive' functions of conflict, which were initially set out by Simmel, may be described as follows: intragroup conflict, if it is kept within limits, may help to maintain the unity of the group by providing a safety valve, or it may serve to re-establish unity; intergroup conflict sets the boundaries of groups, it may maintain a whole social system by upholding a balance of power between various groups, and it may enhance the internal unity of groups which are engaged in conflict. Simmel refers particularly to the

[1] Coser, op. cit., p. 151.

way in which the modern centralised states were formed as a result of warfare, and he notes that estates and classes were also created by conflict. Marx had earlier expressed the same idea: classes engage in conflict, but they are also its product, as fully constituted and conscious groups. In these examples Simmel suggests the influence which conflict may have in promoting social change, and he argues more generally that without conflict a social group can show no 'real life process'. The recent studies of conflict have not emphasised to the same extent the connection between conflict and social change, in part perhaps because such an association is a prominent feature of Marxist theory. The point becomes clear if we consider how little attention sociologists have devoted to the study of revolutionary movements in the twentieth century, except occasionally as advisers on counterinsurgency. Revolution, like war, and perhaps even more than war, brings to the forefront those moral considerations which are interwoven with any kind of reflection upon the social meaning of conflict, the implications and influence of which are not always candidly avowed. However, the impact which revolutionary movements are beginning to have upon social thought may be seen in the recent appearance of new reflections upon the phenomenon of revolution.[1] and in the attention now given to the theoretical writings of revolutionaries, from Mao Tse-tung to Che Guevara, Frantz Fanon, and Regis Debray.

But before we turn to this theme, there are some other aspects of the connection between conflict and the maintenance or transformation of a form of social life which need to be discussed. Simmel, and most of the later writers, have been concerned with clarifying concepts and indicating possible relationships, rather than with asserting correlations. For example, Simmel observed that intergroup conflict would be likely to increase the internal cohesion of the groups involved in it, but he also observed that it did not always do so. To take a current example: the American war in Vietnam is quite obviously not increasing the unity of American society; in fact, it is dividing the society in an extremely bitter conflict. A more general case is that in which defeat, or the likelihood of defeat, in an external conflict produces serious divisions within the group concerned. In the twentieth century, revolutions have often followed military defeat. Yet the association is not constant; there have been defeats without any accompanying

---

[1] Ralf Dahrendorf, 'Über einige Probleme der soziologischen Theorie der Revolution', *European Journal of Sociology*, Vol. 2 (1961); Hannah Arendt, *On Revolution* (New York, 1963); Carl J. Friedrich (ed.), 'Revolution', *NOMOS*, Vol. 8 (1967).

revolutionary struggles, and there have been revolutions without defeat in an external conflict. The Chinese revolution took place after victory. Thus it is far from sufficient to indicate possible connections between the existence and outcome of external conflict and the degree of internal cohesion. Some more elaborate theoretical model has to be constructed which would allow us to make precise empirical statements about the effect of various types of external conflict upon various types of social groups.

The general relationship between conflict and social change also needs to be investigated much more closely. Conflict between groups and within groups may evidently bring about change, or create a propensity to change by unsettling established ways of life. Simmel observed that '. . . in the early stages of culture, war is almost the only form in which contact with alien groups is brought about at all',[1] and many sociologists have attributed to warfare the extension of the scale of early societies, and in more recent times, the creation of nation states. Warfare has been held by some writers to have a major influence upon the development of technology, and thus to contribute to more profound changes in society; while modern war, which affects the whole population of a society and which may be taken to date from World War I, has been credited with important political consequences, from the enfranchisement of women to the extension of social welfare legislation. Equally, internal conflict may bring about important social changes. Marx adopted, as he said, the view of bourgeois historians that modern Europe was the product of class struggles, and he expected new class struggles to result in still more fundamental changes in society; in fact, Marxist political movements in many countries have radically transformed the structure of their societies. Less dramatically, it may be argued that the conflict between organised political parties in the industrial countries, and in some developing nations, has been a major influence in establishing the rights of the individual, and notably the rights of dissent, criticism, and opposition.

One form of conflict which Simmel examined, but which has received little attention subsequently, is competition. Simmel disagreed with the view of the socialists, and of such liberals as J. S. Mill, that the effects of competition were generally harmful, and he emphasised what he termed the 'socialising and civilising function of competition'. 'Modern competition', he wrote, 'is described as the fight of all against all, but at the same time it is

---

[1] Simmel, op. cit., p. 33.

the fight *for* all'; this in the sense that economic competition is directed toward maximum output at minimum cost. Furthermore, 'given the breadth and individualism of society, many kinds of interest, which eventually hold the group together throughout its members, seem to come alive and stay alive only when the urgency and requirements of the competitive struggle force them upon the individual.'[1] Competition, and the whole *laissez-faire* economy of nineteenth-century capitalism, may have been important in promoting economic growth; moreover, the exceptionally rapid development of the American economy may be attributable to the greater scope of competition in the United States. But still we can produce no exact correlations between the extent of competition, or the intensity of the competitive spirit, and the rate of economic growth in different societies. And on the other hand, there are grounds for supposing that competition has other less welcome effects; its civilising influence, which Simmel sees in the manner of Durkheim as the creation of a network of mutual obligations and dependencies, may be counteracted by its effect upon the rate of mental illness and of crime. Again, however, the demonstration of an exact correspondence is wanting.

Simmel, and following him Coser and others, have devoted much of their attention to the positive functions (meaning the *beneficial effects*) of conflict. One of these positive aspects is, as we have seen, that conflict engenders changes which are themselves judged to be on the whole beneficial. But aside from the fact that conflict may also produce changes which are judged to be harmful (a possibility of which we are uncomfortably aware in the nuclear age), there are other aspects of the relation between conflict and change to be considered. It cannot be demonstrated that all change results from conflict, although Hegel's philosophy of history and (with some qualifications) Marx's social theory, and the many theoretical schemes derived from them, assert or insinuate that it does. There may be changes which occur without conflict—the accumulation of scientific knowledge, for example—and which themselves then provoke conflict, as did modern science in the 'battle of the books', in the conflict between science and religion, and more remotely in the struggles among interest groups and classes which were incited by the rise of a new technology. On the other side, there is no warrant for asserting that all conflict produces change. Some kinds of conflict, as Simmel suggested, help to maintain or strengthen an established form of social life;

[1] Ibid., pp. 63–4.

in tribal societies ritualised conflicts seem intended to enhance social solidarity and to reinforce existing institutions.[1] Moreover, it is not difficult to conceive or to suggest instances of a sufficiently protracted and intense conflict within a social group which might produce a stalemate, and impede or halt changes which had already begun.

PROSPECT

The renewed interest in the study of conflict has been determined very largely by practical concerns, and in particular by the desire to find some means of avoiding, or at the least controlling and limiting, war in the nuclear age. This has given rise to a whole new field of inquiry, under the name of 'strategic studies', which is concerned on one side with those conditions and situations which seem likely to result in war, and on the other side with the outcome or consequences of war. A work which reflects better than any other these new interests, and which is illuminating also in the variety of methods which it employs, is Raymond Aron's *Peace and War: A Theory of International Relations*.[2] After discussing those concepts and classifications which are needed in any study of war and peace—power, force, the international system of states, types of war, and types of peace—and considering the determinants of war, Aron turns, in the third and fourth parts of his book, to a historical examination of the global system of states in the nuclear age, and to a consideration of some moral evaluations of war and their political and strategic implications. Several of the subjects treated in the latter part of the book have been widely discussed. One of these is the question of the influence of the level of armaments (or more generally, military preparedness) and especially of an arms race, upon the probability of war. Richardson, whose work on the causes of war was mentioned previously, also constructed mathematical models of arms races,[3] one of which (the runaway arms race) he applied to the periods preceding the two world wars; at the time of his death he was studying the third arms race, which began in 1948, but he had not yet reached any conclusions about the

---

[1] On this see Max Gluckman, *Custom and Conflict in Africa* (Oxford, 1955; New York, 1964) and subsequently *Politics, Law and Ritual in Tribal Societies* (Chicago, 1965).

[2] (New York, 1966.) Originally published in French as *Paix et Guerre entre les nations* (Paris, 1962).

[3] L. F. Richardson, *Arms and Insecurity* (Pittsburgh, 1960).

outcome. It may not be possible to make any strict inferences from such work as to the probablity of an arms race ending in war; but it is reasonable to argue that a stabilisation or reduction of armaments is likely to diminish the chances of war, first because it represents already a measure of agreement between the conflicting nations, and secondly, because it will probably affect the mood of the nations involved—a factor which Richardson considered of great importance.

Another question discussed by Aron is that of an alternative to war as a means of regulating the relations between states, each of which is pursuing its own national interest. He examines two possibilities: peace through law, and peace through empire. Either course would involve a greater or lesser sacrifice of national sovereignty. Peace through law may be conceived, up to a point, as an extension of present international agreements, but its full realisation would seem to require the creation in some form of a supranational legislature, executive body, and administration. Peace through empire would quite plainly involve the loss of independence for the nations incorporated in it; it is also quite unrealisable at the present time, since neither the United States nor the Soviet Union is capable of establishing a universal empire. There is also a third possibility: peace through the balance of power, as it now exists. Here the question is whether, and under what conditions, a stable and enduring balance of power is achievable.[1]

The last of the themes raised in recent studies which I propose to consider here is that concerning the role of war in national policy. Is war any longer a rational instrument of policy, in Clausewitz's sense? Here we are obliged to distinguish between different kinds of wars. Wars of national liberation, counter revolutionary wars, and some others, fought on a limited scale with what are now called 'conventional weapons', may be rational in the sense that the gains may clearly outweight the losses for one side, and that the common ruin of the contenders, though possible, is not necessary. But what of thermo-nuclear war between major powers? Majority opinion throughout the world would probably now consider that such a war would not be rational, that it would entail a common ruin, and even perhaps the extinction of mankind. There are, however, dissenters from this view, one of the best known being Herman Kahn, who has

---

[1] The principal doubts concern the effects of rapid technological advance and of the spread of nuclear weapons.

argued in his book *On Thermonuclear War*,[1] and in later writings, that the cost of such a war in casualties and destruction would not be prohibitive. One new element in these studies is the use of game-theory models as an aid to determining strategy; a use which, in the extraordinary fascination which it has for some social scientists and policy makers, has attracted much criticism. Aron concludes his study of peace and war with a criticism of the spurious realism of these models, and he advocates paying more attention to 'reasonable policy' than to 'rational strategy'.[2] Anatol Rapoport in his *Fights, Games and Debates*,[3] and in a more recent article,[4] while acknowledging that game theory offers a conceptual framework in which strategic analogues of conflict situations can be clearly formulated,[5] points to the limitations of the theory, especially in non-zero-sum games (which are the analogues of many real conflict situations) in which a rational choice cannot be prescribed.

One circumstance which accounts for the rapid growth of strategic studies is the widespread desire to control war in the nuclear age, both on rational and on moral grounds.[6] The same degree of concern, and of moral agreement, does not exist in respect of other forms of social conflict. Hence the reluctance to see revolutions, industrial conflict, and until fairly recently, ethnic conflict, as subjects which might engage the attention of any substantial number of sociologists, or figure prominently in the theoretical models or descriptive accounts of a social system. Hence, too, the uneasiness which becomes apparent when the attempt to investigate such conflicts is made. Revolutions do not fit very comfortably into a conceptual scheme which regards the positive functions of conflict as being to maintain, with minor adaptations, a given social system. Only if a revolution is defeated is the social order maintained; if it succeeds, society is transformed. And whereas sociologists, like other men, are generally *against*

[1] (Princeton, 1960.)

[2] Aron, op. cit., Final Note.

[3] (Ann Arbor, 1960.)

[4] 'Models of Conflict: Cataclysmic and Strategic', in *Conflict in Society*, op. cit., pp. 259–87.

[5] Ibid., p. 277.

[6] There are perhaps minor exceptions. The satirical *Report from Iron Mountain*, L. Lewin (ed.) (New York, 1967), suggests that in some 'think-tanks' and in other circles in the United States there may be greater concern about the horrors of peace; that is, about the difficulty of finding adequate substitutes for what are claimed to be the vital functions of war in the economic, political, sociological, demographic, and cultural spheres.

war and can without any qualms see their studies of war as having the practical objective of limiting or avoiding it, they may be either for or against revolution (and other kinds of internal conflict) and suddenly become aware of the intrusion of moral attitudes and commitments into their inquiry. They may, and do, approach the study of revolutions with sympathy or aversion; they may become advisers to revolutionary leaders, or more frequently to counterinsurgency agencies. This should not deter them from such delicate inquiries, nor should it prevent them from expressing as clearly as possible the point of view which guides their research and writing, and which makes their studies humanly significant.[1] I see little to criticise in the expression 'positive functions of conflict', if it can be taken to cover revolutionary transformations, as well as more gradual changes, or the maintenance of an existing order; and if the contrasting negative functions are defined and given their due importance. What is open to criticism is the view which seems often to prevail that a sympathy with movements of rebellion is somehow more ideological, and a greater threat to sociological objectivity, than is an attachment to the status quo; or more generally, that a preoccupation with social conflict is less scientifically pure than is a concern with social order. For such notions there is no justification whatsoever.

I began this essay by saying that we do not have a sociological theory of conflict. Yet the recent studies of conflict have made an important contribution, not least to sociological theory in a broader sense. The studies of war, at present the most advanced, have begun to amass the kind of historical and statistical knowledge which is essential for any causal analysis, and they have been fruitful in developing models of conflict situations which, for all their shortcomings, are a powerful aid to investigation. If these studies have not yet produced any general theory of war, they have at least made clearer the complexity of the phenomenon, they have identified some of the proximate causes, and they hold out the prospect of an eventual rational control of this form of conflict. The same degree of intellectual effort has still to be

---

[1] The ill-fated 'Project Camelot' illustrates well some of these issues, and its implications have been lucidly examined by Irving L. Horowitz in 'The Life and Death of Project Camelot', *Trans-action*, Vol. 3 (1965) and by Ralf Dahrendorf, *Essays in the Theory of Society* (Stanford, 1968), Chapter 10. It would perhaps illuminate one critical aspect of the project if we were to suppose that there had been another project, officially sponsored and financed by the Cuban government, to study systematically, and with a view to aiding them, the Negro rebellions in American cities.

applied in the study of other types of conflict—class conflict and revolutionary movements, industrial conflict and ethnic conflict— and these phenomena present in some respects greater difficulties because both the practical end in view and the extent to which rational control of them is desired are more ambiguous. Nevertheless, it seems likely that the methods which have been used in studying conflict in an international system could be applied with profit in studying the relations among groups within a society or within segments of a society, so long as we keep in mind the difficulties of judging what is positive and what is negative in different forms of social conflict.

Perhaps the clearest gain from recent studies of conflict is the change which they have initiated in our general conceptions of the nature of a social system. It is no longer possible to place such great emphasis upon social harmony, integration, and equilibrium, or to adopt such a static view of social structure, as has been done in the last thirty years under the influence of structural-functionalism. *Deviance* (one of the sloppiest terms in the sociological vocabulary) no longer seems an adequate category to embrace the varieties of dissent, conflict, rebellion, and repression which occur in all societies and which have assumed such vast dimensions in the rapidly changing societies of the twentieth century. Conflict is an intrinsic part of social life, sustaining, modifying, or destroying the social groups in which it takes place. It cannot be treated satisfactorily as a minor and exceptional form of social relationship, in a brief apologetic appendix to a theory of social solidarity, as has so often been done. Whether we like it or not, we shall have to pay increasing attention to conflicts of interest and doctrine, and to the role of violence in upholding or overthrowing a social system, if we are to explain events and provide the means by which men can make reasonable choices between alternative courses of social action. And on the other side we shall need to eliminate from sociological thought the vestiges of the melting-pot ideology, which assumes that vast inequalities of wealth, power, and enjoyment can and should be harmoniously accommodated without any fundamental changes in the structure of society.

Chapter 12

The Political Context of Technology[1]

In the space of a few decades men have attained, in great measure, a goal which was long anticipated and desired. They have become, in Descartes' phrase, 'the masters and possessors of nature'. A scientific and technological revolution, which continues at an accelerating pace, has already largely accomplished the substitution of knowledge for physical labour as the principal force of production, and we live in the conditions which Marx, over a century ago, saw as the final outcome of capitalist production: 'The process of production has ceased to be a process of labour . . . It is man's productive powers in general, his understanding of nature and his ability to master it, which now appear as the basis of production and wealth.'[2]

Yet the achievement has taken on, increasingly, a problematic character: on one side, because the revolution in production, contrary to the expectations of Marx and of later socialists, has not been accompanied by a social revolution, but has taken place mainly within the framework of capitalist society; and on the other side, because science and technology, after three centuries in which they have been almost universally regarded as the supreme means for solving human problems (above all in the nineteenth-century theories of progress, of which Marxism itself was one version), have now come to be seen by many people as a source of problems which they are perhaps unable to solve. Their continued advance creates as much anxiety, and even fear, as it does satisfaction; and these sentiments have begun to take form in

[1] Reprinted, with minor revisions, from the *New York Review of Books*, XVII (7) (November 1971).

[2] Karl Marx, in the preparatory manuscripts for *Capital*, which were first published in 1939–41 under the title *Grundrisse der Kritik der politischen Oekonomie* (*Rohentwurf*). An English edition of the manuscripts is now available, translated and edited by Martin Nicolaus, under the title *Marx's Grundrisse* (Harmondsworth, 1973).

movements of criticism and opposition. The 'counter culture' emerges as the antithesis of a scientific civilisation.

It is evident, of course, that there was hostility to science and technology (and to their product, industrialism) at a much earlier time, arising in the first place out of aristocratic and religious values; and also that the high tide of the confident Western belief in progress through science has been steadily receding since the end of last century. Nevertheless, the reactions of the present time are on quite a different scale, and they concern more specific dangers. Initially, no doubt, it was the discovery and use of nuclear weapons which produced widespread doubts about the sense of equating increasing scientific knowledge with increasing human happiness. The menace of nuclear war has kept these doubts alive and they have been strengthened by some other unwelcome by-products of technological advance—the population explosion, the pollution of the environment—which are more and more frequently portrayed as alternative forms of an approaching 'doomsday'.[1]

The mistrust of science and technology has ceased to be merely the affair of some traditionalist social groups—of an aristocracy or a coterie of literary intellectuals—who might be seen as struggling to defend an established social position and way of life. It is not even any longer a more general conflict between the 'two cultures', for there has grown up an extensive literature of scientific self-criticism. Dennis Gabor, surveying the course and costs of technological development, writes of 'compulsive innovation' and 'growth addiction', and he urges those who live in the industrial countries to reflect upon ways of making the transition to a 'new stage of civilisation' which would offer *hope without material growth*.[2] Similarly, Anthony Oettinger, in a highly critical examination of the uses of technology in education, refers to 'innovation-drunk schools'.[3] Many scientists now seem ready to engage in collective actions—for example, in the Pugwash Conferences or in the work of the Society for Social Responsibility

---

[1] Eugene S. Schwartz, *Overskill: The Decline of Technology in Modern Civilisation* (Chicago, 1971) quotes from a paper on population growth by Heinz von Foerster, entitled 'Doomsday: Friday 13 November, A.D. 2026', the observation that 'Our great-great grandchildren will not starve to death. They will be squeezed to death'. Or, on the other hand, they may choke to death.

[2] Dennis Gabor, *Innovations: Scientific, Technological and Social* (London, 1970).

[3] Anthony G. Oettinger, with Sema Marks, *Run, Computer, Run: The Mythology of Educational Innovation* (Cambridge, Mass., 1969).

in Science—in an attempt to find solutions for some of the problems which technological development creates.

Yet these attempts themselves raise new problems. It is very widely (though, be it noted, not universally) recognised that science and technology need to be brought under some more stringent kind of control. But how are they to be controlled, and by whom? The answers given to these questions are very diverse and for the most part unconvincing, even in those studies which undertake a more or less systematic inquiry into the relation between technology and society, as distinct from the mass of journalistic and sensational comment in which the whole subject threatens to become engulfed. Their unsatisfactory character is due on one side to the absence, in most cases, of any theory of society which would provide a framework for considering science and technology as social phenomena, and on the other side to the lack of any clearly conceived social end, a desirable form of human society, which science and technology *ought* to help us to achieve. It is idle to blame urban planners, corporation executives (whether public or private), bureaucrats, or miscellaneous others for their misdeeds, when there exists no political consciousness which is capable of defining a form of social life to which we should be aspiring.[1]

Some of these difficulties and deficiencies are exemplified in two major projects of research which have been initiated within the past few years: the Harvard University Programme on Technology and Society, directed by Emmanuel Mesthene,[2] and the Research Group of the Czechoslovak Academy of Sciences, directed by Radovan Richta.[3] Mesthene's book,[4] which presumably reflects the general orientation of the Harvard Programme, makes no pretension to set out from any theoretical ideas about

[1] This issue, to which I shall return, is the main theme of Jürgen Habermas, *Toward a Rational Society* (Boston, 1970). He refers there to '... today's problem of transposing technical knowledge into practical consciousness', that is, into a public consciousness which would make use of ethical and political concepts in formulating social ideas and programmes.

[2] The Harvard Programme began in 1964, and its activities to date are reviewed in the *Sixth Annual Report, 1969–70*. Of the studies published so far those by Mesthene, Oettinger, and Westin will be considered here.

[3] The Czechoslovak project began in 1965. The first studies were published in 1966, and after being discussed widely by both scientists and political leaders they were presented in a revised version in 1968, by Richta and his colleagues, under the title *Civilisation at the Crossroads*. An English edition of the book was published in 1969 (White Plains, N.Y.).

[4] Emmanuel G. Mesthene, *Technological Change: Its Impact on Man and Society* (Cambridge, Mass., 1970).

social structure and social change. It has the appearance of a commonsensical, descriptive account of the impact of technology, avoiding the extremes of boundless enthusiasm or total condemnation and adopting a middle of the road position from which to assess judiciously the costs and benefits of technological innovation, and to reflect upon the social adaptations which will be necessary in order to diminish the former and increase the latter. But behind these statements of the apparently sensible and obvious there is discernible, nonetheless, a distinct point of view—that of the 'end of ideology' school of social scientists. Mesthene assumes a general agreement about social goals, embodied in existing institutions, excludes the possibility of political conflict, and ignores (except for one brief and contemptuous dismissal) the movements of dissent which have grown up during the past decade. With these assumptions he is then able to neglect the social background entirely and to treat technology as an abstract determining force, even though he has remarked earlier in the book that technology is *not* autonomous, *not* independent of society. The problems thus left aside are really the most vital ones, concerning the extent to which technology (not as an abstract force, but as an assemblage of particular kinds of knowledge and as the activities, based upon this knowledge, of distinctive social groups) is dependent or independent in relation to the interests and ideologies of other groups in society.

Mesthene's conception of technology comes out very clearly in that part of the book in which he discusses values. The discussion has several curious features. In the first place, only religious values are considered; and this is bound to seem odd at a time when secularisation is far advanced and many theologians themselves are busy transforming religious into non-religious expressions. More important, however, is the kind of relationship which is assumed between technology and religion; we are told only about the impact of technology on religion, never about the impact of religion on technology. In Mesthene's words: '... the new religious synthesis we seek would ... forge new symbols expressive of technological reality ... a long step will have been taken toward providing a religious belief system adequate to the realities and needs of a technological age'. This is very close to a crude Marxist view, in which the technological basis simply determines the religious superstructure. But if this is the relation to be posited why not proceed to the limit of the Marxist argument and conclude that religious values, as the 'opium of the people', are likely to disappear, or to be emptied of their meaning while retaining the forms, with the further development of technological society? Why not investigate in a more thorough fashion the secularisation of our culture, including the secularisation of theology itself, and the consequences of this process? Alternatively, if it is not meant to suggest that religious values are wholly ideological and determined, if they are conceived as having some independent basis, then their relation with technology should also be seen as potentially critical, and not simply as the legitimation of the technological order which Mesthene appears to advocate.

One consequence or accompaniment of this preoccupation with religious values is a virtually complete indifference to social and political values, even though such values are manifestly more relevant to social change.[1] For example, the student movement, which was certainly an important source of new social values during the 1960s, gets only an oblique reference in a brief comment on 'rebellious youth'. Mesthene sees this rebellion as the outcome of inadequate socialisation; the young generation, he explains, become aware through the mass media of departures from the ideas and norms of society before they can have instilled into them the values which the ideas and norms reflect. It does not seem to occur to him that it may be the values themselves, all too accurately expressed in social norms, which are being rejected, or that there may be reasonable grounds for rejecting them. There is apparent here an obstinate refusal to take political dissent seriously, to conceive that there can be alternative political values from which realistic political conflict may, and should, arise.

Mesthene's general perspective, which assumes that all fundamental political issues have already been settled in American society, proves very restricting when he does raise, in the last few pages of his book, some questions about the impact of technology on politics. He conceives this as involving only a relatively smooth adaptation of existing institutions to the needs of advanced technology, not as offering the opportunity and challenge for a leap forward into a new kind of society. At most he allows that it has brought about an 'enhanced importance of the public

[1] The Harvard Programme as a whole ignores quite conspicuously the field of politics. Among the forty-two projects initiated so far (according to the annual report for 1969–70) there is not one which deals directly with political movements and ideologies. Moreover, in the *Research Review* which is published as part of the programme, only a single issue (for Summer 1969) contains anything on the connection between technology and politics, and then it is a very brief discussion in the familiar context of assumptions about 'stable democracy' in the USA.

sector of society'. But this says very little. Everyone understands that big science and technology (together with military needs) have brought about government intervention in the economy (and also in the more general regulation of social life) on a scale which would have been inconceivable in the era of liberal capitalism. Leaving aside the fact that such intervention by the state is not an unalloyed blessing—is, indeed, from one aspect another problem posed by technology—it should be noted that Mesthene tells us nothing about the *content* of this intervention, or growth of the public sector, which can certainly take place, with very different ends in view, in a Nazi or Stalinist type of society just as well as in a more or less democratic system.

In fairness, it should be said that real political problems do occasionally break in upon these rather abstract reflections. Thus, in discussing the 'needed restructuring of our political institutions' Mesthene mentions the 'strength of privilege and vested interest that will stand in the way'; but the comment is too vague to indicate whether he envisages a genuine conflict of political interests and values, and if so, of which interests, around which major issues. In the same few pages Mesthene considers briefly the opposition which has become apparent between the extension, through technology, of the area of expert decision-making and some traditional ideas of democracy; but his suggestions for dealing with this problem do not go beyond advocating some refurbishing of institutions and procedures in order to make them 'more adequate to the realities of modern technological society', and in this way simply to preserve as much as possible of the kind of democracy we already have.

The attitude to technology which is expressed here, and in the Harvard Programme as a whole, is that of 'responding' to its 'impact'. There is no hint at all that technology, in its varied manifestations, can provide the material for creative political thinking (both critical and positive) which would be concerned above all with ways of getting more democracy, more equality, more widespread human enjoyment. This narrowness of view is particularly evident in discussions of technology in the sphere of information. For the most part the problem is seen as one of reconciling expert administration with our present limited degree of democratic participation, in the context of a widening gap (of knowledge) between the 'experts' and the 'public'. But this conception itself arises in part from the concentration of attention upon the flow of information among experts and specialists, as is the case, for instance, with many of the contributions to Alan F.

Westin, *Information Technology in a Democracy* (published as part of the Harvard Programme), which deal mainly with the value to administrators and managers of new methods of acquiring, presenting and analysing information which will increase the efficiency of 'organisational decision-making'. One consequence of this approach is the neglect of the possibilities for increasing the volume of public knowledge and discussion concerning the state of society. Social scientists, in many cases, contribute to this neglect by thinking of their work exclusively in terms of training new generations of 'experts', and not at all as a means of public enlightenment. Yet it is evident that information on social conditions could be much more widely diffused, and more thoroughly subjected to analysis in public discussions, than is the case at present. A great deal of the work on 'social indicators'[1] is suitable for presentation, in a critical and controversial manner, in regular assessments of the 'state of the nation', on television programmes and elsewhere. Any progress along these lines will no doubt depend largely upon the development of political ideas and a political movement which really aim to extend democracy in all spheres of life; but there is some value, at least, in showing how technology might contribute to a transformation of social life instead of portraying it as an iron cage within which we can only seek to make our cramped existence as tolerable as possible.

Some of these larger opportunities are in fact sketched in the study by Radovan Richta and his colleagues, which appears at first sight to diverge widely from the approach adopted in the Harvard project. In the first place, it begins from a comprehensive theory of society—Marxism—which can provide a framework for the systematic exploration of the relations between technology and the social structure; secondly, it puts the scientific and technological revolution firmly in the context of a specific form of society, namely that which has developed on the basis of a socialist economy; and finally, it deals with all these questions in terms of a social ideal, a future type of society far superior to our present condition, which is yet realistically described inasmuch as the continuance of conflict, uncertainty and change is acknowledged. The idea of a completely harmonious society, according to Richta, was one of the myths of the industrial age. The future civilisation will be characterised by 'more and more vigorous conflicts',

[1] See, for example, *Toward a Social Report* (Washington, D.C., 1969); the new British publication *Social Trends* (London, 1970); and some of the papers in the *Annals of the American Academy of Political and Social Science* (January 1971), 'Social Information for Developing Countries'.

arising out of the work experiences and life-styles of different social groups, and out of the opposition between generations there will emerge 'an ever-renewed, increasingly profound, polarisation of *progressive* and *conservative* attitudes', and a more intense clash of ideas.

Nevertheless, in spite of these obvious differences, there are also striking resemblances between the two projects. To begin with Richta adopts an interpretation of Marxism in which the determining influence of technology is very strongly emphasised; deriving this principally from those sections of the *Grundrisse* in which Marx outlined the development of industrial capitalist society up to the stage of automated production, characterised by the pre-eminence of science as the major productive force. Following, and to some extent amplifying, Marx's ideas Richta distinguishes several phases in the development of modern economic systems, beginning with the introduction of simple machinery, then the use of steam power facilitating a concentration of machinery and workers, followed by the use of electric power and a further concentration. These phases culminate in the system of mass production, based upon a large industrial labour force. The succeeding phase, that of the scientific and technological revolution, carries some of these processes further, introducing new forms of power and a larger stock of more complex machinery, but at the same time it reverses the line of development in one important respect; by making possible automated production it halts the increase, and then tends to bring about a decline, in the size of the industrial labour force and creates a new structure of occupations. Richta sums up this qualitative change by contrasting the 'industrial' or 'extensive' type of economic growth (involving the construction of new factories, improvement of machinery, growth in the numbers of industrial workers) with the 'post-industrial' or 'intensive' type (involving the discovery and use of qualitatively superior productive forces, by a transfer of resources to scientific research and development); and he concludes by arguing that this new kind of economy requires, and is bringing about, a new form of society. The scientific and technological revolution can proceed most easily, and can deliver its benefits most fully, in a socialist or communist society.

Richta, then, sees technology as the determining force in social development[1] and, like Mesthene, virtually ignores political move-

---

[1] This is evident not only in his own exposition but in the kind of supporting comments which he brings; thus he quotes approvingly (p. 30, note 47) the

ments. But the thesis he presents has some contradictory features. While claiming that socialism is the social form which corresponds with a system of production based upon advanced science and technology Richta acknowledges that the scientific and technological revolution has actually taken place most fully in the capitalist societies, whereas the socialist countries are still for the most part engaged in the preceding type of 'extensive' economic development. Indeed, one of the main themes of his book is the need, in Czechoslovakia, with its relatively developed industry, to bring about a change in economic policies in order to move from 'extensive' to 'intensive' growth. But in that case, what has become of the determining influence of technology? In the capitalist societies the 'post-industrial' stage has been reached without provoking any fundamental change in the social system. Conversely, in Czechoslovakia a socialist form of society has been created in the absence of an appropriate technological basis.

These historical problems, which obviously call for an analysis of the political forces at work in society, are not the only ones to emerge from Richta's book. There is also the question of how future changes are to be accomplished. Richta gives the impression that technological change will necessarily engender the good society which he describes in such an appealing way. But if the scientific and technological revolution has left the social system of Western capitalism largely intact, and has created in addition the monstrous problems against which the prophets of doom inveigh, why should we suppose that it will transform society in Czechoslovakia? In fact, it is all too evident that the optimistic and enthusiastic outlook conveyed by Richta's book had *its* source in the new political ideas and movements which came to life in Czechoslovakia between 1965 and 1968; and that the kind of social development envisaged at that time was arrested by another political act, namely the military occupation of August 1968.

As for the possibility of social change in the capitalist countries, Richta refers to it only in passing, and his theory of the development of productive forces merely raises again some well-known problems. For if the scientific and technological revolution has taken place, and the erosion of the industrial working class is

---

remark by J. Diebold in *Jobs, Men and Machines: Problems of Automation* (London, 1964) to the effect that Marxism–Leninism has long recognised technology as a determining factor in social change, and that this idea corresponds well with our experience of the present changes in our way of life.

already well advanced, then there may no longer exist, in an adequate form, that social force which, according to Marx's theory, would revolutionise capitalist society. And what is to take its place? The present-day weakness of radical political thought consists very largely in not being able to answer this question.

It is easy enough to see why writers like Mesthene and Richta should attribute such an overwhelming influence to science and technology, and should neglect, or fail to take seriously, the signs that there may be other forces in modern society which either make for change or stand in the way of change. The impact of scientists and technologists is highly visible; they form powerful interest groups, and they are able to recruit widespread support from other groups because their activities are essential to the goals of economic growth and military strength. At the same time, a scientific and technological outlook has been widely diffused and might be said to predominate in the culture of industrial societies, with the result that although the direction of technological development can be regarded as being determined in a broad sense by political authorities (through the financing of research, etc.), these authorities themselves are very likely to make decisions in a technological frame of mind, supported by all manner of 'expert' advice.

One important element in this situation has been the increasingly scientific and technological character of the social sciences. Ever since the war the notions of 'policy sciences' and 'social engineering' have steadily gained ground, and in spite of much recent criticism the main line of development in research is still (and in some countries increasingly) toward quantitative, policy-oriented studies which are intended to provide technical solutions of social problems. A good recent example is to be found in 'Forrester's Law'.[1] Jay W. Forrester argues, using the particular example of depressed urban areas, that many reform programmes actually worsen the situation they are designed to remedy, because they do not take into account a sufficiently large number of features in the situation. In the case of urban decay Forrester suggests that there is too much low-income housing in the depressed areas rather than too little; the provision of such housing attracts low-income people inwards until their numbers exceed available income opportunities and the level of living declines, with the

[1] This is the title bestowed in an article in the *New York Times* (14 June 1971). Forrester's own article, entitled 'Counterintuitive Behaviour of Social Systems', appears in *Technology Review*, Vol. 73, No. 3 (January 1971).

consequence that there is then a further deterioration in housing and other services. The remedy proposed, for this and other problems, is the construction of computer models of social systems, which would make it possible to take into account a much wider range of factors, to grasp their interconnections, and to foresee more accurately the consequences of intervening in one or other aspect of the situation. Forrester himself situates the problem of urban decay within an ambitious model of the interactions, on a world scale, between population, industrialisation, depletion of natural resources, agriculture, and pollution. I am far from wishing to condemn this approach out of hand. It is certainly preferable to base social policy upon an adequate, rather than an inadequate, representation of a social situation. But the use of computer models has limitations which should restrain our enthusiasm. First, it is by no means easy to determine that all the relevant variables have been included, or to decide upon their relative importance, as demographers have discovered in their attempts to construct models of changes in fertility. Secondly, and much more important in my view, every programme of social reform, even in a limited area—housing, poverty, discrimination— is embedded in the valuations of a social group which is seeking to preserve or to change a particular form of social life. The interests of slum dwellers conflict with those of slum landlords, the interests of the poor with those of the rich, and such conflicting interests are expressed, more or less clearly and vigorously at different times, in political doctrines and political action. Technical solutions are necessarily incomplete; they presuppose a *policy*, derive their meaning from being set within some valuation of what constitutes a good society, and are more or less successful, achieve this or that result, according to the outcome of political struggles.

The appeal of science and technology is enhanced by the relative weakness of political thought, faced with the diversity and complexity of present-day problems, the apparent insolubility of some of these problems, and a prevailing uncertainty about the bases and validity of political judgements. It is very much easier for the critic to concentrate his attention upon a particular evil consequence of technological advance (and to see the remedy in yet more technology) than to work out a comprehensive political view. What scheme of social thought is actually capable of grasping the whole array of problems—nuclear and biological warfare, the population explosion, massive pollution of the environment, exhaustion of natural resources, the totalitarian threat of data banks, the dangers inherent in genetic engineering—and offering, even in principle, a general solution?

The task appears even more unmanageable when we consider how many difficulties even a single one of these problems presents. It has often been remarked that environmental pollution cannot be tackled by any one country alone, for its air and water may be polluted by others. The problem is international. It is the same with population growth. One country, or a few countries together, cannot influence greatly the rate of increase of world population. But if we think in terms of a world population policy immense difficulties become apparent. First, as sober demographers tell us, population management is a very inexact science; we simply do not know enough about the influences upon fertility to be able to plan very precisely the size of population. Even if we could do so there would be other problems to face: population size is closely bound up with considerations of national interest and national power, and it would scarcely be easier to reach agreement on the limitation of population than on the limitation of armaments. Moreover, the attempt to arrive at international agreements and regulations in this and other spheres would create new problems, for the creation and consolidation of an international authority would tend to produce a system of government still more remote from the individual, and a still more impersonal bureaucracy.

Confronted by these immense problems political thought appears still weaker because of doubts about its own validity. Science and technology seem to provide certain knowledge; to a large extent they have become identified with human reason itself. By contrast, the valuations and judgements which constitute political thought appear insecure and tentative; they can easily be dismissed, especially when they take the form of a criticism of established society, as mere 'ideology', and even as an attack upon reason. This character comes out very plainly in some of the more critical studies of technology. Dennis Gabor, for instance, appeals in vague terms for a transition to a 'new stage of civilisation', while Eugene Schwartz expounds a mystical worship of nature. Among radicals the invocation of 'socialism' or 'revolution' all too often takes the place of a serious attempt to work out a political doctrine.[1]

[1] There is a good example, from a different sphere, in Teresa Hayter's *Aid as Imperialism* (Harmondsworth, 1971). After an acute analysis of the ways in which Western aid fails to help the developing countries the author concludes by saying that her negative assessment is based on observation

In spite of all this we can see the beginnings of a change, presaged by the events of 1968. Political dissent has increased, and new political interests have been articulated. Hardly anyone believes any longer that economic growth and technological innovation are self-evident goals, or that the assertion of them must put an end to all reasonable controversy. Thus the way is open for public discussion of the options which are available to men, given the stage of development of science and technology, in deciding the future form of their social life. What is most important is that this discussion should go beyond the speculations of futurologists and the work of individual critics, and should be taken up within radical parties, many of which had themselves succumbed earlier to a purely technological outlook. It is not too much to hope, perhaps, that we have already taken the first steps into an age of intense political debate and activity.

---

of the existing economic and social system: 'Under socialism, and with the principles of international solidarity operating in full vigour, things will be different'. This is not convincing, first because there are obvious problems in the relations between present-day socialist countries, and secondly, because even an ideal socialism could not be regarded as a solution unless some indication were given of the kind of institutions and procedures which would really make things different.

Chapter 13

Reflections on the Student Movement[1]

The student movement became in the late 1960s an international phenomenon which attracted increasing attention as a new form of political action. In many countries it broke sharply with the past: in the USA, where there is no strong tradition of active student involvement in politics, and in some European countries, where student political activity in earlier periods was closely associated with, and generally subordinate to, the aims and doctrines of broader radical movements. Two of the most prominent differentiating features of the present student movement are: first, its claim to be an independent political movement, which is revealed not only in its language and ideas but also in its frequently contentious relations with other sections of the radical movement; and secondly, its concern with the structures and operation of the university itself. These features have led some observers to speak in terms of a growing 'student consciousness' which they liken in various ways to the emerging 'class consciousness' of industrial workers in the nineteenth century. A French sociologist, Alain Touraine, has drawn a precise analogy between students and workers by arguing that in the large French universities of the present day, and notably in a university such as Nanterre which experiences a profound social isolation, the students have become a distinct collectivity in the same way as industrial workers did in the early capitalist factories; and by comparing the present student doctrines with the utopian visions of the early socialists. He carries the argument further by suggesting that the universities in all the technologically advanced societies have become one of the major 'forces of production', so that in this quasi-Marxist sense too the students may be regarded as having inherited the social role of the proletariat.[2] Similar ideas have been put forward,

1 Reprinted, with minor revisions, from the *Universities Quarterly*, 22 (4) (September 1968).
2 Alain Touraine, 'Naissance d'un mouvement étudiant?', *Le Monde*, 7 and 8 March 1968. These ideas are developed further in his book *The May Movement: Revolt and Reform* (New York, 1971).

from a different perspective, by Herbert Marcuse, who largely follows C. Wright Mills in asserting that the industrial working class, especially in the wealthy consumer society of the USA, has lost the desire and the capacity to bring about radical changes in society, and that its earlier role has now devolved upon the young intellectuals, constituted for the most part by university students. In a recent essay Marcuse qualifies this view to some extent by saying that he does not regard the student movement as being at present a revolutionary force, but as an element in American society which may become a revolutionary force in alliance with underprivileged groups, above all with the Negroes.[1]

It is largely American experience, and the interpretation of that experience by American thinkers, which is responsible for this new conception of the students' political role. In Europe the student movement has grown out of the New Left, that is to say out of a revival of a traditional kind of radicalism, which took shape in 1956 with the opposition to the Anglo-French attack upon Suez and the revolt of Polish and Hungarian workers and intellectuals against the Stalinist type of society; and it has retained strong links with long-established labour and socialist movements. In the USA, on the other hand, students were largely responsible for forming the New Left, in the civil rights movement, in the defence of the Cuban Revolution, and in the opposition to the Vietnam War, however much they may have owed in intellectual and political self-confidence to the radical criticism of American society which was launched by an older generation of thinkers in the darkest days of McCarthyism. The reasons for this difference should be plain: in the USA since the end of the First World War there has been no political labour movement, no widely based radical party, which could be the source of a new radicalism, even at a time when many Americans felt a growing unease about the domestic and foreign policies of their country. University students, therefore, assumed a pre-eminent role in expressing this unease, and later opposition; and they have remained the most important element in the radical movement, even after the rise of a militant Negro movement, as provokers of critical ideas, as leaders of mass demonstrations, and as a major influence upon national politics through their support of opposition candidates, most notably in the Presidential campaign of Senator Eugene McCarthy.

[1] Herbert Marcuse, 'Das Problem der Gewalt in der Opposition', in *Psychanalyse und Politik*, pp. 54–6.

The international influence which the American student move-ment has acquired is due very largely to the importance of its political role in the USA, and also to the fact that American students were the first to become involved in a major conflict within the university itself, in the Berkeley Free Speech Movement of 1964. Yet this influence could not have arisen if there had not been some common elements in the situation of students in most of the industrial countries. On one side there are general political conditions: the international repercussions of the Vietnam War; the conflict between races, which is acute in the USA, but which exists in other industrial countries and on the international scene in the relations between rich white and poor coloured nations; the appearance in countries other than the USA (for example, in West Germany) of a form of consensus politics which obstructs the expression of radical dissent. On the other side there are similarities in the universities themselves: the rapid growth in student numbers; the increasing size of universities; the emerg-ence of a more critical, less complaisant, younger generation; the survival, in many countries, of authoritarian or paternalistic forms of university government.

But even if we accept this view of the political significance which the student movement has in the USA, and of the prevalence in many industrial countries of conditions which enhance the im-portance of student movements, this is still very far from requiring acceptance of the idea that the student movement, on an inter-national scale, is in any sense a historical successor to the labour movement. Between the labour movement, early or late, and the student movement, there are immense differences. In the first place, students are not an oppressed and exploited group in society. In some countries and in some universities they may have serious grievances about their economic situation, the facilities available for their work, their relations with teachers and adminis-trators, or the nature of university discipline. But in relation to the rest of society they form a privileged group. They come predominantly from families in the middle and upper strata of society, and after passing through university they are able to enter the most rewarding occupations. The constraints which are imposed upon them in the university, even in the worst cases, are gentle indeed when compared with those which most workers have to endure. Their social situation is far removed from that of most industrial workers, of Negroes in the American ghettos, or of peasants in the underdeveloped countries, and it is absurd to pretend otherwise. Secondly, students are not now, and will not become, a majority of the population. For them a 'revolution of the immense majority' such as Marx and the early socialists foresaw is impossible. As a small minority they cannot expect to do more than provide radical diagnoses of the state of society—in other words, to carry on the traditional function of radical intellectuals—or to become allied with other social groups in a broader movement. In several countries the student movement has attempted to form such alliances; for example, with Negroes and other impoverished groups in the USA, with trade unions in France and in West Germany, but so far without much success. The reasons for this failure are to be found, perhaps, not so much in ideological incompatibilities as in the different social situation of the various groups. Negroes and industrial workers form real or potential interest groups which are engaged in very practical struggles; the student movement is primarily the expression of a more detached intellectual and moral criticism of society. These distinct activities—radical criticism and battles over material interests—have always been associated and have profoundly influenced each other, as the history of the labour movement and of Marxism plainly shows; but the fundamental element in all enduring radical movements has been the real life experience of oppressed and exploited classes. And lastly, students, unlike the working class, or the peasantry, or an ethnic group, lack a stable and continuing membership. The university career of most students extends over a period of three to five years; to be a student is to occupy a temporary position, not a permanent status, in society. This circumstance makes it unrealistic to regard the student body, or the present student movement, as an enduring and stable basis for a radical movement.

There are, however, two other important senses in which the student movement might be regarded as representing a distinct social interest. It may be claimed, first, that students are only expressing more clearly and vigorously the resentments and aspirations of the whole younger generation; that they are, so to speak, the vanguard of a 'party of youth'. For this view there is evidence from a variety of sources. The student movement, particularly in the USA, does seem to be in part a continuation of the un-political revolt of youth in the 1950s which was symbolised in the films, and the life, of James Dean; and there exists at the present time a youth culture, extending far beyond the student movement, which is more distinct within each nation, and at the same time more international in character, than was previously the case in the industrial countries. The causes of this accentuated division between generations are still not clear, although the speed of technological change, rising levels of living, and the growing proportion of young people in the population of some countries, must all have an influence. At all events, there seems to be a new spirit abroad. In many ways it is not unlike that which was evoked in another disturbed period of American history, before the First World War, by Randolph Bourne in his essays on *Youth and Life*, in which he expressed his sense of the growing contradiction between the new possibilities for human happiness and the threat of destructive war. The contradiction is even more acute now; for our technological achievement may in one sense make Utopia no longer utopian, as Marcuse has argued,[1] while on the other hand it makes possible total destruction. It is probable that this contrast is experienced most deeply by young people, and that the revolt of youth, as it is reflected in the student movement, is in some measure a protestation against the brooding menace of that 'blind Fury with the abhorr'd shears'. The most revealing slogan of the revolt is, perhaps, 'Make love, not war'.

The affinity between the student movement and a wider youth culture can be shown also in more specific ways; during the revolt of May 1968 in France, for example, the students were most successful in attracting young industrial workers to their movement, while the trade unions as a whole remained aloof. Nevertheless, I think it would be wrong to conclude that the cultural gap between generations is likely to produce any new political orientation, with a 'party of youth' confronting a 'party of middle age'. Youth is an ill-defined and transitory condition which, like the condition of being a student, is inadequate for the formation of an enduring movement. In fact, observation suggests that in so far as there is disaffection with the established political organisations in some industrial countries it has expressed itself more prominently in a sympathy with new movements and parties based upon ethnic, linguistic and cultural ties, through a revival of diverse forms of nationalism (among American Negroes, in

---

[1] 'Das Ende der Utopie', in *Psychanalyse und Politik*, pp. 69–78. From another aspect Marcuse's own view is still utopian, for although Utopia may be technologically and economically realisable it remains uncertain whether the social relations necessary to sustain it can be developed. An egalitarian and less coercive form of society would make great demands upon human qualities which are still, so to speak, underdeveloped; for instance the qualities of reasonableness and moderation. Moreover, we still lack precise knowledge of the conditions in which new social relations can be effectively established, even where they have been attempted, as in the Yugoslav system of workers' self-management.

French-speaking Canada, in Scotland and Wales), than in any generational bond.

There is one favoured arena in which we should expect the new self-awareness of students as a distinct social group to reveal itself, and that is the university. In its most radical form this self-awareness has been expressed recently by the slogan of 'student power'. Even where the university itself is concerned, however, it is important to notice that student protest has usually been most vigorous and extensive where the confrontation between students and the university administration has involved general political issues; as, for example, at Berkeley, the London School of Economics, West Berlin, Warsaw and Nanterre. Although there are considerable differences between countries it is evident that the vitality of the student movement everywhere depends in some measure upon its ability to express national discontents which find no other outlet. This is most apparent in the USA, where students have led the campaigns against the war in Vietnam, against poverty, and until recently, against the exploitation of the Negro; in Czechoslovakia and Poland, where they have played a prominent part in the struggles for greater political and cultural freedom; and in France, where they provoked a massive revolt against the authoritarian Gaullist régime.

The ability of the radical minority to lead large numbers of students in these campaigns on national political issues depends in turn upon their influence on the campus in relation to problems of the structure and government of universities. The success of the student movement here has been due largely to the fact that it has advocated a kind of equality and participation which appears highly appropriate to the university as an institution. The appeal of such ideas as are expressed by 'student power' (a term which covers very diverse aspirations), and the degree of feeling which they excite, depends of course upon the nature of the existing university structure which students confront. In North America, both in the USA and in Canada, where the ultimate governing body in many universities is an entirely non-academic Board of Governors such as Thorstein Veblen attacked and ridiculed fifty years ago in *The Higher Learning in America*, students, and also university teachers, have urged changes which would lead to greater academic independence and self-government. Some radical student leaders have carried the argument further: recognising that even where effective everyday control of the curriculum, appointments, etc. has passed by custom into academic hands (although substantial residual powers and influence may remain with the Board and the President), participation in university government may still be confined to a fairly small group of senior teachers and administrators, and that a hierarchical and bureaucratic spirit may still pervade the university, they have advocated a more thoroughgoing 'democratisation' of the university. Their views are well formulated in an essay by Tom Hayden which has been republished in the recent pamphlet of the Radical Student Alliance, *Teach Yourself Student Power* (edited by David Adelstein). Hayden writes:

'A company of scholars is a company of equals in the crucial sense that none has a premium on truth, though some may be wiser, more literate ... more knowledgeable than others. Because the faculty has more permanence and more educational training, theirs should be the primary responsibility for the direction of the university. Because education is not a one-way process, because faculty tradition must be balanced by the fresh eye of youth, and because democracy requires popular control over important decisions, students should share with professors in developing the university (p. 50).'

Ideals of this kind have been widely diffused throughout the student movement in recent years, and they have been applied in a variety of different situations. In France, the student opposition has assailed the control of the university by officials of the Ministry of Education and by a small group of senior professors. In Czechoslovakia and Poland, it is much more the control of the university by Communist Party officials which is under attack. In Britain, where some form of academic self-government has been the rule in universities, though not in other institutions of higher education, the student protest has been correspondingly less radical. But in Britain, as elsewhere, the original opposition to the direct external control of universities by appointed boards, politicians, or government officials, has been extended by some student groups to include criticism of indirect, mainly economic, constraints upon academic self-government; and at the same time the idea of a 'democratic university', which was formulated, however abstractly, as an alternative to the 'multiversity' or 'knowledge factory', has been defined in more extreme terms as implying student control of the university. This is, at least, one of the possible meanings of the term 'student power'. In the RSA pamphlet from which I have already quoted David Adelstein makes some proposals along these lines, supporting them with arguments to the effect that teachers are likely to be more attached to the *status quo*, social and academic, and thus less critical in outlook, than their students. It would be difficult, I think, to demonstrate that this has generally been the case; and it may seem an odd sort of argument to bring forward in the context of the present student movement, which has derived a large part of its intellectual sustenance from eminent members of the upper levels of the academic hierarchy, among them Herbert Marcuse and the late C. Wright Mills.

The idea of a 'democratic university' obviously needs a more systematic examination than it has yet received, however useful it may be in a negative sense as a criticism of authoritarian and bureaucratic university structures which are dominated by absentee governors, or by party or government officials. In some respects a university clearly provides exceptionally favourable conditions for the practice of democracy: there is a basic equality among its members, and the nature of university work facilitates government by reason rather than by coercion. Equally, however, the nature of its work, which is scholarship, discovery, and the passing on of an intellectual tradition continually revised, makes it impossible to conceive university democracy in terms of the representation of majorities; it implies, rather, a certain climate of opinion, the existence of a genuine intellectual community, and a style of personal relations, which are all difficult to achieve and to maintain. The term 'democratic university' is perhaps misleading, and it would be better to speak of academic self-government and of participation in a scholarly community. This would be consistent with the idea, which I think is conveyed by Tom Hayden in the passage I have quoted, that the university as a whole should be governed mainly by its teachers, that students should be entirely self-governing in all those spheres which vitally concern them and which do not involve problems of intellectual quality, and that in the consideration of general questions of educational policy in the university students should participate but not govern. It is in pursuing such objectives, and particularly in opposing an external non-academic control over the university, which university teachers have similarly opposed, that the student movement has so far been most effective.

The three aspects of the student movement, as a new radical movement, as the representative of a new generation, and as an interest group within the university, which I have distinguished, are closely related. The issues in one sphere spread over into another: war and preparation for war, which are the major themes of political protest, affect the universities, which provide some of the technological means of war through their research. Some of the problems which radical students are attacking look very similar from these three aspects: for example, the existence of institutional structures which are too authoritarian and too bureaucratic, which deny participation and responsibility to most of those who are involved in them. Because of these interconnections the future development of the student movement is likely to depend to a great extent upon more general political events. If the war in Vietnam were to end the student movement might well lose some of its vigour, especially in the USA, but it would be unlikely to disappear. In most of the European countries its principal role will probably be that of a 'ginger group' within broader radical movements; in the USA it may form the nucleus of a new radical party, although the first efforts in this direction, at the Conference for New Politics held last year, were not encouraging. Everywhere, it seems to me, one of the most important functions of the student movement is to produce a new generation of radical thinkers, and its achievement in this respect we shall not be able to judge for another decade.

Chapter 14

The Prospect for Radicalism[1]

There is evident, at the present time, in all the industrial countries, not only a strong reaction against radicalism but also a loss of vigour and a proliferation of internal divisions in the radical movement itself. Indeed, there has been a very rapid and bewildering fluctuation in the character and fortunes of the new social movements ever since they first emerged in the late 1950s, after the Anglo-French attack upon Suez and the Hungarian revolt. The 'New Left' which developed at that time in the European countries was still deeply involved with traditional radical and socialist movements, through membership of labour organisations and through participation in a community of ideas derived from Marxism and other socialist doctrines; it possessed, therefore, many elements of continuity with earlier forms of radicalism, and particularly with those of the 1930s.

A notable change occurred with the rebirth of radicalism in the United States of America. This began with the civil rights movement of the early 1960s, in which there appeared the two elements which were afterward to dominate the whole movement: the students and the Negroes. At the outset the two groups co-operated in what was essentially a militant reform movement, but divisions soon appeared as the more radical Negroes moved on to 'black nationalism' and 'black power', while the students became increasingly involved in the antiwar movements and in the confrontations within the universities. By the end of 1968 the separation of the two movements was almost complete. At the same time each movement came to represent quite a striking departure from previous forms of radicalism: in one case, radicalism as an ethnic, 'nationalist' movement, loosely connected with ideas about revolution in the Third World; in the other case radicalism as a youth movement, associated with cultural dissent and innovation which encompassed such phenomena as pop and folk music and the cult of 'mind-expanding' drugs.

[1] Reprinted, with minor revisions, from Bernard Landis and Edward S. Tauber (eds), *In the Name of Life: Essays in Honour of Erich Fromm* (New York, 1971).

In the following discussion I shall concentrate upon the student movement, which has an international character and is less specifically tied to American conditions.[1] Some aspects of its development were foreseen and given an intellectual justification by C. Wright Mills, who argued from the absence of a radical labour movement in the United States of America to the need to envisage possibilities of radical change in terms of a cultural criticism animated by the young intellectuals. This American style of radicalism assumed a definite form in the Berkeley Free Speech Movement of 1964, and soon thereafter it spread widely in many countries. Its influence resulted to some extent from the world involvement of the United States of America; without question, the single most important unifying element in the radical student movement has been the opposition to the Vietnam War. But there were also other factors at work. One, which has itself to be explained, was the growing sense of a generational identity among young people in the industrial countries, and the particular feeling, among university students, that with the accelerating technological revolution and the rapid increase in their own numbers which is a part of this process, they were coming to occupy a position of crucial importance in society. Another factor was the apparent decline of some older kinds of radicalism, which manifested itself in what the students regarded as the spread of 'consensus politics', whether this took the form of an actual coalition of parties (as in West Germany) or simply the diminishing radicalism of left-wing parties. During the 1950s there seemed to be spreading in Europe a style of non-ideological politics resembling that in the United States of America, and insofar as this could be attributed to changes in the character and role of the working class in the European countries the conclusion followed that a new basis for dissent and opposition had to be found in other social groups.

The student movement, as the new animator of political conflict, developed with extraordinary rapidity between 1964 and 1968, reaching a climax in the revolt of May 1968, in France. Since then it has suffered a decline. In the United States the principal radical organisation, Students for a Democratic Society, has

[1] Some important features of the Negro movement have been well analysed by Harold Cruse, *The Crisis of the Negro Intellectual* (New York, 1967). Quite recently, the movement has taken another new direction with the emergence of the Black Panther party, which seeks to establish a broad alliance with white radical groups and has proposed an economic programme which is closer to socialist ideas than most of the new radicalism has been.

become divided into a number of conflicting groups; in France the student movement has reverted to the pre-1968 welter of campus sects (largely along the lines of left-wing groups outside the university) and has lost much of the public support it enjoyed for a time; the German SDS has recently been dissolved and its erstwhile leaders have dispersed; in Britain there is no longer an effective radical student organisation. It is possible that this represents no more than a temporary setback. If it is true, as some have argued, that the 'scientific and educational estate' now occupies a crucial place in society and is in the process of elaborating an ideology and forms of political action appropriate to its situation, as the industrial working class did in the nineteenth century, then recent events may be seen as the first tentative steps toward organisation and action of a more durable kind. On the other hand, the decline may correspond with a characteristically rapid fluctuation of mood, interest, and orientation in student movements, resulting from the high degree of mobility of their members.

However we interpret these phenomena it is important to recognise some of the weaknesses of the student movement, which tended to be overlooked in the excitement of the late 1960s when students presented in a dramatic way new ideas and attitudes, helped to produce a much needed revival of intellectual and political controversy, and animated the protest movements. One of the weaknesses arises simply from the fact that the student movement is a *youth* movement. The social influence of a younger generation may be considerable, as Karl Mannheim noted, in bringing a novel approach, a new mode of thought and experience, to the assimilation, use, and development of the cultural heritage which it encounters. But it is highly improbable that the structure and course of development of any society at any time will be determined mainly by the ideas and aspirations of its very young and inexperienced members. In most spheres, the 'young Turks' who bring about important innovations do not belong to the age group of university students, but are in their late twenties or early thirties, having passed beyond the period of confused seeking and striving which characterises younger age groups. Moreover, this kind of innovation is very largely a matter of individual discoveries, rather than an activity of a whole generational group. When we consider the nature of broad social movements and of major changes in the structure of society it becomes apparent that these depend upon quite different bonds from those of an age group— upon nationality, economic interest, class membership, or religious community. Thus, even the argument about the growing importance of the 'scientific and educational estate' as an active social and political group (which I mentioned earlier) concerns the future role of the scientific and academic professions much more than it concerns the students.

These disabilities of the student movement are enhanced by other factors. One is the rapid circulation of members, which renders difficult the maintenance of a consistent political style or organisation. Others arise from the connection between the student movement and some aspects of a wider 'youth culture' including pop and folk music and drugs, which have very little radical significance at all. It is true that these phenomena have sometimes been regarded as forming part of a general movement of liberation, but this is largely a misinterpretation of them. Pop music expresses, generally in the most banal language, the universal doubts and uncertainties of adolescence. It has little critical content, and what it had at the outset has diminished with the growth of commercial interests. The most that can be said for it as a cultural innovation is that it may reflect, especially in such activities as pop festivals, a desire for greater community, or even, in a religious sense, communion, and thus a drift away from acquisitiveness and self-aggrandisement. In folk music there is a larger element of social criticism and protest, but by comparison with earlier periods the protest is vague, ill-formulated, individualistic, and sometimes counterfeit, as in the case of those folk singers who use protest songs merely in order to further their own careers.[1]

The cult of drugs can also not be regarded as liberating; for what enlargement of human freedom can possibly result from making one's mental states and experiences totally dependent upon chemical substances? It is rather the ultimate alienation of one's human powers to a world of objects. Like alcoholism, the use of drugs is an action expressing despair, revulsion, withdrawal from the public world of social issues into a private world of personal troubles and fantasies. It reflects, no doubt, a dissatisfaction with the state of society as seen from an individual point of view, and at the same time a malaise of society itself; but it does not lead to any kind of movement for the radical reconstruction of society.

It is not very clear, at present, how closely these different aspects of the 'youth culture' are related, but insofar as the student movement lays stress upon its own generational character

[1] See the discussion in R. Serge Denisoff, 'Folk Music and the American Left: A Generational-Ideological Comparison', *British Journal of Sociology*, 20 (4) (December 1969).

it is certainly affected by the prevailing outlook of the whole age group to which it belongs; and there is evidently a considerable degree of cultural exchange between the 'hippy' and the 'activist' groups within the younger generation (though more obviously in the United States of America than elsewhere). This mingling of radical and nonradical tendencies undoubtedly adds to the ideological confusion which reigns in the student movement but the confusion is in any case a phenomenon which, on more general grounds, we should expect.

The student movement became active at a time when radical social thought was passing through its still unresolved crisis, which originated in the criticisms and revisions of Marxist thought,[1] in the confrontation with doctrines elaborated by revolutionary movements in peasant societies (for example, in China, in Cuba, in North Africa, and in other areas of the Third World), and in controversies with the exponents of new theories about the nature of modern industrial societies.[2] The students, consequently, drew their ideas from very diverse sources; from the thought and experience of revolutionaries in the Third World as well as from the extraordinarily varied interpretations of present-day society offered by social critics in the Western industrial countries. It is not to be supposed that students themselves are capable of producing a coherent social theory from this mishmash, although they may, as they have shown, raise critical questions and shadow forth a new social outlook which will help to direct the work of critical social thought. Unfortunately, this valuable activity has frequently been perverted into purely political campaigns, carried on with the aid of simple slogans, which have brought the movement into conflict with most of the rest of society, including a large part of the labour movement,[3] and have considerably reduced the effectiveness of the social criticism which emanates from universities.

---

[1] It is impossible, here, to review all the criticisms and reinterpretations of Marxism during the past twenty years. Among the important contributions to this debate are the writings of Leszek Kolakowski, Stanislaw Ossowski, Gajo Petrović and others associated with the Yugoslav journal *Praxis*, C. Wright Mills, Herbert Marcuse, Jürgen Habermas, Jean-Paul Sartre and Eric Fromm himself.

[2] For example, Raymond Aron, *18 Lectures on Industrial Society* (New York, 1967), and J. K. Galbraith, *The Affluent Society* (Boston, 1958) and *The New Industrial State* (London, 1967).

[3] This has occurred in many West European countries, where the radical student movement has had strained relations, and sometimes open conflicts, with socialist parties and with the trade unions. This was particularly evident

The future of radicalism—in thought and action—depends upon whether or not the limitations imposed by the recent predominance of the student movement can be overcome. The student movement has to be seen, and to see itself, as only one section of a growing intellectual movement, best described as socialist humanism, which is directed (unlike most earlier forms of dissent) against a multiplicity of enemies—against capitalism, against technocracy and against totalitarian socialism. In this movement there are several important objectives which students can help, and in some degree have already helped, to attain. The first is to equip themselves—and this applies above all to those in the social sciences—as effective critics of society. The second is to establish this critical, and so far as possible radical, outlook securely enough for it to persist and develop outside the university, in the scientific and professional occupations which students will enter. The third is to defend intellectual freedom and autonomy in the universities, or to re-establish it in those societies where universities have fallen under the domination of businessmen, civil servants, or party officials. In this area, though, I think the main responsibility falls upon university teachers, and it has been their defection in many cases which has thrust an impossible burden upon students. There is a further objective, closely connected with this, which is to examine carefully and thoroughly what are the alternatives to the 'multiversity' or 'knowledge factory'. It is somewhat surprising, in view of the importance which students themselves attribute to their opposition to bureaucratisation, that there has been so little serious consideration of what needs to be done in order to create a human atmosphere in the university, and to restore its character as a community of scholars in which critical thought can flourish unhindered—if indeed that is what is wanted. One necessary step would obviously be to limit the size of universities, another (in many countries) to reform the system of university government; but beyond this there is the task of thinking profoundly about the proper character of universities in the twentieth century, in the context of a rapid expansion of higher education of very diverse kinds, and at the same time experimenting with different forms of organisation. Far from aiding this process of reflection

---

in West Germany in 1968. In the United States the gulf between workers and students has been even more marked; the most recent illustration is the demonstration of New York construction workers against the peace movement.

and transformation, some student activism in the last two or three years has seemed more likely to destroy the universities, by its contempt for intellectual life, its intolerance of divergent opinions, and its obsession with purely political questions. This has been extremely damaging to the radical cause, not least because no good society is conceivable without universities, or equivalent institutions, in which men can practise and exemplify free intellectual inquiry for its own sake.

Even if intellectual dissent flourished, as it began to do in the 1960s, and even if it took shape in a coherent critical theory, as it has not yet done, this would still be inadequate for the transformation of society. In order to bring about radical change there is needed a social movement which embodies the practical experiences and interests of large numbers of men. In most of the West European countries the labour movement still occupies this place, and outside the labour movement there can be no radical politics. There are, in fact, many signs that this movement is itself becoming more radical again—the rapid extension of a general strike in France in May 1968, which, far more than the student movement, threatened the Gaullist regime; the wave of militant trade union activity in Italy at the end of 1969; the increasing militancy of workers in the most technologically advanced industries in many countries; the considerable revival of interest in the ideas and practices of workers' control. It is not at all improbable that the intellectual radicalism in the universities and the new orientations in the labour movement will come together to produce great social changes in the course of the next decade.

In the United States of America it is much more difficult to foresee the development of a broad radical movement. Since the end of the First World War there has been no mass labour movement committed to bringing about radical changes in the structure of American society. Is it conceivable that this should change now, in conditions of growing prosperity and declining trade unionism? There are, as radicals have frequently pointed out, many groups in American society which do not share in its material advantages, and which constitute potential nuclei of opposition. Some of them, notably the Negroes and the Mexicans, have engaged in increasingly militant, though not necessarily radical, action. There is also a revolt of at least a considerable part of the younger generation against the condition of American society. But the American working class remains largely aloof from any kind of radical politics. I do not think this state of affairs will change quickly. Nevertheless, if the present intellectual dissent, and the various opposition movements, could be brought together in a political organisation—a new radical party—it does not seem impossible that such a party could eventually attract many workers to its policies and actions, especially those workers in the more advanced industries, who are likely to have a growing interest, in the United States of America as elsewhere, in directing more fully the work process in which they are engaged. These possibilities can only be tested in practice; at all events, the endeavour to create a new radical party would offer greater hope than a continuation of the present fragmented dissent and sporadic protest.

Equally difficult is the assessment of possible changes in the Soviet societies of Eastern Europe. It is clear that there has been, since 1956, growing intellectual dissent, and it can scarcely be doubted that the kind of social outlook which was formulated by Czechoslovak intellectuals and students during the socialist renaissance of 1967–68 would also find expression in the other Soviet countries if the opportunity presented itself. We should note, however, that in the instances where there has been a radical movement in these countries—in Hungary and Poland in 1956, and in Czechoslovakia in 1967–68—it has arisen out of a conjunction between intellectual dissent and working-class, trade union opposition to the regime. If there is to be progress, on the basis of an economy which is already collectivised, toward a socialist society in which men are genuinely liberated, not subjected to the rule of censors, party officials, and the secret police, then both these elements will be necessary—the intellectuals who demand freedom to speculate and criticise, and the workers who demand control over their working conditions and a real voice in the determination of social policy.

In all modern radical movements there has been this close link between ideas and interests, most fully developed when a theory of society such as Marxism becomes inextricably involved with a powerful social movement. The contribution of radical intellectuals to this process is both negative and positive. On one side it is to show, in a critical way, the character of existing society; its injustices, limitations, and conflicts. This work of criticism, when it becomes sufficiently widespread—when the established order is largely deserted by the intellectuals—is one of the elements which prepare the way for a new society. But it is not complete unless it can also show the possible directions of change, interpret the emerging social movements, and prefigure the new social order. It has to accomplish the work which Marx, as a young man, set himself when he wrote: 'We develop new principles for the world out of its own existing principles. . . . We may sum up the outlook of our Journal (the *Deutsch-Französische Jahrbücher*) in a single phrase: the self-knowledge (critical philosophy) of the age about its struggles and aims.'

This positive vision, the development of new principles out of existing principles, is what appears weakest and most obscure in present-day radical thought. If we search out the reason for this weakness we can hardly fail to reach the conclusion that it is above all the disillusionment with socialism, which began at the end of the 1930s and has been intensified by the development of the Soviet version of socialism since the end of the war, through the closing years of the Stalinist terror to the *Realpolitik* of the military occupation of Czechoslovakia. Radical thinkers have now to criticise both capitalism and socialism as existing forms of society, and they are often tempted to direct their main criticism against industrialism itself. The idea of an alternative form of society becomes faint and shadowy, because what was once the ideal——socialism—now exists as a problematic reality. What we have to do in order to meet this situation, as some are already attempting, is to rethink socialism, both in terms of the institutions appropriate to an egalitarian society,[1] and in terms of the social movements and political actions which are capable of bringing it about without the disfigurement which it has suffered from violence and repression.

[1] I have in mind, particularly, the serious study of problems of management and participation in large-scale industry, of reforms in social administration which would bring the social services more under the control of those affected by them, of changes in educational institutions which would diminish the authoritarian elements in them and provide a better early experience of self-government. Too little thought has been devoted to the possible forms of new institutions, and too little attention has yet been given to the available practical experience of more egalitarian types of organisation, such as workers' self-management, communities of work, and some community development projects.

Index

Index

About the Author

T. B. BOTTOMORE taught sociology at the London School of Economics from 1952 to 1964. He then spent three years as Professor and Head of the Department of Political Science, Sociology and Anthropology at Simon Fraser University at Vancouver, and since 1968 has been Professor of Sociology at the University of Sussex. He is well-known for his work on Karl Marx, for intimate knowledge of European sociology, and for his outstanding textbook, *Sociology: A Guide to Problems and Literature,* as well as for such books as *Classes in Modern Society.*